MW00331153

The Latinx Guide to
GRADUATE SCHOOL

The Latinx Guide to
GRADUATE SCHOOL

Genevieve Negrón-Gonzales and
Magdalena L. Barrera

DUKE UNIVERSITY PRESS   DURHAM AND LONDON   2023

© 2023 DUKE UNIVERSITY PRESS
All rights reserved

Designed by Matthew Tauch
Typeset in Alegreya and Bitter
by Westchester Publishing Services

Library of Congress Cataloging-in-Publication Data
Names: Negrón-Gonzales, Genevieve, author. | Barrera,
Magdalena L., [date] author.
Title: The Latinx guide to graduate school / Genevieve
Negrón-Gonzales and Magdalena L. Barrera.
Description: Durham : Duke University Press, 2023. |
Includes bibliographical references and index.
Identifiers: LCCN 2022039694 (print)
LCCN 2022039695 (ebook)
ISBN 9781478019671 (paperback)
ISBN 9781478017035 (hardcover)
ISBN 9781478024309 (ebook)
Subjects: LCSH: Hispanic Americans—Education (Graduate) |
Hispanic Americans—Graduate students. | Universities and
colleges—Graduate work—Social aspects. | Education,
Higher— Social aspects—United States. | BISAC: SOCIAL
SCIENCE / Ethnic Studies / American / Hispanic American
Studies | EDUCATION / Schools / Levels / Higher
Classification: LCC LC2670.6 .N44 2023 (print) | LCC LC2670.6
(ebook) | DDC 378.1/5508968073—dc23/eng/20221011
LC record available at https://lccn.loc.gov/2022039694
LC ebook record available at https://lccn.loc.gov/2022039695

Cover art: Illustration by Adriana Arriaga.

We dedicate this book to the up-and-coming
Latinx/a/o scholars and practitioners.
¡Ánimo!

Contents

180   6 Navigating Personal Relationships in Graduate School

205   7 Life after Graduate School

Acknowledgments

This book is a labor of love. While it may be clear that this project was motivated by our love for our former, current, and future students (the Latinx scholars coming up behind us), it is also the product of the mentorship we received from those who paved the way before us. We want to thank our students, who have shared with us their lives and academic journeys as well as their dreams and struggles. We were motivated to write this book because we believe in you so deeply.

In particular, we want to acknowledge a group of emerging scholars whom we have had the honor of teaching and working alongside. These scholars are current and/or recent Latinx/a/o graduate students who read an early draft of this book and provided critical feedback that helped us improve it in countless ways. Thank you Alonzo Campos, Erika Carrillo, Leslie Clark, Alicia Garcia, Mario Gonzalez, Luz Jiménez Ruvalcaba, Lucia Leon, Elisa Romero-Heaps, and Carolina Valdivia. We are grateful to you and excited to see all you will contribute in and outside of the academy in the coming years.

We also want to thank a group of our colleagues who provided feedback on an earlier draft. They drew on their own experiences mentoring and supporting students to help us improve the book, and some of them provided consejos so that our readers can learn directly from them. These colleagues are colegas in the truest sense—sources of inspiration, collaboration, and radical camaraderie in the academy. Thank you Leisy Abrego, Ursula Aldana, Jack Cáraves, Esther Díaz Martín, Jonathan Gomez, Susana Muñoz, Yolanda Padilla, Katy M. Pinto, Gina Perez, Simon Weffer-Elizondo, and Pat Zavella.

We also want to thank Dulce Martinez, our graduate assistant and MA student at the University of San Francisco, who provided us with invaluable support and feedback throughout the writing process. Thank you to Kathy Coll, a colleague and friend, for planting the seed for us to write this book.

I, Genevieve, also want to thank my women of color writing group, who provided me with support and motivation to keep writing, even through the pandemic: Monisha Bajaj, Dana Wright, and Kimberly Williams Brown. I would also like to thank my family—Jason, Amado, and Mayari—who, thanks to COVID-19, were never more than a few feet away while I was working on this book because we were all working and learning from home together for a year and a half. Thank you for sharing the desk, joining me for lunch on the porch, and encouraging me to keep going. I would also like to recognize and thank my parents—Mary and Henry Gonzales—who always encouraged a love of learning, emphasized the importance of education, supported all my educational pursuits, and cheered me on every step of the way. Last, I want to thank my friend, colega, and coconspirator Magdalena Barrera. Magdalena, there could be no better collaborator on this book than you. Thank you for being a continual source of inspiration and camaraderie over the past decade.

I, Magdalena, would like to express my deep appreciation for Marcos Pizarro and Lilly Pinedo Gangai, incredible thought partners in developing culturally resonant academic programming for Latinx/a/o students at San José State University (SJSU). Thanks also go to SJSU's Office of the Provost for supporting the development of this manuscript. I offer abrazos to the friends who cheered me on as I tackled both this manuscript and a new chapter in my career: Erlinda Yañez, Marcelle Dougan, Anne Marie Todd, and Katie Wilkinson. Thank you to Enrrigue Barrera for being such a loving father and for always offering unwavering support, encouragement, and friendship. I could not have completed this project without the love and support of Ryan Pinto, who calmly weathered the dramatic highs and lows of my writing process, reminded me to get up and stretch when I was hunched at my desk for hours, and made sure I had something warm and spicy to eat every day. Finally, thanks to Genevieve Negrón-Gonzales for being such a wonderful collaborator and friend. Genevieve, I admire you as someone who consistently shows up, walks the walk, and demonstrates how to foreground a commitment to social justice through everything you do— always with good energy and humor. I hope we always keep this conversation going.

Last but not least, we want to thank Gisela Fosado and Alejandra Mejía at Duke University Press, for believing in this project from the start. We would also like to thank the anonymous reviewers whose support and thoughtful feedback made this text even stronger, as well as Ideas on Fire for copyediting and indexing a 100,000-word manuscript. Turns out we had a lot to say about grad school!

Introduction

YOU THOUGHT YOU WERE BUYING A
HOW-TO BOOK BUT ENDED UP GETTING
A LOVE LETTER, MANIFESTO, AND
FLASHLIGHT

Perhaps you are picking up this book because you are considering the possibility of graduate school. Maybe you feel a bit panicked because you think you should have read this a couple of years ago, before you started your program or when you were deciding to go to graduate school. Maybe you are a mentor or professor or advisor to students who are attending or considering graduate school, and you are reading this book because you plan to assign it to them so that they can have their feet on the ground as they navigate the academy. The intention of this book is not to lay out a blueprint for success or a cheat sheet of how-tos but rather to document some of the unwritten rules about graduate education that are relevant to Latinx students because they fundamentally shape our experience.[1] One of the ways that educational privilege is preserved, replicated, and transferred from one generation to the next is that those who know *know*, and those who don't know don't know what it is that they don't know. The academy thrives on this dynamic of unwritten rules and carefully guarded information. One of our main goals in writing this book is to demystify and clarify elements that are a part of the process of navigating graduate school that Latinx students often do not know because, for most of us, we are the first in our families to walk this path.

Moreover, we are often made to feel less than, undeserving, and like we are impostors in a place where everyone belongs except us. That dynamic can make it difficult to ask questions, to seek clarification, or to find mentorship—because needing to ask for help further intensifies the feeling that we do not belong or do not deserve to be here (something we discuss at much greater length in chapter 2). The university was not meant for people like us; the history of higher education is steeped in legacies of slavery, white supremacy, sexism, and elitism. Undoing that legacy is much bigger than this book, but our hope is that by using our foothold as two people who have been able to squeak through the slight crack in that door and push it open more widely, we are able to help shape how Latinx graduate students navigate the academy so that more of us can get in, get through, and get out, using our education for the betterment of our communities. The charge is grandiose, but as Latinx academics we know that everything we do is political and race-laden. This book, then, is simultaneously our love letter to Latinx graduate students, our manifesto, and an indictment of the academy that pushes us out and pushes us by. It is also a flashlight you can keep in your pocket to pull out when the road ahead is dark and the path is uncharted.

Equal parts how-to, personal reflection, and academic musing, this book is for Latinx/a/o people who are considering going to graduate school, about to start graduate school, or in graduate school. We were inspired by Kerry Anne Rockquemore and Tracey Laszloffy's *The Black Academic's Guide to Winning Tenure—without Losing Your Soul*, which served as an anchor for both of us in our early years on the tenure track. While our book was written with one particular community in mind—the Latina/o/x community, particularly those who are first-generation college students— we believe it likely has resonance for others as well, particularly those who occupy other marginalized positions in our society, including women, queer, and trans students, Latinx students who are not first-generation, and so on.[2]

Through years of working with students in both formal and informal capacities as professors, advisors, and mentors, we have identified common challenges and key questions shared by many Latinx and first-generation students. These experiences have inspired us to adopt more helpful techniques and refine our approaches to working with students in a way that pushes them forward in their work in a humane, culturally cognizant manner. This book that you hold in your hands was born of those experiences and our hope that the skills we have developed in supporting Latinx graduate students over the past decade can be useful to a broader set of students. We also see this work in the tradition of other critical books in the tradition we come from, such as *Telling to Live: Latina Feminist Testimonios*, which maps the navigations of Latina feminist scholars and their journeys through higher education for the purpose of imagining a new way of being.[3] We draw on this tradition, and the scholars and thinkers and activists and organizers who not only came before us but cleared the path for us. We, very humbly, see ourselves as a part of this long history of Latinas, women of color, and other oppressed groups who tell our stories, look out for each other, and work each day to bring about a new reality.

This book came about because a mutual friend and colleague, Kathy Coll, asked each of us if we knew of any books or materials to pass on to a soon-to-be Latinx master's student who was just about to start in the Migration Studies Program at the University of San Francisco and needed some grounding and preparation. Kathy, in an offhanded way, said to each of us, "I knew that if there was such a book, that you would know about it. And if there's not, you should really write it." And now we have.

El Comienzo: How This Book Came About

Given that less than 3 percent of the professoriate is Latina, we tend to see each other, find each other, and know each other when we are on the same campus. When the authors of this book met at San José State University (SJSU) in 2011, one was a tenure-track assistant professor in Mexican American studies and the other, in the last stages of her PhD program, was teaching classes in the same department as an adjunct professor. Through this connection, we began what would become a now decade-long conversation about teaching, supporting, and mentoring first-generation Latinx graduate students. On virtually every campus, professors of color become de facto mentors to students of color, especially on campuses where the number of faculty of color is small. As junior scholars finding our footing in the academy with our graduate experiences still pretty fresh in our memories, we felt a profound responsibility to our students—those who were in our classes, those whom we advised in the graduate program, and those who found their way to our offices because they were looking for mentorship or just a point of connection. We began to talk about how to engage with intention and purpose. Our commitment was rooted in our own experiences as first-generation Latinas in the academy, and we continually wrestled—both on our own and together—with how to do this work. We were the products of elite graduate programs that had shaped us in positive ways but had also broken us down. We had both considered walking away at various points along our graduate journeys. Both of us had the kind of professors, advisors, and mentors whom we wanted to emulate and also those whom we vowed never to become. We grappled with the need to balance the structural and institutional inequalities that shaped the educational lives of our students before they ever stepped foot on a college campus alongside the demands of institutions of higher education that were never meant to be accessed by people like us (much, much more on how the academy is an institution steeped in white supremacy in chapters 2, 3, 4, and, well, you know, the whole damn book).

In this process, we struggled to articulate—for ourselves and for our students—the idea that we had the potential to try to remake the university by remaking ourselves through it; we did not need to replicate the racist, classist, heterosexist, and elitist ways of academia as a rite of passage or collective penance that others should suffer because we had to suffer. Painful graduate school experiences that break students down are often seen as the process necessary to produce rigorous scholars and skilled practitioners. We were committed to rigor and solid training, yet unconvinced that trauma was a necessary part of that equation. We began to consider—on our own, in conversations with each other, and in our broader professional and personal networks—how to be the kinds of professors who could both have the hard conversations with students that hold them accountable to a higher standard and also be the professors who always have an open door and a willing ear. We saw it as our responsibility and privilege to model a kind of cariño which insists that these politics of care are not something superfluous but rather lie at the heart of our pedagogical practice as teachers and mentors, as well as at the heart of our intellectual identities as researchers and professors. It is also about ánimo, not simply a blanket encouragement to go to graduate school but a thoughtful encouragement that you can do the hard things your heart calls you to do.

Over the years, Magdalena Barrera (or Barrera, as her students often call her) earned tenure and promotion to associate professor at SJSU in the Department of Chicana and Chicano Studies and then was promoted again to full professor, the highest faculty rank possible. In the midst of writing this book, she was appointed to serve as inaugural vice provost for faculty success at SJSU. Genevieve Negrón-Gonzales (or Profa, as her students often call her, even though yes, technically not correct Spanish because

Profe can be both masculine and feminine, but you know how nicknames stick) secured a tenure-track position at the University of San Francisco in the School of Education and was awarded early tenure and promotion to associate professor. Through these years and transitions, the conversations continued as we taught cohort after cohort of students, learning from our mistakes, piloting new ideas, seeing what worked well, and honing our mentorship, teaching, and professional practice.

In this work, over the years, we have seen Latinx graduate students struggle. There are numerous structural and institutional barriers that cause this to be so. We work with students who struggle in graduate school because they never learned the proper mechanics of a research paper or how to formulate a thesis statement. We have watched as students struggle to remain true to themselves and their roots, wondering if the only way they can succeed in the academy is to put their heads down, tame their accents, and abandon their radical ideas in service of something less controversial and more palatable to mainstream academic audiences. We have counseled students through the moments they considered leaving their programs because of the racist comments of classmates and when feelings of isolation and **impostor syndrome** became too much to bear. As we continued to see Latinx students struggle through graduate school, it was also clear that to truly understand what was happening, the experiences of our students had to be contextualized by the broader educational apparatus through which they were positioned as learners. In other words, we cannot talk meaningfully about the struggles Latinx graduate students have within the structure of graduate education if we do not analyze these in light of their experiences as students of color in an educational system that spans from preschool through college in which they are pushed out, pushed back, and pushed on by a system that was not set up for their success.

Through these years of mentoring and teaching, we also have seen students who thrived in their graduate programs, producing scholarship that has moved their field of study as well as the grassroots work on the ground. We have worked with students who graduated with a stronger sense of self, propelled by a responsibility to do good in the world and the knowledge that they were situated to do so. We watch our students go on to work with other students as professors, graduate instructors, mentors, and teachers, noticing how they formulate new ways of being in the university that are based on principles of collaboration rather than competition. We know that this is, indeed, the way that we make a new university for the generations of scholars that come after us.

Our Journeys to Graduate School

Genevieve Negrón-Gonzales: Una Herida Abierta, Affirmative Action, and the Path to the Professoriate

When I started college, I planned to be an elementary school teacher. I spent most of my childhood imagining myself as a kindergarten teacher (well, when I was really small, I wanted to be a nun, but that is a story for another time), but landing on a college campus in the midst of a racial justice fight recalibrated that plan, my educational trajectory, and my life in general.

I grew up on the US-Mexico border in southern San Diego County in a city called Chula Vista. Gloria Anzaldúa famously wrote that the "U.S.-Mexico border *es una herida abierta* where the Third World grates against the first and bleeds."[4] I grew up on this "open wound" that is the U.S.-Mexico border at a moment in which the wound was quite raw. I was in high school when Proposition 187, which sought to prohibit undocumented immigrants from accessing public goods and services, including health care and public education, was put on the ballot in California, passed by voters, and later thrown out by the courts. Proposition 187 was part of a legacy of racial propositions put on the state ballot in the 1990s, in an expression of racial anxiety over the "browning" of California.[5] This was also the era of Operation Gatekeeper at the US-Mexico border, a Clinton-era policy that sought to further militarize the border and criminalize migrants. As a teenager who grew up in the context of a pro-poor, pro-migrant ethos rooted in our identity as a Mexican Catholic family, I was politicized through this dark moment in California's history. I got involved in political activism in my teenage years, and followed my older sister to UC Berkeley.

I graduated from high school in the spring of 1996. Months earlier, the UC Regents (the governing body of the University of California system) had passed SB1 and SB2, which dismantled affirmative action in the UC system. A couple months after I stepped onto the UC Berkeley campus as a first-year student, California voters approved Proposition 209, which dismantled affirmative action in all sectors statewide. Coinciding with the start of my college career, this confluence of events meant that I was the last class admitted under affirmative action policies to UC Berkeley (making me a proud beneficiary of affirmative action), and I was entering a campus that was enmeshed in a racial justice fight. I had been in school for only a couple of months when activists occupied the clock tower at UC Berkeley on election night. When I got home that night (I did not get arrested), there was a voice mail from my mom that went something along the lines of, "Mija! I saw the kids chaining themselves to that clock on the news and I know you are out there! You better call me back!" If there was a graphic novel recap of my undergraduate years, it would be that scene: me listening to messages from my worried mom wondering why I had not picked up and whether I had chained myself to something or if I was just in class.

The fight to save affirmative action and the subsequent and related fight to preserve Ethnic Studies at UC Berkeley shaped my undergraduate years, crystallized my political analysis, and helped me realize that while I was not sure what profession I would choose, it would be work done in the service of racial justice and attempting to address the oppressive structures in our society. I was fundamentally shaped by the experience of being on the UC Berkeley campus as affirmative action was being dismantled; I was there during this infamous year that the law school (then called Boalt, now called Berkeley Law) admitted one Black student. By the time those four years were up, I had had enough of the campus, enough of academia, enough of privileged white people, and I was sure that my graduation would signal the last degree I would earn. The idea of returning for an advanced degree was not anywhere in my consciousness. Graduate school was not something that people in my social/political circle talked about; continuing my education was nowhere on my radar. I had gotten a college degree, made good on my promise to make my parents' sacrifice worth it, and was done.

After graduation, I went to work full-time at the nonprofit organization where I had worked part-time for the last two years of undergraduate school (I had a job through my entire undergraduate career). I was doing work that was meaningful to me, developing curriculum and conducting political education workshops with young people, when I began to think about returning to school two years after graduating with my bachelor of arts. I decided to apply to graduate school not because I was after the degree but because the work I was doing surfaced questions that my eighty-hour-a-week struggling nonprofit worker schedule did not afford me the mental space or the analytical tools to really grapple with. I began to think about graduate school as a way to push pause on this work, have some space to think about the questions that were coming up around the development of political consciousness and the building of social movements, which I would then use to come back to the organization to do the work better and smarter. I had spent the previous seven years building community in the Bay Area—my life and my partner and my political community were here—so I did not consider relocating for graduate school. I looked at programs around the Bay Area and decided there was only one that really interested me. I applied and waited for a decision. For me, the decision would not be which graduate program to attend. The decision would be made for me: if I got in, I would attend; if I did not, I would keep on with my nonprofit work and figure out how to prioritize the reflective and analytical space I was hoping graduate school would provide. I got in, with a fully funded fellowship. As my dad says, "If it's free, give me three!" I am my father's daughter and am never one to pass up a deal, which meant that my acceptance, with a fully funded fellowship, cemented my decision to enroll in the MA/PhD program at UC Berkeley in Social and Cultural Studies in Education.

At the time, I did not know anyone with an advanced degree aside from professors I had as an undergrad. To be honest, I did not understand that a PhD was a research degree. I did not imagine I would ever be able to be a professor. The MA/PhD sounded good to me because I figured if I couldn't handle it—if I wasn't smart enough or couldn't put up with the white people any longer or felt like it was not useful to my broader political aims—then I could leave after two years with an MA in hand and go back to the work I had been doing before, having lost nothing. The details of those years will come out throughout the book, but a few things happened along the way that are probably useful to know at the outset. I walked across the stage on graduation day with a six-month-old baby in my arms and her four-year-old brother's hand in mine. My son was born a couple of weeks after I finished the MA (I did not even attend the ceremony). Getting pregnant with my daughter is what gave me the ganas to finish my dissertation. She was due on November 15, so I told myself I would have a full draft done by October 31. Because she was my second baby, I knew what it meant to have a newborn; I did not think I would be able to come up with any original insight or analysis while sleep-deprived and caring for a newborn (thus the writing needed to be done), but I also knew that I would spend long hours sitting, nursing, and holding a baby (and therefore revising a complete dissertation would be possible). I was mistaken for janitorial staff at UC Berkeley when I was a few weeks away from completing my PhD. Very pregnant when I was assembling my dissertation committee, I was told by a faculty member that she only works with students who are "really serious" as she showed me the door; the implication that a pregnant Chicana could never be a serious student was thinly veiled. I thought about quitting many, many times. The urgency I felt around the issues I was researching and writing about, as well as my love for my students, made me stay the course, and I secured a position at the University of San Francisco's School of Education in 2013. I earned early tenure in the spring of 2018 and currently serve as associate professor in the School of Education, affiliate faculty in the Migration Studies program, as well as the chair and founder of the University Task Force to Support Undocumented Students.

Magdalena L. Barrera: A Journey to and through Elite Institutions

I am a third-generation Mexican American from suburban Chicago; my grandparents migrated from central Mexico in the 1910s, finding work in the railroad industry and factories of the US Midwest. My parents were born and raised in Chicago's richly multiethnic Italian, Chinese, and Mexican neighborhoods and, through my dad's military service, lived for a time in Germany. By the time I came along, our family had settled in a predominantly white suburb, where I was often the only Latina in my K–12 classes. Though at times my family was only tenuously middle class, my parents made sure that school was my only job. Having inherited my mother's love of reading, I aspired to become a famous novelist like my idol Sandra Cisneros. Her novel *The House on Mango Street* changed my life when I stumbled upon it at my local bookstore during my senior year of high school, because it was the first time I had ever read a story told from the perspective of a midwestern Mexican girl like me.

I became aware of college at a young age, having seen my mother take courses at a local community college through the years. Though my older sister was accepted to a four-year institution, she chose not to attend, so from age twelve I began to feel even more acutely my mother's desire to see one of her daughters earn a college degree. My mom worked as a support administrator at a research laboratory and observed how people with advanced degrees were accorded more respect. As a result, she often intoned, "Because you're a woman and a minority, you need a master's degree!" It sounded like good advice, but everything I knew about college came from *Class of '96*, a TV show about six friends in their freshman year.

I was accepted into the University of Chicago in 1993 with a full-tuition scholarship. Unprepared for the rarefied academic world I was entering, I soon found myself struggling with impostor syndrome. UChicago prides itself on being a "great books" school, and the professors' pedagogical style was more suited to teaching advanced graduate students than novice undergraduates. I enrolled in courses like Classics of Social and Political Thought mainly because the titles sounded grand and promised to impart things that an educated person should know. I was quickly lost, struggling to plow through Adam Smith's *Wealth of Nations* without falling asleep. Meanwhile, my peers seemed to know how to take reading notes, talk to faculty, manage their time, and attend office hours. Though I eventually found my footing, I developed the terrible and persistent habit of procrastinating on my writing out of fear of failure.

I double-majored in English, pursuing my passion for literature, and Latin American studies, which enabled me to learn about the legacies of race and colonization that shaped my family history. Ultimately, two support systems helped me attain my bachelor's degree in 1997: First were the close friends I made in our Latinx student group, who were my primary social circle and source of emotional support. Second were my mentors, Curtis Marez, the only Chicano faculty member in English, and Yolanda Padilla, a doctoral student in the department. With their support, I applied for a Summer Research Opportunity Program and completed my first independent research project, and then was awarded a Mellon Minority Undergraduate Fellowship (now known as the Mellon Mays), which prepared me for the graduate school application process.

After graduation, I traveled with my then boyfriend to Mexico City, where I dreamed of writing the Great Chicano Novel. Instead, all that happened was that I ran out of money, broke up with the guy, and returned home to apply to graduate school. Thanks to my research opportunities and friendships with grad students, I thought I understood what grad school entailed. Yet just as with my college applications, I had no idea what kinds of questions I should ask about doctoral programs; all I knew was that I wanted to study the writings of women activists within the Chicano Movement. To my surprise, I was accepted with five years of funding into the highly competitive PhD program in Modern Thought and Literature (MTL) at Stanford University.

When I arrived at Stanford in 1998, I learned that MTL had an informal peer mentor system. My assigned buddy was, like me, a first-generation Chicano student. He invited me to coffee and started the conversation by asking, "So, what's your background?" I was about to tell him about growing up amid the cornfields of suburban Chicago when he completed his question by rattling off a list of theoretical lineages: "Do you consider yourself post-structuralist, postmodernist, postcolonial . . . ?" Panicked, I gulped, "Um, I'm not sure yet." His question was my first indication that graduate school meant not just learning specialized knowledge and the research and writing skills required for a PhD but also adjusting to the significant class, language, and identity shifts that are inextricably bound up with the process.

My undergrad research skills and successes quickly faded once classes began. I found that faculty often gave assignments ("write a reading response") without providing any specific instructions. My voice was drowned out by the droning of the self-appointed superstars, students who tried to impress everyone by brutally critiquing each reading. Meanwhile, I was struggling to complete the densely theoretical readings and figure out the author's argument, not to mention clarifying my own response to it. With time, I began to see through the posturing of others and to develop a system of reading, note taking, and preparing for class—a system I developed through trial and error because those skills, while absolutely essential, were never explicitly discussed in any class. Rather, it was through my peers in the program that I learned to navigate the hidden curriculum of graduate school.

With time, I found success in my classes because the assignments and readings came with clear deadlines. However, I became unmoored while writing my dissertation, as I had no idea how to harness my self-discipline and create accountability structures to make progress on my research. My faculty were encouraging but hands-off, assuming that I knew what I was doing. Looking back, I should have asked for more direction, but I was loath to admit that I needed help. Three of the four years I spent working on my dissertation consisted of struggling with writer's block and avoiding my faculty advisors. I was so burned out by this journey that I lost interest in pursuing a faculty career; my limited experience as a teaching assistant was nothing great, and I feared that I would wither under the pressure to publish. I entered an existential crisis, wondering what the past seven years meant now that I no longer wanted to be a professor.

I applied for a postdoctoral teaching fellowship at Stanford because it was renewable for up to three years and thus afforded me a window of time to find an alternative career path. I will forever be thankful for that experience for two reasons. First, I learned that if I did not file my dissertation by December 2005, I would have to reapply for the fellowship—and truly, that was the only reason I was able to break through my writer's block. I couldn't afford to lose that opportunity. So in the week between the end of our training and the start of full-time teaching, I completed one and a half remaining chapters of my dissertation and drafted the conclusion. It was finally done! I had a *Shawshank Redemption*–like moment of holding aloft the completed draft, still warm from the printer, and sinking to my knees, crying with relief. Second, the fellowship's training and pedagogical practice helped me see that I had a passion for teaching and that perhaps I would enjoy a faculty career if it were at a teaching-centered institution.

All these years later, I am the first woman to be promoted to full professor and to have served as department chair of Chicana and Chicano Studies at SJSU, a **Hispanic-Serving Institution (HSI)**. As we completed the first draft of this book, I entered a new phase of my career, stepping into a senior leadership role supporting faculty success and working to recruit and retain teacher-scholars who reflect the diversity of our students. I have found incredible meaning working with and learning alongside SJSU students, many of whom are first-generation students from working-class and immigrant backgrounds. They inspired me to take on a new area of research centered on the mentoring and retention of historically underrepresented students and faculty in higher education—and that is what drives me to contribute to this book you hold in your hands.

Latinx/a/os and Higher Education: ¡¿Pa' Qué?!

Every semester, we teach, mentor, and become academic "ninas" to first-generation Latinx students who are passionately invested in their education—students who likely share many similarities with you who are reading this book.[6] Like them, perhaps you have been galvanized by scholarship that enables you to analyze your lived experiences and connect your family and community histories with a larger socioeconomic context. Perhaps you are deeply committed to developing projects that enable you to apply that knowledge in ways that matter to you. To be clear, you have overcome tremendous odds: You may be part of the 9 percent of Latinx students who enrolled in a four-year institution directly after high school. Or you may be part of the 42 percent of Latinx high school graduates who start off at community colleges, only 5 percent of whom make the jump to a four-year university. Upon graduation, you will have joined the 13 percent of Latinxs with a bachelor's degree.[7]

Yet even that figure elides notable differences within our communities. For instance, since 1980, Latinas have earned degrees at higher rates than their male counterparts.[8] In another example, educational outcomes tend to be better for Cubans and Puerto Ricans than for Mexicans and Central Americans.[9] Not surprisingly, class and citizenship status have tremendous impact on educational attainment among Latinxs; one study finds that among Chicana/o/x students, 51 percent of those in the highest income range earn at least one degree (associate's or higher) versus only 7 percent among those in the lowest income range.[10] Sixty percent of Latinxs in higher education are enrolled at Hispanic-Serving Institutions, and 63 percent are clustered in just four states: California, Florida, New York, and Texas. Undocumented students face serious and significant barriers in most states, hindering their access to higher education. These figures demonstrate that Latinx students face massive underrepresentation across many institutions and regions.[11] Further still, Latinxs in higher education tend to be concentrated in the social sciences and education, with significantly fewer going into science, technology, engineering, and math fields.[12]

Making your way through this educational pipeline, you may find that while you are hungry for more, you are feeling exhausted by the overall journey—and no wonder. Perhaps you have felt the financial strain of paying for your education while also contributing to your family's household income. Maybe you have faced a longer time to complete your degree and have accumulated more debt along the way. Indeed, maybe even as you aspire to an advanced degree, you are having a hard time envisioning yourself continuing along the path because you see so few faculty who share your ethnic background and cultural values—after all, Latinxs make up just 5 percent of the professoriate nationwide.[13] Perhaps most significant is the much broader challenge we all face in bridging our home/cultural values with those of our academic institutions. Most universities are ill prepared to draw upon Latinx students' many strengths, causing you to wonder, as we did multiple times throughout our own journeys, "¿Qué estoy haciendo aquí?"[14] As a Latinx student, you may find yourself exerting great intercultural effort, a term that describes the additional energy that you feel like you have to put into making yourself fit in with your campus culture.[15]

In short, the academy was not created for people like us. As numerous scholars before us have elaborated, the modern-day university was built for the sons of the wealthy elite, and the institution itself was built with the wealth accumulated by dispossession through the violence of colonialism, slavery, and wage exploitation.[16] This fundamental truth about the institution is one that we have to be comfortable talking about explicitly and plainly if we are to join its ranks. It does us no favors if we forget that the history of the university is steeped in elitism and exploitation. The question, then, is what does it mean to permeate this institution as a literal and subjective outsider—one whose identity and subjectivity are historically crafted through otherness? Why make the decision to willingly enter an institution that is historically crafted to exclude us—and continues to perpetuate this dynamic through both formal and informal processes of marginalization?

There are the easy and prescriptive answers, of course. There are certain jobs for which an advanced degree is required. There are some fields in which how far you can climb is constrained by the degree that you have. Some sectors require a skill specialization that can only be accessed and obtained through graduate education. Thus, there may be concrete reasons for seeking an advanced degree that have to do with professional aspirations and the necessary credentials. These are valid reasons that drive many to graduate education.

There are also other answers to the question of why we willingly submit to graduate education, despite knowing that it is often a hostile environment for people like us. What does it mean to claim as our own a site we have been told could never be ours? I (Genevieve) was talking to my mentor once, a woman of color slightly older than myself, who had been hired at her R1 university job as a spousal hire. A spousal hire is, in short, when a job candidate who has been made an offer of employment negotiates an employment offer for their spouse as a condition of their acceptance. This mentor, who was nothing short of an academic superstar in her field, told me about the experience of being the "trailing spouse," meaning she was not the targeted hire but rather the spouse who was negotiated in. I asked her whether that experience made her feel like she was less than, under a microscope, unwanted but tolerated. She laughed, and said, "I loved how they underestimated me because you can't imagine how shocked they were when I excelled." I have held onto that statement for years. This attitude sums up what it means to claim space that we were never intended to inhabit: to look the powerful in the eye and say, "We will not apologize for being here, and we rightfully claim our place at the table." The power in doing so is tremendous.

¿A Dónde Vamos? A Road Map of the Book

What is in store for you as you read this book? It is organized into seven thematic chapters that address aspects of the hidden curriculum of higher education and graduate school that are most critical for first-generation Latinx student success. Thus, rather than a chronological step-by-step organization ("in year one, you should . . . in year two, your focus should be . . ."), we highlight the key navigational areas we find critical for development in graduate school. The chapters build on each other yet also can be read individually in whatever order is best for you. Also, because of its thematic approach, this guide provides essential insights that apply to scholars who are interested in or already enrolled in a master's or doctoral program. It needs to be explicitly stated that this book has an inherent humanities and social sciences bias. This is not to say that those in other areas, including the hard sciences (biology, physics, etc.) and engineering, cannot learn something from this book or that they do not experience the same obstacles that students in the humanities and social sciences do; it is simply to acknowledge the background of the authors and how that creates an inherent bias in how we have written this book and what advice we give. Magdalena Barrera has a PhD in Modern Thought and Literature from Stanford University and taught in Chicana and Chicano Studies; Genevieve Negrón-Gonzales has a PhD in Social and Cultural Studies in Education from UC Berkeley and currently teaches in a School of Education. Thus, while we hope (and believe) that Latinx students of all disciplines can find helpful information in this book, the disciplines we were trained in and that we teach in shape the way we come to this topic and have also shaped the kinds of students we have worked with.

On a practical note, you can read this book from front to back, you can flip to the sections that feel most relevant, or you can read it in pieces. As you read, don't skip the sections you assume do not apply to you or that you think you do not need. We have done our best to highlight the principal areas of navigating graduate school that we think all Latinx graduate students need to be thinking about, improving on, and considering in terms of their development and practice. We include what we do because these are the areas we have seen students struggle through, a struggle that sometimes is exacerbated by their own inability to realize the need for improvement or skill development. Our invitation is to read, reflect, and act in each of these areas.

Chapter 1 lays the foundation for readers who are considering graduate school by posing the important question, "To Grad School or Not to Grad School?" We explain the primary differences between master's and doctoral programs in the humanities and social sciences, and how each degree functions as a different kind of tool for your career. As part of that discussion, we encourage those who are thinking about applying to truly reflect, before committing the effort, time, and money to these programs, on whether research is the tool you need to accomplish the things that you hope to do. We go on to discuss the relationship between theory and practice, dispelling the notion that real work takes place in the community rather than in the classroom while also holding onto a critical approach that reifies advanced degrees as the only way to get ahead. We provide an overview of financing a graduate education, sharing concrete warnings while still providing a non-fear-based orientation to making it work. The decision to pursue a graduate education is different for people who are racialized in the way Latinxs are and who are first in our families to attend college; we attempt to tease out these nuances in the discussion of how to think about the decision to enroll in a graduate program. We end by covering the nuts and bolts of the application process, particularly the importance of crafting a strong statement of purpose that helps first-generation scholars envision their educational narrative in a way that powerfully sets the tone for the work that lies ahead of them.

Chapter 2, "Learning to Be a Grad Student," builds on chapter 1 by providing a framework by which students can develop a graduate student identity. As a first-generation student, you are not a blank slate; you arrived at this point precisely because you honed concrete skills for academic success, in and out of the classroom, that enabled you to earn your bachelor's degree. There are also many things that you likely did not learn as an undergraduate that will be essential to your success as a graduate student. This chapter helps you understand the different expectations faculty have of undergraduate and graduate students so that you can identify new skills that you may need to purposefully cultivate. We also explore the relationship between graduate school and the political and social justice–driven commitments that often motivate us to pursue an advanced academic degree. We discuss impostor syndrome and share strategies for combating the feeling that you are not good enough or out of place in your program. One of the most critical tools to regain your sense of confidence is to identify your mission, the vision you have for yourself, your family, and your community that you would strive for no matter what kind of degree program or career path you found yourself in.

Whereas chapter 2 takes a theoretical or broader view of developing a graduate student identity, chapter 3, "Essential Skills in Graduate School," addresses best practices for undertaking the day-to-day work of an emerging professional writer and researcher. This chapter provides techniques for reading at the graduate level, enabling you to move past the summary-driven work that often happens at the undergraduate level to a deeper level of scholarly engagement that is expected of graduate students. It also explores what it means to write at the graduate level and how to embrace your identity as a scholarly writer. Part of that journey is learning to manage and work around the writing anxieties that not only first-generation Latinx students but in fact all writers must confront. An important part of the writing process is the ability to distinguish between critique from faculty advisors and other interlocutors that may be hard to take yet necessary for strengthening your writing and argumentation versus that which is only meant to tear you down—and, as a flip side, becoming wary of empty praise. At the core of these advanced reading and writing skills is cultivating effective time management and structures of accountability. We share strategies to help students who work part- or full-time while in their degree programs and address the critical difference between being in your courses (meeting deadlines set by others) and working independently on your theses/dissertations (meeting deadlines largely set by you). Finally, we suggest some guidelines for managing your social media use, with an eye toward your overall mental health and well-being, and overall presence, thinking strategically about your professional future.

Now that you understand the essential skills of advancing your research, chapter 4, "Unwritten Rules of the Academy: Navigating the Gray Area," delves more deeply into some of the intricacies of academic life that may be a bit less obvious to the naked eye. This chapter begins by laying out the unwritten rules of the academy, particularly modes of communicating, interacting, and carrying oneself that can feel elusive, confusing, or surprising for first-generation academics. In this way, this chapter acts as a translator of academese. These insights are especially helpful when it comes to attending conferences and developing your professional networks, as we help you understand the purpose of conferences, how to make them work within your finances, and how to maximize your time. We also discuss social media as it relates to how we present ourselves in the world, and in academia.

Chapter 5, "Navigating Professional Relationships in Graduate School," prepares you to think about and manage the professional relationships that are critical to your success in graduate school. For many of us, the interpersonal aspect of navigating higher education can prove to be especially challenging, as the norms and mores of academic culture can differ radically from the cultural and familial values with which we were raised. In this chapter, we share best practices for communicating with faculty advisors. Building on the advice of experts like Kerry Rockquemore, we emphasize the importance of cultivating a network of mentors who, taken as a whole, provide you insights into every aspect of your graduate journey and beyond. At the same time, and given the lack of Latinx representation among university faculty, we share advice regarding the possible need to mentor your mentors, particularly when they have not worked closely with historically underrepresented students. To that end, we encourage you to think about mentorship broadly, considering not just faculty but also your graduate student peers who may also have pointed advice and strategies for success. Cultivating positive connections among the others in your program is critical.

Chapter 6 focuses on a different kind of essential relationship, the intimate and personal relationships with people you love. "Navigating Personal Relationships in Graduate School" focuses on the personal and family connections with people you are dating, long-term partners, extended family, and even your children. A conversation about how we navigate these personal and intimate relationships in the context of graduate school is particularly critical for first-generation scholars and is often skipped over when we talk about graduate education because the de facto assumption is that graduate students are single and unattached. This chapter makes space for those conversations and also strategizes how to navigate the terrain when it feels that family culture and grad school culture come into conflict with one another.

Chapter 7, "Life after Graduate School," explores what happens after you complete your degree. While this may feel very far away, it is important to understand the intricacies of the academic job search both for those who are pursuing work in the academy and for those who are interested in pursuing a career outside of the academy and have questions about how to use their degree, whether it be a master's or a doctoral degree. We emphasize the need to thoughtfully prepare for the next stage of your journey and to identify the concrete skills gained in your graduate program so that you can demonstrate your potential for success in multiple career fields.

While we believe it is important to openly describe the very real challenges Latinx students face as they pursue advanced degrees, we also feel that it is critical that we never lose sight of our collective power to positively transform the academy by undertaking the work that we passionately pursue. Thus, we conclude on a more hopeful note, encouraging you not to feel overwhelmed by the information. Rather, empower yourself with it by approaching the academy with a clear-eyed sense that it is only one of many tools that can enable you to do meaningful, socially responsive work. We emphasize that there is no blueprint, no single way to "do" graduate school that applies uniformly to all Latinxs. Getting into graduate school is not an end in and of itself; we must work toward our degrees always with an eye to charting a path for what comes after and work to find meaning both inside and outside academic institutions. We firmly believe that in doing so we have the power to transform higher education and make it more attuned to the needs of Latinx communities. We can only achieve that end if we accept our collective responsibility to mentor others along the way. Ultimately, there is tremendous power in reflecting not only on what we do as Latinx academics but also on how and why we do it. This book aims to prepare you for academic success and to envision an academy that is of and for Latinx and other marginalized communities.

A Note on Voice and Narration

All of the chapters in this book were collaboratively written by the two authors, resulting in "four hands on the keyboard"—borrowing from Alejandra Marchevsky and Jeanne Theoharis's vision of coauthorship as collaborative practice—working to deepen ideas through dual voices that represent the interdependency that is valued by our community and enables us to thrive academically.[17] However, each chapter was spearheaded by one author, and therefore is written in that author's voice. At the start of each chapter, you will see a note that says, "Though collaboratively written, this chapter was principally drafted by [author name], thus the use of *I* in this chapter refers to her." We chose this approach because we drew heavily on our own experiences as graduate students and faculty members, and we wanted to write in a way that was collaborative but also clear on who was speaking. Chapters 1, 7, and the conclusion were written by both authors, so the use of *I* shifts and is noted in the text accordingly.

Similarly, you will see sidebars throughout the book with little pieces of advice, called "Consejos." These are short pieces of advice from Latinx scholars in the field that we solicited for this book. We asked these scholars, who are experienced in mentoring, teaching, and supporting Latinx graduate students, what advice they would offer to you all. We are excited to include their consejos throughout the text and feel confident that hearing the reflections and advice of this broader group of Latinx scholars will be helpful regardless of where you are in your graduate school journey. In addition, at the end of this book, you will find an appendix of resources for undocumented students, authored by a colleague with a background in that experience. Thus, this is "A Note on Voice and Narration," but it is also a reminder of the collectivist ethos that lies at the heart of this book. None of us would have gotten here without the support of others, and we take that seriously. It is who we are as a community, and it is what we inherit as our responsibility. We hope you read each chapter, and every consejo, with an understanding that there is a whole crew of us Latinx professors who are cheering you on.

One last note on the writing: at times, we intersperse Spanish into the text. Some of us grew up speaking Spanish and some of us did not. Speaking Spanish is not a marker of Latinidad, both because Spanish itself is a colonial language and also because one of the main reasons many of us do not speak Spanish, or do not speak it fluently, is because it is so debased and devalued in our society. This debasing also means that for many of us, speaking Spanish in an English-dominant society is an act of resistance. It is with that spirit that there is Spanish sprinkled throughout the text.

One Final Note: "Se Hace Camino Al Andar"

One last note on our approach, both as writers of this book and as professors and mentors to Latinx graduate students. There is a famous line from a poem by Spanish poet Antonio Machado: "Caminante, no hay camino / se hace camino al andar."[18] This is a road we have made by walking, a path that was forged by the sister scholars who preceded us and that will continue to be (re)made by those who come after us. Like many other societal institutions—housing, health care, finance, the criminal justice system, you name it—universities are steeped in an elitism that was not made for us and is not set up to foster our success as Latinx people; this is not something we will debate. It is also not something that we will belabor; this is the pond we are swimming in, the context we are operating in, and the sector we have chosen to fight from. Operating in this environment requires us to walk a fine line: complaining about how unjust the academy is can trap us in a place in which we feel disempowered and believe that the mountain is unclimbable. At the same time, failing to acknowledge the inherent bias in the institution can make us feel like we are flattened under the weight of it all, which we often are told must be the result of our own shortcomings and deficiencies. We walk a line between these two, acknowledging this undeniable context yet also claiming our power within it. We are honest and clear-eyed. We do not believe that you need to play the white guy's game to get ahead, but we also know that because we work twice as hard to get half as far, exceeding expectations is our only choice.

This book is written with that idea in mind. We face an impossible conundrum: little is expected of us because of who we are and where we come from, but the expectations by which we are measured are increasingly elevated, requiring us to prove our worth over and over again. We are blamed when we stumble on this booby-trapped path. The only way out of that is to have our eyes wide open, to prepare for the path ahead, and to support one another in that journey. What that means in terms of our approach in writing this book is that we endeavor to tell it like it is, to be pragmatic, and not to make excuses. We take this approach not out of some sort of aim to make you all suffer because we have suffered but rather to rewrite the script on what we can expect of our Latinx students. We can be great. We can move mountains. We can write cutting-edge theory, conduct critical empirical studies, and move our disciplines. We can and we will.

1 To Grad School or Not to Grad School?

If you are picking up this book, you may be in the process of exploring a graduate degree, you may have already decided to go to graduate school, or you may be currently enrolled in a graduate program. Whatever stage you are in, this next sentence is for you: approach graduate school with intentionality and purpose. Grad school is not something to stumble into because you have nothing else going on or do not have a clear professional path in mind. Nor is it the universally logical next step after completing your undergraduate degree or what you should do because you assume the more degrees, the better. Now, if we lived in a country in which people could access college education and pursue advanced degrees for free, our advice would be very different. But the decision to enroll in a graduate program is a major financial commitment and, as a result, should not be taken lightly. I am not saying you need to have everything figured out or know the topic of your dissertation before you show up for orientation, but you should approach the decision to enroll in a graduate program with a clear sense of why you are doing this and whether it makes sense for your personal and professional goals.[1]

Genevieve recalls growing up in the 1980s and how, as a first-generation college student, her conception of what college would be like was largely based on the television show *A Different World* (a spinoff of *The Cosby Show*). Not gonna lie—there are similarities, but not as many as she had hoped for. It may be helpful for you to spend some time considering the conceptions you have about what graduate school will be like and teasing apart these fantasies from reality. This is particularly relevant for those of us who have no frame of reference for graduate school because we come from families and communities in which we are the first. It is easy to imagine graduate school as long, wide-open days spent reading books on a grassy knoll on campus, having deep conversations with friends at a coffee shop late into the night, journaling and writing and playing with ideas and getting feedback on these ideas from smart professors who push your thinking forward.

Here's the good news: graduate school can totally be that. Yet it is important to inject less appealing elements into that image as well. You may have to work a part-time or full-time job to pay the bills because graduate school is expensive, and even students who are funded (more on that later) often find that the stipend offered is too little to actually live on. Graduate school can be isolating for students of color; being one of few or being "the only" can feel hard in the abstract but be truly emotionally and intellectually draining when it becomes your daily reality. There is the reading on grassy knolls, but it is accompanied by the stress of trying to get it all done and attempting to figure out how to prioritize what you focus on because there is no way you can read carefully the way you did as an undergrad. There are the deep conversations in coffee shops with friends, but there are also the difficult interpersonal dynamics that make those kinds of relationships complicated at times, when you are up for the same departmental award or graduate student assistant position. There are the meaningful connections with professors, but there are also the interactions with professors who make your path difficult, are not interested or prepared to be good mentors, or are biased against you because of what you look like or how thick your accent is.

Look, we are not trying to sour you on the experience before you even submit your application. We want you to find a way to navigate graduate school that feels whole and empowering and intellectually stimulating to you—that is why we are writing this book. At the same time, if you come into graduate school with an unrealistic expectation of how it will be, you may find yourself disappointed and consider throwing in the towel. We think it is good to know that even in the best circumstances, navigating graduate school will likely be a mixed bag. There are spaces and moments in which you can truly pursue your intellectual and political passions and forge deep and meaningful personal connections with other scholars. Yet this all occurs within the context of an institution that is steeped in legacies of racism, white supremacy, and patriarchy, and so it is important to consider the real implications of what that means on a day-to-day level for a Latinx student forging a path within that environment.

One of the main considerations when approaching a decision about graduate school with intentionality and purpose is what work you really want to do and whether this degree and/or title is necessary to do that. For some, this consideration may be very easy. You want to work as a social worker, therefore you need to get your master's in social work. You want to be a doctor, therefore you need a medical degree. In these situations, it is easy to approach your degree program with intentionality and purpose. You are getting the degree so you can pursue that professional path. But it is possible that the consideration of what you want to do and whether this degree and/or title is necessary can be more complicated than in those examples. Genevieve remembers meeting with a master's student who was talking about her desire to apply to doctoral programs; when asked what she wanted to do professionally long-term, the student replied, "I want to be a leader in my community." But there are so many ways to be a leader in one's community! And let us say clearly that the forward march toward an advanced degree makes sense when you consider the ways that we as a community have been systematically and institutionally locked out of graduate pathways. The desire to go to graduate school and earn an advanced degree is for many an act of resistance. I want to be really clear when I say that: yes, it is an act of resistance and should be celebrated as such. At the same time, resistance comes in many forms, and pursuing a graduate degree simply as an act of resistance and to be a leader in one's community is an unnecessarily limited way to approach this decision.

You may think, "But I don't know what I want to do professionally yet." Here is a suggestion: explore. Make some plans, take some jobs. Figure out what you love, what you are good at. Save money if you can, so that there are more options available to you should you need them in the future. Some folks may tell you that if you do not go to graduate school right out of undergrad, you will never go back. In our experience, this is false. You will go back if you decide to do so; in many fields, having work experience makes you a stronger candidate or may even be required. There is so much to be said for exploring various paths and possibilities. Work experience will often strengthen your candidacy as a prospective graduate student because it demonstrates that your scholarly interests are rooted in real-world experience. Remember that graduate school is not your only option, may not be necessary given your professional path, and is not the only way to resist. Do not just go to graduate school because you are not sure what you want to do after you graduate with your undergraduate degree; this approach does not resolve the problem of what you will do professionally but just delays it. Given the cost of graduate education in this country, it is an expensive delay.

If you find that graduate school is the logical next step for you because you have asked yourself what you want to do and if this degree is necessary for you to be able to do that work and the answer is a resounding yes, then fantastic! Such reflection means that you are approaching the decision to pursue graduate school with intention and purpose. On the other side of things, you may feel the pull to work instead of going back to school to pursue another degree. This pragmatism is a common experience among first-generation and working-class students. You will need to figure out if graduate school is something you can pull off financially (more on that later in the chapter), but keep in mind that it is important to approach these considerations with a balance of aspiration and reality. You need to pay the bills, but you also deserve to pursue your dreams. We hope there is a way to do both, and for many it involves creative solutions like working and saving up, working while in school, or side hustling. Be thoughtful and intentional, and don't abandon your pursuits simply because work pays and school costs.

Something that can creep into Latinx students' decisions about whether to pursue a graduate degree is the issue of where the real work is done. Anti-intellectualism sometimes runs through community-oriented spaces—the notion that the real work is done in the community because the ivory tower is always bullshit and will never be anything but bullshit that encroaches on and exploits the work that happens at the grassroots community level. This idea is unhelpful. It simultaneously disregards the reality that the university has played an important role in activism and the development of social movements around the world throughout history, and it also renders invisible the important work that some folks in the academy are engaged in through partnership with people on the ground. It acts as if there is nothing of value we can learn in and through university spaces, which is particularly debasing the place of Ethnic Studies and its affiliate fields (African American and Black Studies, Chicana/o/x Studies, Puerto Rican Studies, Central American Studies, Native American Studies, Asian American Studies, etc.). It also reifies the dichotomy between the community and the academy even as many people breach that line daily.

And yet . . . this sort of anti-intellectual sentiment makes sense. The academy has a long and well-documented tradition of unethical, problematic, and elitist behavior against low-income communities, communities of color, and other marginalized and oppressed communities. This legacy is often coupled with an implicit or explicit hierarchy—the idea that those in the academy or with fancy titles know more and know better and are the ones who are doing the work with real value that others should accommodate. The perpetuation of these actions and ideologies often lies at the root of that sort of anti-intellectualism; it is a response to this kind of practice and ideology and is a thinly veiled representation of distrust of and disdain for the elitism of the ivory tower.

Here is where we stand on this topic and where we hope you land as well: on the question of where the real work happens and whether it is more important if the work happens on the ground in the community or in the ivory towers of the academy, we say, "Ya basta." Important work happens in both places because the challenges ahead of us are broad and large, requiring multiple points of engagement. Why are we talking about this here? Because if there is any part of you that is considering graduate school out of an elitist belief that the university is the only place where you can make an impact or engage in meaningful work, check yourself. There are real, and compelling, reasons to pursue a graduate degree. But institutional prestige is not one of them. And if the idea of doing the work to bridge this constructed divide between the academy and the community speaks to you, embrace it! This is a worthy endeavor, one that is at the center of many (most?) worthy scholarly pursuits.

Two Reality Checks If You Are Considering a PhD:
Finances and the Academic Job Market

If you are considering enrolling in a PhD program, get your pen and start taking notes because this discussion is especially for you. It is important for us to speak honestly and explicitly about two things that are often overlooked in conversations about doctoral programs: finances and the academic job market. These are often overlooked because white middle-class culture dominates the academy, and for white and middle-class people, these considerations are different than they are for Latinx/a/o first-generation students. While we address finances again later in this chapter, this section addresses how to think about the question of finances in the context of the academic job market, and so it is most relevant to those of you who are considering doctoral degrees.

The academic job market is unique—a topic we revisit in chapter 7, but we raise it here because it relates to the professional aspirations leading you to pursue a doctoral degree. As explained above, one sound reason to pursue a graduate degree is because your professional aspirations require it. There is a bit of an asterisk on that point if your professional aspiration is to be a university professor, because it is very difficult to get a job as a university professor (taken up in more detail in chapter 7). The reason for this is worthy of more space than we can devote here but rests largely on these two realities:

1 Universities are increasingly relying on **adjunct** (temporary) instructors rather than hiring full-time, tenure-track professors.[2] This reliance is a result of adjunct faculty being more appealing hires because they are paid less, often are not given benefits, and can be fired at any time. This is a hallmark of the **neoliberal university**.

2 Though the number of full-time, tenure-track positions continues to shrink, doctoral programs continue to admit large numbers of students. This results in a glut in the market: there are far more people with PhDs than there are full-time, tenure-track professor job openings.

The intersection of these dynamics means that, unlike many other career paths that require professional accreditation, licensure, or specialized degrees, being a professor is a professional path that is very difficult to access even when you have the appropriate and required degree. Thus, pursuing a doctoral degree is the equivalent of going to dental school without assurance that you will ever be able to work as a dentist.

Is this trend unique to the academic professions? No. There are many sectors of employment that are difficult to break into; for example, consider all those who want to go into acting but do not get cast or those who aspire to be professional athletes but never break through to that level of play. While the academy is not unique in this situation, it definitely stands out (the previous examples are rare—how many people truly aspire to be professional athletes?) and is, moreover, a costly investment. And while we will not talk deeply about the neoliberalization of higher education here, it is a worthwhile area of study to understand the institution you seek to enter. You may be wondering why institutions continue to admit so many doctoral students, even though there are fewer and fewer jobs as professors. The answer is multifaceted, but without a doubt, a meaningful part of the answer is that they can make money by doing so, and higher education is a business.

The financial element of this conversation comes in at this point. The broad picture is that graduate school is expensive, and if your career goal is to be a professor, you will likely pay a lot of money for your degree but not actually be able to find fairly compensated work as a professor, if you get a tenure-track job at all. Reread that if you need to, and sit with that reality as long as necessary before we move on to make sure that you really let it sink in. The odds are stacked against you.

Now, there are two ways that we can take this information, which are principally inscribed with racial and class dynamics. The first approach is shaped by people who say that you absolutely should not get a PhD and anybody who tells you otherwise is selling you a bag of lies and is intentionally out to deceive you and set you up for disappointment. They cite the reality that there is a shrinking number of positions for professors and a glut of PhDs on the market competing for those positions. Those who are in this camp say you should never, ever go to graduate school to get a doctoral degree unless you are fully funded to do so and will not have to pay out of pocket for your degree.

Fair enough. They make a good point, and you can see from the previous conversation how we can take that at face value and say that it is good advice to follow. But remember, you are reading *The Latinx Guide to Graduate School*, and this conversation is a little bit different for us. Genevieve came across a blog post a few years ago that, despite all our efforts and recruiting friends to help us, we have not been able to find again. It was by a young woman of color who wrote about this dynamic and then talked about her own negotiation of it. We wish we could locate it again so we could quote her and give her credit, but essentially this is what it comes down to: she says that people like us don't do anything because we have a guarantee that we will get a job as a result of it; we know deep in our bones that nothing is guaranteed to us. People of color do not get jobs that we deserve all the damn time because of racism, xenophobia, our accents, the way we wear our hair. She contends that the dominance of the "Don't go to grad school because you will never get a job, which means it's a sham!" chorus is rooted in an entitled white identity: essentially people who cannot believe they do not get the jobs for which they are qualified. She argues that people like us pursue dreams with no guarantees all the time because it is the only way we operate; the reality of what white supremacy robs from us all the time means that we do not have an entitled sense of what we are owed. I may be riffing on her argument and adding a bit of my own here; I can't quite remember (I read it years ago just once and could not find it again as we prepared this book manuscript—why oh why did I not bookmark it at least?!). But the point here comes down to the following:

- We do not know what we are going to get and we take risks all the time.
- There is definitely no guarantee of getting a professor position upon graduation, and anybody who enrolls in a doctoral program should be very aware of that.
- There are more reasons to pursue a doctoral degree than simply your job prospects. Accessing education is liberating—we know this! Education can be personally, politically, and intellectually transformative. There is so much that is so beneficial about learning that goes beyond what job you are being prepared for. So, if you can access that sort of education in a realistic and nondamaging way for your financial situation, perhaps the pursuit of a doctoral degree is not a terrible idea.
- The most important point is that you should have your eyes wide open. The terrible state of the academic job market is not something you should learn about three years into your program. You need to make the decision that makes the most sense for you, and that decision is likely shaped by who you are, where you come from, and where you are going.

Identifying the Right Program(s) for You

Okay, so let's circle back to the emphasis on intentionality and purpose. One of the most important things to do when embarking on the journey to grad school is to understand the many different types of degrees out there. When you are the first in your family to pursue an advanced degree, it is not always so clear. The key question is to ask yourself, "What do I want to do?" Starting from this vantage point is critical because, ultimately, a graduate degree is not an end in and of itself. You have a master's or doctoral degree . . . so what? Rather, a graduate degree is a tool that enables you to go on to do something else. That is, it prepares you for a longer-term career. So please spend some time answering the "¿por qué?" that your family is likely to ask you over and over again when they find out you are "still" in school. There are many different directions this can go, and the answer is unique to you. Here are some examples:

- I want to advocate for children who have been separated from their families at the border.
- I want to develop a strong knowledge base and specialized network to create programming at my local community health center.
- I want to be a college academic advisor to students of color.

There are so many degrees to explore—many of these you may have heard of from the letters you see after someone's name. Let's start with different kinds of master's degrees:

- Master of arts (MA): specialized knowledge in a wide range of humanities, educational, and social science fields.
- Master of science (MS): fields in science, technology, and engineering.
- Master of fine arts (MFA): advanced training in the fine arts, such as creative writing, fine arts (painting, sculpture, photography), music, dance, and theatrical performance.
- Master of business administration (MBA): technical training for people in business or management fields.
- Master of public administration (MPA) or public health (MPH): preparation to become a community, nonprofit, or government leader or to shape public health policies in your community.

Across this range, master's degrees are typically two-year programs that consist of a series of courses that prepare you to write a master's thesis, an independent research project (or creative work, if you're in an MFA program) that demonstrates your mastery (get it?) of a particular subject.

And then, to add even more options (or confusion), there are the doctoral degrees:

- Juris doctor (JD): training for folks who are interested in pursuing legal careers.
- Doctor of medicine (MD): what your family probably considers real doctors, the ones who treat physical ailments.
- Doctor of education (EdD): a doctoral degree specific to the field of education that is generally more practitioner oriented than a PhD in education, though it culminates in a doctoral dissertation.
- Doctor of philosophy (PhD): an advanced research degree that is available in a wide variety of fields (humanities, education, social sciences, STEM, and beyond) and is generally meant to prepare you for a university-level research and teaching career or to be a thought leader in a given area of specialization.

Doctoral degrees often command the most respect because they tend to be intensive programs—for example, a JD is the shortest, at three years, while an MD is often four years of study plus several more years of specialized, hands-on training. The length of time to complete an EdD depends on the institution but can be anywhere from three to five years. Depending on the program and your funding situation, a PhD could take anywhere from four years to . . . well, let's just say many more. The average in humanities and social science fields tends to be about seven years—but I (Magdalena) once dated un sabelotodo who started his PhD program when I was a college freshman; by the time he finished, I was already a tenured professor (picture me taking a long sip of tea with a raised eyebrow). To be fair, the guy was very intelligent, which just goes to show that all kinds of unexpected life circumstances (financial, familial, physical, emotional) can impact time to complete your degree. Ultimately, your degree is your degree, something to be proud of no matter how long it takes to get conferred. So, all this is to say that the time it takes to complete a PhD can really vary and is often impacted by financial constraints.

If you're going to make a commitment to spend two or more years of your life pursuing an advanced degree, make sure you know what you are getting into and that your degree program is a match for your long-term interests. With so many choices, how are those of us who are first generation supposed to figure this out? One way is to conduct informational interviews with a variety of faculty, mentors, and folks who currently occupy the kinds of positions to which you aspire. If you're not familiar with it, an informational interview is a meeting where you ask working professionals focused questions about their work and their career journey. An internet search for "informational interviews" will provide you with lots of advice on how to reach out to potential interviewees and sample questions to ask. These discussions can generate powerful insights that will help you understand the different ways the people whom you admire reached their current positions—often with surprising detours along the way.

"When's the Right Time?" and Other Common Questions

Three questions frequently emerge when you are considering graduate school. And—spoiler alert—the answer to each is the same: it depends!

When Is the Right Time to Apply?

There is no one answer here. Some people feel primed to head to graduate school directly after completing their bachelor's degree, without any break; these are the students who apply to grad school in the fall of their last year of college. Some undergraduates find their way into programs such as McNair Scholars or Mellon Mays Undergraduate Fellowship, research programs that seek to increase diversity in higher ed by providing students with the support and mentorship to pursue their own independent research project. Oftentimes, to signal their success rate, these programs strongly encourage students to follow this direct path from undergrad to grad school without a break. Other people choose to wait a year or two before applying; meanwhile, some take several years, or even decades, before the timing feels right or they home in on the questions and issues that inspire them to seek an advanced degree. Wherever you fall on this spectrum, here are some issues to consider:

- Going directly after earning your bachelor's

  PROS: You will obviously be in school mode, and so starting a graduate program next fall will not feel like an enormous shift in your routine. Likewise, if you are used to living on a limited student budget, your lifestyle will not feel dramatically different in grad school.

  CONS: Burnout may become an issue. Anecdotally, many of my peers who did not take time off before grad school ended up doing so at some point during their program; some paused temporarily, but others stopped entirely, either switching to different programs (for example, leaving a PhD program in cultural anthropology to pursue a law degree) or leaving grad school altogether. Sometimes they hadn't taken the time to really make sure this was the right long-term commitment. Additionally, as mentioned previously, some disciplines prefer that you bring some professional experience before jumping in, so a lack of experience could be a barrier in terms of admission.

- Waiting one or more years to apply

  PROS: You get a break from school and can use the time to reflect on your interests and motivations to continue and to allow more time to research your many options. You may also be able to work in a job that enables you to tuck away some savings that will help you in grad school. Also, you bring more life experience, which adds to the perspective you contribute to your program and class discussions.

CONS: The longer you wait, the bigger the adjustment becomes to return to a student lifestyle. This transition may be a particular concern if you are in a job that enables you to live comfortably or support family members; leaving a solid income stream to live on a grad student stipend—if your program even pays one (more on that below)—can be a real challenge.

I (Magdalena) took a year off between college and grad school—primarily to have an actual break from being in school nonstop since kindergarten. My mom was concerned that I was going to abandon my doctoral aspirations to instead marry the sabelotodo I had been dating for several years. I'm glad I had the short break because it was just long enough to help me miss the intellectual interactions of being in class, give me time to retake the Graduate Record Exam (GRE; I'll get back to this story in a bit), and prepare stronger applications for grad school.

Do I Need to Earn a Master's before Applying to a PhD Program?

The answer really depends on your particular experience and the programs that interest you. Technically, you do not need an MA to enroll in a PhD program. In my doctoral program, for example, successfully submitting a qualifying paper (a substantial, independent research paper written in the second year) qualified students to continue in the program and opened the door for them to request a formal master's degree. I actually never got around to doing this, so my CV lists my bachelor's and then jumps to my PhD. You may want to consider an MA program, however, if you are making a major switch in disciplines (say, you were a business major but are now interested in sociology) and want to get the foundational training in that new field. Or if you know that your academic skills need further strengthening, then a master's program can be a great way to dip your toes in the waters of grad school and make sure that you are making the right investment of your time and energy. Additionally, some programs may require you to have an MA before applying to a doctoral program.

Do I Need to Move for Grad School?

Like the other questions, the answer depends on your specific family and financial circumstances. You may be a caretaker or critical financial contributor to your household, and moving away may not be a tenable option. Perhaps you are settled in your career path and are interested in attending an evening master's program to advance to the next level professionally, so, again, moving may not be feasible. Maybe you live in an area with multiple universities within commuting distance, so you have some options for the degree programs that interest you. All of these are absolutely legitimate reasons not to move. That's not to say that there are no significant adjustments you'd have to make to enroll in programs close to home; you still have to help your family and friends understand this new phase of your education. We return to that topic in chapter 6.

If you are able to move away, you may find a greater number of opportunities to pursue specialized training. Look at it this way: say you want to conduct research on voter participation within BIPOC communities. You may live near schools that offer both MA and PhD degrees in political science, but they may not have any faculty who specialize in that area. If you have your heart set on becoming an expert on this topic, then you may want to consider more distant programs.

I often meet with students who are nervous about moving away from home because they worry about the risk of regretting the decision for any number of reasons. I get that. It takes real guts and preparation to make a long-distance move, at any stage of life. But remember that for every negative "what if?" there is a positive one: What if you move from the West Coast to the East Coast and totally fall in love with your new city? What if you make incredible community connections in your new location? What if you have the best of both worlds: pursue a degree far from home and then return for a great job near your family? This is not to discount the very real reasons you are hesitant to pick up and move, and you should consider those seriously. Maybe you are queer and unsure about moving to a very conservative small town. Maybe you are undocumented, and boarding a plane raises security concerns for you. In short, be honest with yourself about what is possible given your circumstances, but also don't limit yourself unnecessarily.

Looking back on my journey, moving from Chicago to the Bay Area, where I did not have immediate family, at the age of twenty-three was a critical experience, especially as a young Latina trying to find my way in the world. It gave me the confidence to know that I could establish myself in a new place, make friends, and feel at home somewhere so different from where I grew up. This lesson served me well years later, when I was a thirty-five-year-old assistant professor making the difficult choice to end my first marriage. I had the opportunity to move to Austin, Texas, for a year to pursue my research—and I had the courage to launch a new chapter of my life in a different place, precisely because I knew from experience that I would make connections, build community, and handle life on my own.

Do Your Research before Signing Up for a Professional Research Degree

Let's say that you've done your homework and conducted at least three informational interviews and have confirmed that an MA or doctoral degree is the right choice for you. This decision means that you are aware of the massive shift required to go from being a good student (someone who earned a bachelor's) to becoming a professional scholar (a recipient of a master's or doctoral degree) who produces new knowledge and makes an active contribution to intellectual debate. Okay, great! Now you are ready for the next step, which is to start researching specific programs. Meet with a faculty mentor (You do have faculty mentors, right? If not, you need to get some, and we'll explain why later) and ask the following kinds of questions: What programs have faculty who work in my areas of interest? What programs produce cutting-edge work in the areas that interest me? What programs have a good reputation for supporting students? You can also look up the authors whose work you admire and find out where they got their training.

To enter this discussion, be sure to understand the difference between a discipline and a field. A discipline is a broad branch of knowledge taught at an institution—for example, English, history, or education. Within every discipline are fields or subspecialties—so, to use the previous examples, these could include things like contemporary Latinx literature or Puerto Rican history. Just because a university offers a discipline you are interested in does not mean it will be the place where you can develop your interests in a specific field. You will need to carefully think through the kinds of topics and issues that you want to spend years exploring, because these will shape your career prospects.

Once you have homed in on the area(s) that interest you, the next step is to start looking into different programs. Look up each program online: What does the university program say about itself and its priorities (mission statements, for example)? Does it offer courses in the kinds of topics that interest you? Who are the faculty in the program and what do they currently work on? How accessible and organized is this information online? (That can also tell you something about how on top of things—or not— certain programs are.) Does the program have social media accounts and, if so, how does it portray itself there? What events, announcements, and community highlights does it share? If possible, visit the campus in person; you may even be able to sit in on a class to get a feel for the kinds of work you would be doing.

Aside from first impressions, check to see if the program offers any of the following general information in the form of online FAQs (frequently asked questions):

- What is the admissions process? What size, on average, is the incoming cohort?
- Is any funding offered? If so, do students get the same package? If not, how do students typically pay for the program?
- Is there funding for professional development? Are students in the program eligible to apply for funds to attend conferences or other cv-building activities?
- What is the average length of time students stay in the program? What do students go on to do or what kind of academic placements do they get?
- Does the program or university offer any formal mentoring (faculty-student or student-student)?
- What kind of scholarly community (research and writing groups, for example) does the program offer?
- Does the campus offer support services (such as programs at the writing center) for graduate students?
- Do students tend to live on or off campus? What is it like to live in the area?

CONSEJO #1   If you are thinking about graduate school, find out what opportunities your college provides for undergraduate research. I went to UC Davis, which had a program meant to encourage students from underrepresented backgrounds to learn more about what research entails and possibly pursue an academic career in research and teaching. I was matched with a faculty mentor who guided my research and was a great support throughout the graduate application process. I subsequently learned about the Summer Research Opportunity Program (SROP), which allowed me to spend a summer working with a faculty mentor at the University of Chicago. It was a phenomenal experience—not only did I have a good relationship with my mentor, I was part of a cohort of dynamic students of color from all over the country, many of whom became good friends and part of my support network. These programs prepared me for research and enabled me to get to know two faculty members very well, and they both wrote letters for me. If such programs aren't available to you, look into doing an independent study or becoming a research assistant with a professor in your field of interest.

Yolanda Padilla, School of Interdisciplinary Arts & Sciences, University of Washington, Bothell

---

As a Latinx student, you also may want to consider more specific aspects of campus life that will shape your experience:

- Is this campus a Hispanic-Serving Institution? What are the current racial demographics of faculty and students, both in the program you are considering and at the university overall?
- Is there a Latinx/a/o student center on campus? Are there Latinx/a/o student organizations?
- Is there an undocumented support center, task force, or even coordinator at this campus?

This sort of information is sometimes available on a public-facing institutional research site (a campus office tasked with collecting critical data) or can be requested from the admissions office. As with the first-impression info above, you also may want to check out the social media content of Latinx-focused centers and student organizations on campus to gain a sense of how the Latinx campus community is faring or to locate a current Latinx/a/o student to learn more about the racial climate on campus.

If you are having difficulty locating online answers to the many questions above, you can reach out to the program's **graduate advisor** and current students to ask those questions. You may find that you get slightly different information from different sources: the official university line on a website is probably going to be different than the real talk among current students. In fact, many programs appoint one or more current students to serve as representatives who are prepared to field questions from potential applicants, so do take advantage of the insights they can share. Websites and glossy brochures may portray a certain image, but no one will give you the real-deal info like current students. You can ask the department to connect you with a student or contact students via social media or personal/professional contacts. Don't skip this important part of the process—students can give you an honest sense of the disconnect (if there is one) between how the program presents itself and what it is like to be a part of it.

In addition to talking with the program's graduate advisor, you can reach out to faculty with whom you are interested in working. There are many things to consider about the professors in the program whose work interests you, starting with where they are in their career. One important clue about their career stage is their title. **Assistant professors**, referred to as junior faculty, are professors who do not yet have **tenure** and are early in their academic careers. By contrast, **associate professors**, or midcareer faculty, do have tenure and are typically better established in their fields than assistants. Meanwhile, **full professors**, or senior faculty, have been promoted to the highest rank of the profession and may have leadership roles, such as **department chair**.

These distinctions matter because they impact how you might work with them. Say you enroll in a program to work with a particular assistant professor who goes on research leave or departs to work at another institution. Is there another faculty member in the program who can guide you? Or say you dream of working with a renowned superstar professor—their name would look great on a letter of recommendation, but they might not have the time and attention to advise you meaningfully. Or maybe they are an associate who will be on **sabbatical** or who has just taken on a new leadership role on campus to get promoted to professor, so they are not accepting new advisees at this time. For these and many other reasons, you will likely have to work closely with multiple faculty over the course of your time in the program; don't expect one single professor to meet all of your needs and interests.

To gain a sense of where potential faculty mentors are, reach out to them via email. We provide a template for doing so at the end of this chapter. Reaching out can feel scary, but it is an important exercise because—remember—you need this critical information when you are committing years and money to your educational ambitions. When you reach out to prospective faculty mentors, you will learn more about their current research interests, whether they are taking on new students, what they think makes for a successful applicant to the program, and what they view as the strengths of the degree program. Better to know all this going in than to enroll in a program and discover it is not at all what you expected it to be. Keep in mind that you may send that email inquiry and not hear back for any number of reasons, none of which have anything to do with you. The faculty member may be too busy to respond at the moment, or your message might have gone to their spam folder. Do not let a lack of response crush your dreams. Reaching out is an important part of the learning process.

The Finances of Grad School

The next part of your research is figuring out how much this degree will cost. And here you will see our recurring theme in this chapter: it all depends—in this case on the type of program and institution. The matrix in table 1.1 provides an overview of the typical costs and funding packages.

There are a few things to note here. First, on the public institution side, there are differences between in-state and out-of-state tuition; the rates are lower for in-state students because they have established residency (i.e., at least one year of living) within their state. Second, on the private side, this only includes **nonprofit institutions**, because you should under no circumstance attend a **for-profit institution**.[3] There are other differences that come with attending a private institution versus a public institution—be sure to explore this and ensure the program you find is the right fit for you. Finally, you may notice in table 1.1 that the master's degrees do not have information on funding packages—and that is because it is very rare to find an MA program that offers full funding in the way that many doctoral programs do.

The bottom line: graduate school is expensive. Not only is it an investment in your long-term career, but it's a choice that you will live with for a long time because getting specialized research training in humanities and social science fields is not something we do because we plan on making bank. You will likely be taking out loans to make this happen—even when you are on full funding. For example, here was my experience: I applied to

TABLE 1.1 Typical yearly cost of graduate tuition and fees

	TYPE OF INSTITUTION	
TYPE OF PROGRAM	Public	Private
MASTER'S PROGRAMS	Average: $11,000/year	Average: $26,000/year
DOCTORAL PROGRAMS	Average: $11,000/year TYPICAL FUNDING PACKAGE: Two years of teaching assistantship Competitive fellowship opportunities Funding is often department-based, so different disciplines may offer very different levels of support. Also, funding within the cohort may differ (some may receive better packages than others).	Average: $44,000/year TYPICAL FUNDING PACKAGE: Depends on the program and institution. Support at an elite institution is likely to be generous (e.g., five years of funding plus a summer). Support at a small private school is likely to be slimmer. Funding is often the same within the cohort.

four doctoral programs and was accepted into two—one public and one private institution. The private one offered me five full years of funding, meaning a tuition and fee waiver plus a $20,000 stipend to live on. The public school offered two years of fellowship . . . and that was it. I immediately felt at home with my would-be fellow grad students at the public school and loved the city it was in and the general atmosphere of campus. I received advice to ask the public school if they could match the funding of the private; they tried but ultimately could not do it. So I made my decision about where to go to grad school based primarily on the funding— which worked out for me, fortunately, because I got connected to a great academic community and a big-name school. But I had no idea how to assess those benefits at the time. In any case, the private institution was in a notoriously expensive area of the country and the living stipend was only $20,000, so I had to take out additional student loans to make ends meet. And I paid those loans for the next ten years, making minimum payments at first and then increasing as my salary allowed. All this is to say: even when you have a best-case funding scenario, grad school still costs, likely long after you complete the degree.

Another important point on the theme of "graduate school is expensive" is this (and buckle up, because this may feel a bit harsh): graduate school requires a great deal of time and money. If you are not at a place in your life in which you can be serious and make graduate school a priority, you should seriously reflect on whether this is the right time to apply. You can maybe get away with not reading or faking your way through class discussions as an undergraduate, but this is not the case in graduate school.

So how do grad students make this work? Here are the variety of means:

- Tuition remission: some institutions waive tuition and fees for graduate students. As noted above, this is done primarily for doctoral students as part of a broader funding package.
- Fellowships and grants: yearly competitive funding opportunities that may be internal (institution-specific) or external (foundations or agencies that seek to support scholars who are underrepresented in their fields).
- Teaching assistantships: assisting faculty with teaching a course, grading student work, and/or leading discussion sections of a course for a given term.
- Research assistantships: supporting faculty research during the term.
- Unsubsidized student loans: federal loans that are not based on financial need; usually your institution determines the amount you can borrow.
- Paid jobs: working on or off campus for an hourly wage.
- Credit cards: avoid this method at all costs, as it can lead to negative long-term implications for your overall finances.

You may look at this list and think, "Cool, I'll get a job to help pay for grad school." We want you to be aware of the realities of working while taking coursework and doing independent research. Having an on-campus job can be a great way to build connections at your institution—especially if you work at a library, research institute, or cultural center—and can help you transition quickly between class and work. However, know that the institution may set limits on how many hours you can work; on many campuses, for example, there is a cap at twenty hours per week. Working off campus at a job that is not connected to your schoolwork has pros and cons. On the positive side, an off-campus job can provide a nice break from and outside perspective on the petty dramas of campus. On the downside, however, your off-campus managers may be less understanding or supportive of your academic schedule, and you may feel less inclined to focus on school-work if your off-campus job is particularly demanding or requires a major mental shift after work.

A special note to our undocumented readers: You already know that you are deserving of far more resources than you are eligible to apply for as a result of xenophobic, racist laws and policies. Because finances related to undocumented students vary so widely by institution type, geographic area, and field, there is little we can say that is universally true about what it means to navigate the finances of graduate education as an undocumented student. What we will say is that you should navigate this as you see fit in terms of disclosing your status, but there are some programs and institutions that are trying to do right by undocumented students. The one universal truth is that the best resource on this question will be other undocumented graduate students. Tap into networks online and in your area and ask questions about what institutions in which locations are doing a good job funding and supporting undocumented graduate students. (In fact, while we have your attention, please check out "UndocuGrads: Undocumented and Applying to Grad School (FAQs)," the appendix to this book written specifically for undocumented Latinx students navigating graduate school. The contributor, Professor Carolina Valdivia of UC Irvine, has worked in this area for many years and is an incredible resource on this question.) And for those of you who are reading this and who are not undocumented, make sure you are using whatever foothold you have in the institution to stand in solidarity with your undocumented colleagues.

Putting Together Your Application

Okay, you have done your homework and have found one or more programs that are a good fit for your interests. Now it is time to apply. Plan ahead so you have enough time to pull together the different application components and solicit feedback from trusted mentors before you submit. You do not want to be doing this at the last minute. Your writing sample and statement of purpose are particularly important and must put forward your best self and represent your best work. Applications to most graduate programs include the following components:

- University application form and application fee: this form collects standard information about you so that an application profile is created in the university's system. Fees can range from $55 for a master's program at a public university to $120 for a doctoral program at a private institution. However, many schools offer fee waivers, so look up that information online or ask the graduate admissions office directly. Note: you may find that fee waivers are (ridiculously) only open to citizen students. If that is the case, and you feel comfortable doing so, reach out to someone in the office or a faculty member who is a potential ally, explain your situation, and ask if an accommodation can be made.
- GRE score: the Graduate Record Examination is like the SAT for graduate school; just under four hours long, it tests your verbal, math, and analytical skills. Programs that receive a high number of applications sometimes use GRE scores to weed out applications. Most master's programs do not require the GRE, but many doctoral programs do. The cost is about $200, though there is a GRE Fee Reduction Program for those who can demonstrate financial need. (Various logistics involved in taking the GRE can present barriers for students for whom having a government-issued ID is a problem—perhaps because they are undocumented or transgender. Make sure you carefully review the ID requirements of the testing center before the morning of the exam.)[4]
- Academic transcripts: official copies of your academic record sent directly by the school(s) you attended to the institution(s) to which you are applying. You should request transcripts from all of your undergraduate institutions—so if you transferred from community college, don't forget to request the transcript from that school as well. Many schools charge a small fee ($10–$20) for official transcripts, as well as additional fees for rush processing, so make sure to request these well in advance of your application deadlines.
- Statement of purpose: a three- to four-page (double-spaced) essay in which you explain your interest in the program and outline your preparation for grad school. We have much more to say on this below.
- Writing sample: A fifteen- to twenty-page (double-spaced) sample of your best academic writing—again, more on this shortly.
- Letters of recommendation: three confidential letters of recommendation from faculty who are familiar with your work.

Let's pause here for a moment: as you can see, applying to one doctoral program can cost upward of $350. This is not meant to dissuade you from applying—and there is so much to say about the signals these fees send about the kinds of folks who typically can afford to apply to graduate school in the first place and the testing systems that prey upon hopeful applicants—but rather to make you aware of this so that you are not surprised by the cost.

From that above list, there are two key opportunities to share your vision of who you are: the statement of purpose and the writing sample. We'll walk you through those now.

Statement of Purpose

In this brief essay, your aim is to tell the members of the admissions committee (typically, four or five professors who teach in the graduate program) who you are; what your scholarly interests are and why; your academic background and preparation for advanced work; and why you are a good match for their program. This statement is probably the most critical piece of your overall application—and that is good news, because along with the writing sample, it is absolutely under your control. To craft a strong statement, you will need to draw on the soul-searching you engaged in when deciding whether to apply to grad school. Revisit questions such as:

- Why do I want this degree? What courses, faculty, or experiences inspired me to be on this path?
- What courses, faculty, or program features interest me the most?
- Where do I want this degree to take me professionally?
- How will my unique personal and academic experience add value to the program?

This final question asks you to take stock of what you bring—while you don't want to overstate or exaggerate your strengths, this is not the time to be humble! You are needed in higher ed, and you are entitled to pursue an advanced education. The programs you are considering would be lucky to have you; your prospective peers and faculty will learn from you as much as you learn from them. Enter the writing of this statement with a strong sense of self. If this is hard to do, ask people who know you well—whether faculty mentors, friends, or family—to describe how they see you and your accomplishments.

There are four basic sections (let's be clear: not four paragraphs, but four multiparagraph *sections*) to this document. Dr. Anthony Ocampo, a sociologist at Cal Poly Pomona, outlines them in a helpful way: (1) introduction, where you share an interesting factoid or anecdote, followed by a clear statement of your general interest and long-term goals; (2) your previous academic and research experience, or how you have been preparing for this degree; (3) a description of the specific topic(s) you want to study, and why (i.e., the field within the discipline); and (4) why this particular program is a good fit for your interests—for example, particular professors with whom you want to study or a special focus or initiative within the program.[5] Some applications will want you to address specific questions in the statement of purpose, so pay special attention if this is the case. You must answer all parts of the prompt.

Once you have written a draft, reach out to faculty mentors for feedback on the content of your statement, and identify someone (a friend who is a strong writer or someone at the writing center on your campus) to help you proofread it extra carefully—because, like a résumé, your statement of purpose should be flawless. Allow time for the editing process: develop your draft, let it rest a day, then revisit it with fresh eyes, and allow your faculty/editors time to provide their feedback and time for yourself to digest their suggestions.

If there are weaknesses in your record—say, a semester when your GPA took a dive because you were dealing with a family emergency—you can address it briefly in one or two straightforward, unapologetic sentences, then turn to focus on the lessons learned and/or how you bounced back from the experience. If you took time off after college, then highlight how your work and life experience will enhance what you bring to the program. Let your uniqueness and personality shine through this document.

Writing Sample

Your writing sample should be a fifteen- to twenty-page (double-spaced) academic paper. It's best if your sample is (a) a research-based essay and (b) on a topic similar to the one that you want to pursue in your graduate education. If you were lucky enough to be in a research program like McNair Scholars or Mellon Mays Undergraduate Fellowship, then you should already have an independent research paper to use as your writing sample. If your best example is longer than twenty pages, either edit it down or add a note to the first page indicating which pages the committee should read. If you do not have an academic paper that is long enough or on a topic you will pursue in grad school, then look back through previous assignments and choose a paper that you received high marks on. You may have to expand on it and further polish it for it to serve as a writing sample.

Whatever you use as the basis for the sample, include a cover page that identifies it as your writing sample. I have seen writing samples where applicants have scanned a class assignment, including the instructor's marginalia ("good job!") and final grade/feedback at the end of the paper—perhaps hoping that another professor's positive commentary will boost how an admissions committee views the samples. Unfortunately, this approach comes across as sloppy. If you are using a past assignment, remove the typical info that goes in the corner (date, professor's name, class number, etc.) and replace it with a cover page that looks more professional. This is important because you want to show the committee that you submit work that is polished and have tailored your materials for consideration to their program. In this way, you can send a strong signal of the high quality of work that you will do as a graduate student.

Requesting Strong Letters of Recommendation

Throughout this chapter, you have seen references to faculty mentors. Here is the reality: it is best to lay the groundwork for cultivating faculty mentors and references while you are an undergraduate. If you are still working on your bachelor's, then below are some ways to build these critical connections if you haven't already done so. And if you have been out of the undergraduate level for a while and/or never had faculty mentors or lost touch with them, no need to panic. It may take a bit of work, but you can (and should) rebuild such connections.

If you are still in school, get to know your professors by putting your best efforts into class and attending office hours to discuss course topics and your career interests. As professors, we can assure you that faculty often do not remember who earned an A in their class but rather who put in their best effort to engage with course topics and materials. It may be hard to believe, but faculty are just people: some may be easier to connect with than others (and let's face it, some are total jerks), but don't let one or two bad professors put you off from connecting with the rest. Allow them to get to know you and your interests. As you build relationships with professors, it is helpful to mention that you have graduate school aspirations and that you hope to ask them for a letter in the future. (Here is your opportunity to ask these potential recommenders if they have any advice as you explore graduate programs.) After you graduate, try to stay in touch with them through office visits (if you still live near campus) or emails every six months or so, letting them know what you have been up to, what you have been reading, a news article that reminded you of their class, asking how they are, and so on. If you have been out of school for a while, there is no time like the present to do this kind of outreach. You can send an email reintroducing yourself, reminding them which course(s) you took with them and when, and describing your interests in pursuing a graduate degree.

Laying this groundwork is so critical because it will make it easier to identify faculty recommenders whom you can approach for a letter of recommendation. You should set up a meeting with or visit the office hours of these faculty to discuss your academic goals, career ambitions, and your research into different programs. Then take a deep breath and ask the most important question: "Would you be willing to provide me with a strong letter of recommendation for grad school?" The keyword is "strong." It is a scary question to ask because they might say no—but better to have a no than a lukewarm letter that does not do your application any favors. I have sometimes turned down former students' requests for a letter of recommendation because I did not know them well enough to write a strong letter. I have also been taken aback by receiving an email that says, "Student from years ago has listed you as a recommender for the master's program in X at University of Somewhere," when the student has not even talked to me. How do they know what I will write? Do I even have enough to say or the time to write it? Please do not put any of your professors in this awkward situation. You need to talk to them and make the formal ask before listing them in your application (more on this in chapter 5).

If you don't have three faculty you feel you can approach, does it mean you should give up on applying to grad school? No, but it does mean you will have to be vulnerably creative in reaching out to former professors. When I was assembling my applications, I knew I could count on a strong letter from my faculty mentor who supervised my honor's thesis—but that concluded my list of potential recommenders. I had done well in my Portuguese language course, and so I asked that instructor, who agreed, much to my relief. But I still needed one more recommender. There was an English professor who had given me very positive feedback on an essay

I had written in his course, but I hardly knew him and felt too shy to ask. Meanwhile, all the other pieces of my application were ready to go, thanks to the support of Yolanda Padilla, a Chicana doctoral student who had been mentoring me in the application process. Over coffee one day, I quietly admitted to her, "I might not apply to grad school because I'm too nervous to ask that professor for a letter." Yolanda gave me a verbal chanclazo: "What? We have worked *so hard* to get your applications ready and *all* that's left is to ask for *one* more letter? Email him *right now! Just do it!*" Taken aback, I was like, "All right, Jesus!" and made the ask. He agreed—and I finally had the whole package. I always laugh when looking back on that moment; I'm so thankful Yolanda pushed me out of my fear of rejection.

One last thing I'll say about choosing recommenders is that applicants who do not have strong connections with faculty sometimes ask work supervisors or colleagues to provide letters of support. Unless you are applying to a practically oriented program or it is explicitly suggested, we do not recommend this approach because even though they may mean well, these folks are not usually in a position to discuss your academic strengths and experience. In my department's master's program, applicants who have only one faculty reference are asked to submit one more letter from a professor before we will admit them to the program.

Once you have three professors who have agreed to provide you with a letter of recommendation—again, do not list them as your recommenders before gaining their formal consent!—be ready to provide them with all the background information they need, including:

- Your current application materials: unofficial transcripts, résumé, draft of your statement of purpose, and so on
- List of the programs you are applying to, including links to websites, and why you are applying to them
- Due dates for each program and instructions on how to submit the letter
- List of courses you took with them and how these influenced your current interests, as well as samples of your past coursework (if you have them)
- Anything special they should highlight in the letter (for example, a particular assignment that is related to the topic/method you want to pursue in grad school)
- Information on what you have been up to since you took a class with them

Sharing these materials will save them much time and effort, and it goes a long way to helping them bring their letter to life with specific examples of the kind of work you are capable of doing.

Finally, remember to send polite reminder emails one month in advance of the due date, then two weeks before, and one week before if they have yet to submit their letter, because professors are busy and often procrastinate. You want to make sure that your letter does not fall through the cracks. Once they submit it, a handwritten thank-you note will show your appreciation. Once you hear back with a decision from the schools, tell them the outcome. In fact, let that be a way to continue the process of staying in touch with your faculty supporters over the years, because academia is a small world, and a broad professional network can open great opportunities.

Get Organized and Allow Time for the Process

Are you exhausted yet by the prospect of applying to grad school? Looking back on where I was in the fall and winter of 1997, working on my doctoral applications, I am amazed that I got through this intense process when I understood so little about academic culture and what I was getting myself into. My hope is that you, having read all this, will be in a much stronger place and can proceed with confidence. While it is a lot of work to put all these elements together, the good news is that most schools ask for the same materials, so you can now apply to as many schools that interest you and/or that fit your budget.

Given the scope of work, you can likely see the need for time and the danger of rushing into the application process, as you might waste time and energy applying to programs that are not a good fit or waste money by submitting a haphazard and less than stellar application. Engage in **backward planning**: starting with the date your earliest application is due, work back for each step of the process:

- Submit one week early, to avoid technical issues
- Final review and proofreading of your materials
- Remind faculty recommenders to submit their letters
- Solicit feedback on your statement of purpose and writing sample, and incorporate edits

- Order your transcripts
- Draft your application documents
- Meet with faculty to discuss the programs that interest you and to request letters of recommendation
- Prepare for and take the GRE
- Research the variety of programs out there
- Conduct informational interviews to think carefully about whether a research degree in the humanities or social sciences is the right pathway for you
- Engage in serious soul-searching about your intellectual and career interests

I will share a final story on the theme of "Do as I say, not as I did": when I was in the fall of my last year of undergrad, I decided to take the GRE. My boyfriend at the time—the sabelotodo—kept asking me, "Shouldn't you be studying for the exam?" Overly confident, I was like, "Yes, I have time. Leave me alone." One week out, we were at a bookstore, and I decided to get a GRE guide. They were all variations on the title *30 Days to the GRE!* Not one was *One Week to the GRE!* Suddenly it dawned on me that I might not know what I was doing. Sure enough, my first attempt earned a mediocre score. This experience was my clue that I needed more time to prepare for grad school, and I took the next year to do so. I knew applications were generally due in January, so in early December, I opened the information packets (this was back in the days of paper) from the programs I was interested in. The first one was the History of Consciousness doctoral program at UC Santa Cruz. The deadline? The very next day! Sighing, I set that packet aside—a missed opportunity due to lack of organization and working off a very vague notion of "applying to grad school" without identifying specific steps (the most basic of which is *know the deadlines*). I did take the time to study for the GRE, though, and that round turned out much better because I had taken so many practice exams. (I also give credit to the Virgen de Guadalupe because I took the second GRE on December 12 and wore a T-shirt bearing Ester Hernández's artwork of La Virgen doing a badass roundhouse kick.)[6]

The moral of the story is that you can get into grad school and find career success without going through the specific steps offered in this chapter. But the process can be a lot less stressful and something you enter far more mindfully than I did.

What to Do When the Decision Letters Arrive

Applying to graduate school can tax you emotionally, financially, intellectually, and socially. Like all other times during which you are putting your heart and soul into something that leads you to be judged by others who will also be making a decision about your future, the process of applying may stir up a wide range of feelings. So, before we wade much further into the conversation about what to do when the decisions come in, let us lay out some important reminders. The decisions you get, regardless of what they are, are not a reflection of your intelligence, worthiness, or promise. Grad school is not the only way to further yourself, your career, or your development. Your worth is not determined by the titles you amass or the credentials you accumulate. More school is not the marker of more intelligence. For real. Read that, read it again, and then read it again. Add your own mantra. Read your own mantra, read it again, post it on your bathroom mirror, and read it again. Lather, rinse, repeat. We do not say this in a glib or offhand way. Our people get repeated messages about how we are not good enough or smart enough. When you put yourself forward for judgment, as you are required to do when applying to graduate school, it can be easy for all of those insecurities to bubble back up to the surface—especially when we know there is a very real correlation between having an advanced degree to your name and your long-term salary prospects and job stability. As you wade through this process, and certainly as you start to hear back from programs, remind yourself of these truths. Also remember that you do not have any control over what responses you receive once you reply—you can only control your reaction to them.

In this section, we cover the most common scenarios that you may encounter once you begin to hear decisions on your graduate school applications, how to understand what they mean, and how to navigate them.

I Got into Multiple Programs! How Do I Choose?

Congratulations! If at all possible, and you have not done so already, visit the schools. There is nothing quite like feeling a program out in person—getting the vibe of the campus and surrounding community, meeting with current students and faculty, and picturing yourself there. Remember that this is a place where you will spend the next two (for a master's) to eight (for a doctoral degree) years of your life. Ultimately, it will be up to you to decide what factors are most important. You may consider prestige

(Will graduating from this program help me secure the job I want after I graduate?), finances (Is one program more affordable than another?), faculty mentorship (Who will I work with at this institution and will that mentorship contribute positively to my educational experience and development?), location (Is it near family, community, established networks?), or your general experience in the program (Do people seem happy there? Is there support for first-gen grad students? Is there a community of Latinx students?). These are a few of the considerations that may make one program rise above another, but there may be others; this is a deeply personal question. We partially list these here because there is nothing wrong with picking a program because it allows you to live near your dad as he gets older or to decline a program because the students seem stressed, unsupported, and unhappy. Most importantly, not everything has to be a calculation around prestige. Consult with folks whom you know and trust and who know you. It is a great idea to consult with mentors in your field to get their advice, but also talk with other folks outside of academia who know you, who know the contexts you thrive in, and who can advise you on that basis as well.

I Was Accepted—without Any Funding. What Can I Do?

Before you apply to a school, you should have a sense if funding for the programs you are applying to is the norm, unlikely, or uncertain. How to proceed will depend heavily on the answer to that question. Generally speaking, it is always fine to contact a program you have been admitted to and let them know that you are excited about your offer of admission but that you are having difficulty figuring out how to cover the funding gap and wonder if there are any other funding opportunities you can apply for. They may tell you that there are additional scholarships available or stipends that students can apply for (like **teaching assistant** positions or **graduate researcher** positions). If there are additional options you can be considered for before you have to commit to a program, go for it. If there are teaching assistant or graduate assistant positions, ask what percentage of students get those positions and how many are available. In some institutions (typically larger public universities), many students fund their education through securing these sorts of positions, while in other schools these are not part of the culture. There are longer conversations to be had about the exploitation of graduate students as workers, and how the academy relies on the low-wage labor of graduate students to do the teaching work required to keep the university running. There have been some notable student protests, strikes, and work stoppages in recent years that also call attention to these exploitative practices.

When asking about other funding opportunities, do not overpromise anything. For example, do not contact each of the four schools you were admitted to and let them know they are your top choice if you get some funding. As we have said elsewhere in this book, academia is a small place, and being dishonest does not land well. In short, do not hesitate to tell programs that you have financial need and ask them to engage you in a process of exploring untapped opportunities. At the same time, do so with honesty and integrity; once the chips have all landed, you can figure out your best options. There is also the possibility of negotiating funding from a program if you have a competitive offer from another institution. While it may not always be possible, sometimes institutions are able to free up money if they really want you, but they are not authorized to offer those funds unless you enter into a negotiation process. The negotiation should be done carefully and respectfully; if you find yourself in this situation, seek out the advice of a mentor to walk you through this.

I Was Accepted—but Something Major in My Life Changed. What Are My Options?

Let's say you are accepted to a program that you are excited about, but then something big happens: you get a new job you are really happy in, your professional plans change, you get pregnant, your mom gets sick and you need to move back home, or any other number of things that get filed under the label "life happens." The most common move in this scenario is to ask if you can defer your acceptance. A deferral means that you are still interested in the program, but you are unable to start during the term for which you applied and are asking to begin the following year (or term). Applying for a deferral as opposed to just declining the offer of admission can be beneficial if you just need a bit more time, because it generally means you do not need to go through the admissions process again (and perhaps means you do not need to pay an application fee again). If you are 100 percent sure you are no longer interested in the program, you can simply decline your admission. If you think you might remain interested, or if the conditions you are grappling with may change again (your mom gets well, for example), then a deferral may be the best option.

Deferral is not an option for every program at every campus. Be aware that oftentimes, even if an offer of admission can be deferred, offers of funding cannot. This means that while you may be given the option to put your admission offer on hold for the following year or semester, any funding (scholarships, grants, fellowships, assistantships) is not guaranteed to be offered when you decide to enroll. Many of those awards are decisions made year by year from a specific budget amount, so the school will need to recalibrate any offer in the context of the new cohort/admission cycle. So deferring an offer of admission if there is funding on the line is not a decision that should be taken lightly—but entering a graduate program if you are unsure it is the right move is also not a good idea. As with other feedback, talk to trusted mentors if you are considering deferring.

I Was Wait-Listed. What Happens Now?

Though it can feel like it, being put onto a waiting list is not always a rejection. An offer of a wait-listed spot means that you could not be admitted in the first round of admissions, but space may open up in a later round. There are a number of reasons that someone can be pulled off the waiting list, including that another person has declined their offer of admission. If you get a waiting list offer, you may be asked if you would like to be on the waiting list or not. Don't let your ego get in the way: if you want into that program, say yes. It is also a good idea to clarify if there is anything else you should attend to while you wait to hear if there will be space in the program for you. At most institutions, a wait-listed applicant is excluded from applying for fellowships or teaching assistantships, but it is worth asking. It is also appropriate to ask if there is a certain date by which wait-listed applicants can expect to hear back; if enrolling in that program would require a move or other logistical concerns, you may want to impose a personal deadline at which point you choose to move on. If you are balancing a wait-listed offer (perhaps from a school that is higher on your list) with an offer of admission (perhaps from a school lower on your list), you may need to make a hard decision. It is best to err on the side of caution: take the sure thing rather than holding out for a spot on the waiting list. It is not unheard-of for a student to accept an offer, then get pulled off the waiting list at another institution and decide to go with the second offer (therefore, retracting their intent to enroll at the first university). Explore the implications of this carefully; there may be lost money involved, and if you venture into this territory, do so as carefully, clearly, and respectfully as possible to avoid damaging any relationships in the process (have we not mentioned, one million times, how small academia is?).

I Was Rejected. Should I Give Up?

It is hard to get rejected. Go back to the start of this section and reread what we wrote, as well as your own mantra. It is only natural to spend some time being disappointed or feeling sad. Feel your feelings, but also keep them in perspective. If you are rejected, some would advise you to simply try again the next round—and yes, you should, but with a couple caveats. First, reassess the programs you applied to and consider if you need to make any changes to that list. Did you apply only to big-shot, highly competitive programs? Did you apply to programs—or even a discipline—that are not matched to your interests, and reviewers saw that? (The master's program that Genevieve directs get applications every year from people whose professional plans do not align with the program, and who get rejected. It doesn't do anyone good to be in a program where they do not sync with the mission.) Reconsider your list of institutions and consider your rejections from that standpoint.

The second thing to reconsider is your application materials. Did something in your application materials give admissions folks pause? Go back through your materials and enlist trusted colleagues to help you determine whether there is any tightening you can do. Are there spelling errors or other typos in your materials? Did you accidentally use the wrong name of the institution? (We have seen this copy-paste fail more than once.) This is also a time to consider if your letters of recommendation are helping—or possibly hurting—your application. You likely waived your ability to see the letters themselves, and it is not good academic etiquette to request copies from your recommenders, but you can reach out and let them know you were not admitted and ask if they have any feedback that you can consider when you reapply. You may be able to get a sense in these conversations if any of your recommenders are less than enthusiastic (if so, ask a different letter writer in the future), and you also may get a new perspective on your materials.

Third, consider whether there are any gaps in your profile as a prospective student and try to use the time between application cycles to fill those as best as possible. Genevieve explains: A former student of mine applied to PhD programs right out of his undergrad degree (I warned him that his lack of work experience was going to make this complicated). Despite his strong academic record, he was not admitted to any of the programs he applied to. He decided to build up his professional profile, and in doing so realized he really loved the work he was doing. This experience helped him redefine what he wanted to focus a doctoral dissertation on. He reapplied, three years out of undergrad, and was admitted, with funding, to several top programs.

Your pivot may not be this dramatic, but consider how additional professional or volunteer experience may bolster your application. You have been given more time to make yourself a stronger candidate; do not just wait around until you can apply again. Instead, use that time to make it harder for them to turn you down. So, yes, if you were not admitted and you still want to go to graduate school, you should prepare yourself to reapply. And for many, many scholars, the first rejection in the grad school application cycle is a mere bump in the road that they forget about when they receive their eventual admissions offers. Even if you did not want this bump, take advantage of it: use the time to improve your materials so you are an even stronger candidate for the next round.

Reflection Questions

1 Why are you considering a graduate degree? What are your professional and personal goals, and how does this degree align with them? What impact do you hope to have on the world, and how will this degree program help get you there? Have you considered other pathways that may lead to those same goals?

2 What strengths do you want to communicate in your application materials? Who are you, and why are you a strong candidate for these programs? Why are you pursuing a research degree in this particular discipline and field?

3 What are the major considerations for you in terms of picking programs? What is important to you—personally, intellectually, socially, financially, and as related to your family and social networks? What is important to you in a graduate program?

4 What elements of your application will be easy to pull together? Which will take more effort? What is your timeline, based on the deadlines of programs you are interested in, and what benchmarks will help you meet those deadlines?

5 Who can you reach out to as a potential letter writer? Do you know anyone (a faculty member, a current graduate student, a career counselor on campus) who can serve as a mentor and advisor as you navigate this process?

Sample Email Inquiry to Potential Faculty Mentors

Send individual emails to each professor; do not address multiple professors at the same school with one email![7]

Dear Professor _____,

My name is _____ and I am interested in applying to the [MA or PhD] program in [Name of Department]. I recently graduated with a BA in [major] from [University of X], and my next goal is to _____. Your work on _____ has inspired my interest in studying _____ because _____.

Would it be possible to schedule a brief [in person/phone] meeting to discuss these interests, as well as a few questions I have about the possibility of applying to your program?

Thank you for your consideration, and I look forward to hearing from you.

Sincerely,

[your name]

2 Learning to Be a Grad Student

In the spring of 1998, I was biding my time at my $8 per hour temp job, living at home in the suburbs, and going out clubbing in the city with my friends on Friday and Saturday nights.[1] It was not the most intellectually stimulating lifestyle, but I was happy to have a regular paycheck, fun work colleagues, and the city of Chicago, where my boyfriend and college homies lived, just a half-hour drive away. Once my graduate school applications were submitted in December, I put them out of my mind, focusing my energies on work and socializing.

One day in March, I left work early due to terrible allergies; I popped some antihistamines and promptly fell asleep. I woke up around 5:30 p.m., when I heard my mom arriving home from work. She checked the answering machine, and I heard a muffled voice on the message playback. Suddenly, she began yelling for me; half-asleep, I stumbled downstairs to see what was going on. "You just got admitted to Stanford!" she shouted, jumping up and down. The message was from the doctoral program director, letting me know I was being admitted to the PhD Program in Modern Thought and Literature. I was filled with disbelief and stood there, mouth agape. My mom hugged me and said, "Let's go to dinner to celebrate!" Barely able to breathe through my sinus congestion, I told her that I wasn't feeling well, and we could celebrate tomorrow. "Oh, no," she countered in her mother-knows-best tone, "it's not every day that my daughter gets accepted to Stanford. We are going out to celebrate!" And a little while later, sniffling but happy, I was being toasted with a glass of sparkling wine.

My mom had it right: when your acceptance news comes in, savor the moment and do something to celebrate! You are on your way to becoming one of the growing numbers of Latinxs who earn advanced degrees. This moment alone is already a significant accomplishment. It's not that being accepted into a graduate program makes you better than you were before; rather, you should celebrate having the courage to step boldly in a new direction where likely few, if any, in your family have ventured.

As you get closer to new-student orientation and the first day of class, however, reality will start to sink in. Alongside the excitement about the new courses you'll take, professors you'll learn from, and friendships you'll forge, there may also be a nervous feeling in the pit in your stomach and a growing set of questions: Am I ready for this? Will I be able to handle the work? What will the other students be like? What exactly have I gotten myself into?

This chapter provides some real talk about how to prepare yourself for this new stage of what is not only an educational journey but also a professional and personal one. At the heart of it are two core ideas. First, graduate school is a process that socializes you into a profession, and so it is natural to feel unbalanced as you enter this new phase of your educational journey. The nerves you may feel are a normal part of the process that most everyone experiences. Second, know that while your core concept of self will inevitably change as part of this process, it is possible to merge your home/cultural identity with your academic identity. Holding these two ideas in mind, let's begin.

Getting Your Act Together: Grad School Begins before Classes Start

After my acceptance to Stanford, I spent the next several months daydreaming about my upcoming grad student life and finding ways to casually mention, "I'm moving to California in September to start a PhD program," wait for people to ask where, nonchalantly shrug, say "Stanford," and then bask in the congratulatory comments. That was about as much prep as I did because I had no idea what graduate school would be like, other than I would spend a lot of time reading. There are a few things you can do to ease yourself into the transition. These suggestions appear at the end of this chapter in the form of a checklist.

Visit Campus, if Possible

This step is especially important if you are uprooting your life to begin a program far from where you currently live. I was fortunate in that both doctoral programs that offered me admission paid for me to fly out for a campus visit. During these visits, I was able to tour campus, get an overview of offices that support graduate student success, meet with my prospective faculty advisors, and connect with current students. It was a critical way to gain a sense of what my life would be like at those places. Even if you are enrolling in a program close to home, it is still a good idea to spend a day on campus taking a tour and engaging in similar meetings. You can reach out to the department's graduate advisor for recommendations of whom to speak to. If you are transitioning to a new academic field, this visit is also a great time to connect with current students and faculty to ask whether there are particular readings, methods, or tools you should become familiar with prior to starting the program. Be aware that summer is a time when faculty are off contract and away from campus at many universities, so a springtime trip is a better idea than a summer one.

Figure Out Where You Will Live

Again, this is an important step if you are moving any distance. On my campus visits, I toured grad student housing as well as the neighborhoods preferred by students who opted to live off campus. I applied for campus housing at Stanford but was disappointed to discover that I had been assigned a shared graduate dorm room—originally meant to be a single-occupancy room—with a lottery system for kitchen access. I did not want to return to my college days of sharing a bedroom with a roommate, so I got connected to another new Latina grad student who already lived in the Bay Area and had found a great two-bedroom apartment in a nearby town. We lived together for two years and became part of a tight-knit group of Latinx students in humanities doctoral programs.

Even if you are not moving far, you may want to reassess your current situation: Do you have a dedicated, quiet space where you will be able to focus, store your books, and do your work? If not, what adjustments might help facilitate that? If you do, that's great—and maybe some reorganizing and light redecorating (frame your bachelor's diploma and hang it near your work space) can help to mark the transition to this new phase of your education and make an old space feel new. If you are not transitioning into a full-time program but rather will be pursuing your graduate degree in the evenings or on weekends while other responsibilities in your life remain constant (work, family, etc.), you may not be contemplating moving or new space. Instead, think about how your new responsibilities will come into contact with your existing life and how you will make space—physically and emotionally—to take on this new area of your life.

Preview Your Day-to-Day Course Schedule

Before you begin your program—even ahead of orientation—take a peek at the upcoming class schedule, read the course descriptions, and look up the faculty and the assigned texts in courses you might take. In this way, you can start to gain a sense of what the initial weeks and months will be like and visualize the rhythm of your new student life. When you look at an individual class, the work may seem intense but doable. Looking at multiple courses will help you gain a clearer sense of when assignments pile up and will help you anticipate what adjustments you may need to make to stay on top of your academic work.

Prepare Your Work Schedule

If you plan to continue in your current job while starting a new degree program, you should engage in serious reflection about the feasibility of maintaining your current schedule. If you work full-time, you might have to switch to part-time work, even temporarily, while you adjust to graduate school and give yourself the time and energy to be fully present in your classes. Similarly, if you work part-time, you may need to reduce your hours or ask to change your schedule to accommodate your coursework. Consider if there are schedule alterations that can support your new school obligations—could you work longer Mondays so you can take Tuesdays off? Is it possible for you to work from home at times so that you can cut down on your commute? Even if no changes are possible, it is helpful to spend time getting your head around your new daily and weekly schedule.

Remember that being in school does not consist only of time spent in class. Many out-of-class activities are central to academic success: reading and note taking, looking up materials at the library, writing, attending office hours, connecting with peers to work on assignments together, to name a few. There is also the commute to consider, especially if you need to get to campus during rush hour. Again, what might need to shift to account for these different aspects of being in school? And how will you have those conversations with your supervisor to help them understand why you may need some accommodations in the coming months?

Rethink Your Relationship to Time

Time can feel very different depending on whether you are entering a graduate program directly after graduating with your bachelor's or are returning to school after many years of working full-time. As we discussed in chapter 1, if you begin a graduate program soon after completing a bachelor's, you may still be in tune with the rhythms of the academic year. By contrast, when you have been out of school for a while, you will need to get reacquainted with the habits and routines that served you well as an undergraduate. The longer you have been away and with more life events under your belt—perhaps you have launched your career and/or started a family—you will likely find that there are bigger disruptions to your normal routine.

Oftentimes, work schedules dictate our sense of time—for example, working weekdays from 8 a.m. to 5 p.m. forces us to use evenings and weekends to run errands, spend time with loved ones, pursue hobbies. However, graduate school—doctoral programs, in particular—often entails long stretches of unstructured time, and it will be up to you to manage your time effectively. Time-management techniques are discussed much further in chapter 3—but for now, the point is that time feels different in grad school. It is helpful to get your head around this reality.

Gather the Tools You Need

As you learned in chapter 1, grad school is a long-term commitment, so make sure you have the tools you need to do the work. These include, among other things:

- Hardware: A reliable laptop with long battery life for writing your papers and doing your research. It is also great to have a tablet and stylus, which can make it easier to read and mark up PDFs, though it's not necessary if money is tight. A printer is a good investment. Perhaps invest in noise-canceling headphones to help you focus, especially if you live in shared housing or plan to study on campus.
- Software: Word processor (most academic writing and editing is done in Microsoft Word); citation software (more on this in

chapter 3); a note-taking app; a PDF markup app; and specialized software needed in your particular discipline, such as qualitative coding software. Before you buy these programs, check with your new campus, as you may gain institutional access or be eligible for student discounts to help defray the costs.

- A cloud-based backup system for your documents: graduate education is filled with horror stories of students who lost months or years of research due to an unfortunate coffee spill or a stolen laptop. Side note: begin developing a clear file-naming system (assignment-class-date.doc, for example) and folders (organized by year or class) to keep track of all your documents.
- A sturdy backpack or messenger bag to tote your things to and from campus: ideally, this bag should be water-resistant and lightweight, as it will be weighed down with your laptop, papers, readings, and doodads.
- Work space: a desk, comfortable chair, adequate lighting, reliable internet.
- Basic office supplies: pens, highlighters, sticky notes, planner, and notebooks.
- Leakproof tumbler for water, coffee, or tea throughout the day and lightweight lunch bag.
- Comfortable shoes to get you around campus.

Prepare Your Day-to-Day Life

In addition to the technical supplies, you will need to think about the big-picture aspects of your life:

- Overall physical health: medical and dental checkups, as well as an updated vision prescription, if necessary. Get refills on any medications you may need. Maybe you have been uninsured or underinsured in the period before you go back to school. If that is the case, figure out your options for student insurance through your new campus, which is a good way to get caught up on health needs and checkups.
- Overall mental health: find out what support is available through your medical insurance, if you have it, or the student health center on campus. Most universities offer psychological and counseling services in the form of group and individual counseling. These

resources are valuable, and there is absolutely no shame in taking advantage of them; far from being a sign of weakness, seeking counseling is a strong, proactive step toward developing a healthy perspective and coping mechanisms for life's challenges. There may be dedicated groups for graduate and/or Latinx/a/o students, offering spaces to reflect with others who share our identities (more on this in chapter 5).

- General self-care: a plan for physical activity, a meditation app to help you decompress and/or fall asleep at night, continuing any hobbies that help you destress, and keeping nonacademics in your life as a reminder that grad school is not everything.

- General financial plan and monthly budget: be mindful of daily expenses so that you can minimize credit card debt. Also, consider the finances you may need before starting your program; for example, if you are relocating, organize first and last month's rent, a security deposit, funds to rent a moving truck, and so on.

- Meal planning: if your budget does not have room for buying lunches on or near campus, then you'll need to prepare healthy meals ahead of time and pack them in a lunch bag, along with filling snacks to keep up your energy throughout the day.

- Commuting: think about how you will get to campus, whether via public transit, a bike, or reliable car (you may need a campus parking permit). How will transportation routes and traffic impact the time needed to get to and from class?

Prepare Your Personal Relationships

You are not the only one who will be making a transition to grad school: your family, friends, and other close relationships will experience this change as well. Take the time to walk them through your typical schedule, explaining that even though you're not in class all day long, you are still going to be engaging in schoolwork during other parts of the day and on weekends. With family who live nearby, you may have to start managing expectations, setting boundaries on when you are available to talk or attend family gatherings. When it comes to friends, let them know that you may have to be very focused on school at times and unavailable to hang out on certain days. And with romantic partners and children, you need to similarly manage their expectations by explaining what you will be working on and how your time and attention will be changing while you are establishing yourself—especially when there may be social events or campus talks and workshops that are important to attend to create a strong support network on campus. For more suggestions on how to navigate personal relationships, check out chapter 6.

Looking back on my own experience, I can see that many of these discussions were mitigated by the sheer geographical distance between my family and me once I moved across the country—not to mention that coming from divorced parents who were financially stable, I didn't have the type of extended family that had traditional get-togethers or in which I played a caretaking or financial role. Meanwhile, most of my close college friends were very understanding because they also were considering grad school, and the close friends I made after moving to California were all pretty much graduate students like me. You may have a very different set of considerations depending on your personal circumstances.

Even simply reading through this list and reflecting on a couple of these bullet points will go a long way to helping you navigate the transition to graduate school with greater ease.

Am I Good Enough to Be Here? Confronting the Culture of Academia

Back to 1998: I moved to California in early September, after two bittersweet going-away parties hosted by each parent for their respective sides of the family (a benefit of having divorced parents: twice the celebrations). My boyfriend at the time accompanied me on the four-day cross-country move. After he returned home, I had a couple of weeks to settle into my new apartment, bond with my new roommate, and figure out how to get to the grocery store, local shops, and campus. The first day of the fall term arrived before I even knew it, and I recall the nervous butterflies as I walked onto Stanford's impressive, golden-hued main quad, my book bag filled with fresh school supplies and a new student ID in my pocket.

Those early days were marked by a roller coaster of emotions. I was excited about my new classes, intrigued by the readings, in awe of my professors, and happy with the new friendships I was forming with other grad students, most of whom were also first-generation students of color. On the other hand, I was plagued by massive waves of self-doubt, as I described in the introduction to this book. I felt intimidated by many of my classmates, who seemed wise, wealthy, and worldly, and even more so by my professors, so erudite and aloof. The same readings that intrigued me also filled me with frustration when I found myself reading the same passages multiple times because I couldn't understand the jargon and convoluted construction—I concluded that I must not be smart enough to understand it. And I dreaded having to submit my writing assignments; I felt sure that my professors would immediately see the lack of sophistication in my ideas. They would see that I had been admitted by mistake.

You may already know the term for this feeling: impostor syndrome, a term coined by psychologists Pauline Clance and Suzanne Imes in 1978 to describe the intense self-doubt that high-achieving people experience when they question their competency or suspect that their success is due purely to luck and not their own hard work.[2] Impostor syndrome occurs quite commonly within academia, especially for scholars who are historically underserved and minoritized.[3] It is a terrible and debilitating feeling that may arise for any number of reasons, most likely because we do not see many Latinx/a/o people in positions of authority or who can serve as role models for navigating academic institutions; moreover, we rarely get to see our communities and histories reflected in mainstream curricula.[4] Because there are so few Latinx/a/o scholars in the academy, we often end up feeling like permanent guests in the campus spaces we rightly inhabit.[5]

Once the impostor syndrome set in, I placed great pressure on myself to overcompensate. For example, during class discussions I would scramble to think of something brilliant to say, but then when I could not think of anything that seemed worthy, I would remain silent and disappointed in myself—especially when a classmate later voiced the very idea or question that had occurred to me. Or while listening to someone speak, I would nod along as if I were thinking, "Oh yes, of course," when in reality I had no clue what they were talking about. I would also hold on to my writing too long to make it "perfect" (spoiler alert: it was not perfect, ever) and thus escape critique. Impostor syndrome often held me back from asking clarifying questions about the assignments we were given and the esoteric references being bandied about. At times, it made me wonder if I was even capable of completing the doctoral degree I had dreamed of attaining. To be completely honest, there are times even now, years later and as someone well established in my career, when I experience impostor syndrome in some situations—but I'm better at recognizing it, calming my mind, and finding ways to contribute to conversations and projects by asking good questions and focusing on the skills I have and the things I do know. All of that comes with time and perspective.

Another factor that contributes to impostor syndrome is that we may have internalized the deficit ideologies about Latinx/a/o families and cultures that are perpetuated throughout our schooling, as well as in popular culture more broadly. We receive constant messages—directly and indirectly—telling us that we are not as smart, that we are lazy, that we are not strong writers or innovative thinkers, that we do not have the capacity to be scholars. The fact that so few of us pursue advanced degrees is taken as a sign that we are collectively not good enough rather than the purposeful outcome of systems and structures designed to deny us educational opportunities.[6] And the "compliments" that are parsed out—for example, being told, "You speak English so well!" when English may be your first language, so of course you do—are in reality racist **microaggressions** that chip away at your self-confidence over time.[7]

Moreover, it is hard to feel at home in academia because higher education has its own particular culture—ways of talking, behaving, dressing—that is rooted in upper-middle-class customs and tastes. Many of the students in your program may come from families in which one or more generations have received graduate degrees, and so if they seem more at home with academic culture, it's no surprise: their parents and grandparents have passed down this culture to them, so of course they feel at home in it. There is a longer conversation about this, and in particular the ways that this intersects with professional dress and appearance, in chapter 4. No matter what stage of our journey we are on, when academic culture is very different from your home culture, you continue to reflect on your ways of being and appearance. The message here is not to change who you are, how you dress, and how you speak. Rather, we want you to understand that when you feel different or incapable of doing the work, it is not because you do not belong but because academia has its own culture—aspects of which you are free to take or leave, as you desire.

Grad School Is a Process and a Performance

Graduate school is more than a place or a finite set of years in your life. It is a process, quite literally. We often imagine this process to be linear: get admitted to a grad program, learn all the things, then graduate—ta-da! The reality is far more complex; you undergo dynamic and interactive adaptation over time. In fact, there is a concept for this: **socialization theory**, which is the idea that students pass through different and distinct stages of development, from anticipating what grad school will be like, to learning the formal procedures of grad school, then becoming aware of the informal or unspoken expectations, and onto a final stage in which they fuse their personal and academic identities.[8] The bottom line is that as with the impostor syndrome, many graduate students feel anxious and unbalanced when starting grad school and as they advance to each new level. Think back on your own experience: the things that you found confusing or challenging when you first started college became easier or felt more natural by the time you graduated. Similarly, once you are in grad school, just because you completed your coursework doesn't mean you magically now know how to write a thesis. Socialization theory is a reminder that each phase brings its own new set of learnings—and this can be unnerving.

So why doesn't it seem like others are anxious? Well, it's either because (a) they are overconfident and arrogant, or (b) they are bluffing, trying to fake it until they make it. Here is an example. One day in my first term in grad school, I arrived early to class and struck up a conversation with the woman next to me. At one point, she asked, "What did you think of today's reading?" I don't know what led me to drop my guard, but in that moment, I cheerfully admitted, "I have no idea. I didn't understand any of it." Her eyes widened and she said, "I am so relieved to hear you say that! I thought I was the only one who doesn't understand anything in this class!" Her energy immediately picked up, as though a heavy burden had been lifted. In turn, I was relieved by her reaction, because it confirmed that there wasn't something wrong with me—the reading really was hard. There we were, two first-year grad students convinced that we were the only ones having a hard time, when really everyone in that classroom shared the same anxieties, whether they were willing to admit it or not.

Here's where the performance aspect comes in: a lot of what you may see in other students is a type of know-it-all posturing that they use to cover their own self-doubts. This performance comes in many forms:

- Snarky, cutting responses to someone who is being vulnerable in processing ideas aloud
- Insisting that "everyone" knows [fill in the blank theory or scholar]
- Eagerly agreeing with anything the professor says, or "contributing" to discussion by restating the professor's words
- Rushing to be the first person to respond to a professor's question and going on an endless monologue to show off how much they know

- Offering nothing but critique and tearing down the work of other scholars
- Playing devil's advocate mainly to push people's buttons and seem like an independent thinker
- Generally acting superior and above it all

Don't fall into their trap. When people act this way in class, it is tempting to get sucked into the drama and respond in kind. Instead, just look at them and imagine your abuelita saying, "¡Ay, pobrecito!" They are not at home with themselves and are desperate to impress others. They do not realize that the point of being in grad school is to further your learning; if you already knew it all, you would be teaching the class, not taking it. And guess what? The professor who is teaching it may know a lot, but even they certainly do not know it all, either. I wish I could tell you that academia does not reward this behavior, but the truth is that it often does. Even so, see it for what it is, recognize that this is not about you, and keep it moving.

Remember that what makes the deepest, longest-lasting impression is not a one-off brilliant remark but rather consistent effort and deepening quality over time. That is what people will know you for: someone who is authentically engaged and intellectually open. It also helps to find community with other grad students who are willing to open up about their experiences and support each other in acclimating to grad school. A lifesaver for me was getting involved in the Latinx student center on campus (Stanford's El Centro Chicano), which offered social, academic, and professional development programs centered on Latinx students. It also was a space where I found opportunities to mentor undergraduates, which was a meaningful way to give back to other students and to stay connected to a broader community on campus. If you are enrolling at a school that does not have that kind of center, then it is all the more critical to connect with other students of color across the disciplines so that you can keep each other motivated and provide space to engage in real talk about the intensity of the experience. Figure out what will anchor you—maybe there is a student-parent group, a queer graduate student colectiva, a woman of color support circle—and invest in that space and yourself as a member of that space. If there is nothing like this, consider convening something.

When you are a first-generation student, these relationships provide you with the understanding and validation that you need to persist. I remember taking a class called Contemporary US Feminisms with Dr. Sharon Holland in my first year; she was a badass queer woman of color who forever earned a place in my heart because on the day we discussed Gayatri Spivak's important and challenging essay "Can the Subaltern Speak?," she broke the nervous energy at the start of class by joking, "I hope somebody can *please* explain this essay to me!" We laughed together, relieved that the professor acknowledged the difficulty of entering this notoriously complicated text. Professor Holland assigned weekly writing responses, and she marked our work with a check (adequate), a check-minus (not so much), or a check-plus (outstanding). Week after week, I kept getting checks. Finally, one day, on a paper about Puerto Rican entertainer Iris Chacón—which, by the way, ended up becoming the basis for my first publication[9]—I earned the coveted check-plus. I was so excited that when I saw my friend Marisol in the hallway after class, I ran up to her, waving the paper above my head and shouting, "Sharon Holland gave me a check-plus!" She threw her arms around me in a celebratory hug; she had taken the class the year before and knew how hard it was to earn that mark. I share this story because it is those moments of being real with others that will make all the difference and help you block the negativity of the people desperately performing grad school greatness.

Cultivating Your Grad Student Identity

How do we as Latinx/a/o scholars not lose our way in academia? How do we learn to navigate institutions of higher education in ways that enable us to do meaningful work without abandoning the values and cultures that make us who we are? The reality is that graduate school will change certain parts of you, but just that—parts, not all, of you. This result is inevitable because you will grow in so many ways in response to the concepts you learn, the vocabulary you pick up, the tools you use, the people (peers and faculty) with whom you are in conversation, and the places you may travel while in graduate school. In fact, if you come out of your graduate program as the exact same person you were when you entered, then you probably did not learn much at all. Beyond your campus life, you will become a slightly different version of yourself based on life experience alone. So why would you expect two or more years of grad school not to have the same effect? You are living and evolving, right?

That being said, some of the changes may take family and friends by surprise, and you may get unwelcome commentary from them at times. Here's an example: in my fourth year of grad school, *Band of Brothers*, a television series based on the true stories of a heroic World War II battalion, premiered on HBO. I watched the first episode with my mom while she was in town for a visit. At dinner a few days later, I tried to start a conversation with her and her husband about why World War II stories continue to be so popular in television and film. At one point in our conversation, I observed, "Many of these programs seem so jingoistic." My mom's husband halted the conversation with sudden laughter: "'Jingoistic'? That sounds like a word to describe Santa Claus!" Later, as we walked out of the restaurant, my mom pulled me aside, whispering, "Please don't tell me you're becoming like [the sabelotodo], showing off with your twenty-five-cent words." (In other words, don't use fancy words just to make others feel small.) Her words stung. I hadn't used *jingoistic* to show off; it was simply a word I learned from my readings. Moreover, why would she think I'm the type of person who would purposefully act that way? There were also times when I called home and would describe my grad school stress, and my mom would sarcastically sigh, "Yes, it must be so hard to wake up at noon and read a book," in effect reducing my concerns to a form of first-world problems. Looking back, there were probably many unspoken factors shaping that interaction, perhaps envy of the opportunity I had to be in grad school or feeling subconsciously threatened by my educational advancement even while she outwardly cheered me on.

For as long as Latinx/a/o scholars have been navigating academia, they have been reflecting on this aspect of the first-generation student experience. While there are times when you will feel different and maybe even conflicted or anxious about the gap in experience between you and other family members, this does not need to be a source of friction; it is possible to develop ways of sharing with your family the things you are learning and the opportunities and challenges you are finding. In fact, you likely have already developed ways of navigating this experience, having learned to **code-switch**, or alternate between different ways of speaking, in effect compartmentalizing how you speak or behave in different life contexts. We code-switch, for example, when we mix English and Spanish as we speak; similarly, we code-switch when we are in class, talking with the professor and fellow students about the readings, and outside of class, when a younger cousin asks for help with their homework, and we explain a challenging concept in terms they can relate to.

In fact, bridging your home and academic life in these ways means living in a state of **nepantla**, a term Gloria Anzaldúa uses to describe liminality and in-betweenness, always straddling two cultural worlds.[10] Nepantla, she explains, is the source of our creative powers. As nepantlerx/a/os, we learn how to not only exist but thrive in different cultural spaces and code-switch as needed. It is exhausting work, no doubt, but it enables us to bring the best of each of these worlds into the other. Especially for first-generation graduate students, being in nepantla is a source of strength, because we bring a critical eye to the inequities and assumptions that are so common in academia and are able to ask, "Why are things done this way? Why do people act this way here?" Ultimately, this in-betweenness enables us to work to change academia for the better by sharing our values and perspectives in the work that we are here to do.

You can and should anchor yourself in your broader political and community commitments that inspired you to be on this pathway. Before you begin your first day in the program, take time to develop a personal mission statement to guide your journey and remind you of the intentions you entered with for times when you feel you have lost your way, are unmotivated, or are uninspired. Ask yourself, "What do I really want to do once I get this degree? Who am I doing this for, and why? To whom am I accountable?" You can write a two- to three-sentence statement along the lines of: "I am pursuing a [MA/PhD] in [your field] because I want to contribute to conversations about [list the issues or topics most meaningful to you]. I hope to apply my degree by [career goal] and serving [populations or communities that have shaped you]." This mission statement may change as your progress advances and long-term goals become clearer, but always keep a version of it where you will see it regularly (a file on your computer, a page pinned to a corkboard, etc.).

Also remember what grad school means—and does not mean—about you. Just as we can internalize failure and messages rooted in deficit thinking, we also run the risk of internalizing our success, telling ourselves, "Well, I graduated and they [family members or other students of color] didn't because I worked hard and they didn't want it as much as I did." In other words, do not buy into the individualistic, meritocratic ideologies that perpetuate the notion that it is possible to "pull yourself up by your bootstraps." Surely you did work hard, but success is only meaningful in community, recognizing the people on and off campus who support us and contribute to our success. Maybe you didn't have parents who graduated from college and could thus give you advice about how to do well academically—but did your mom come through with a home-cooked meal when you were feeling down? Did your tío slip a $20 bill into your hand when he heard you were low on gas money this week? We may not always have the traditional social capital to give us a running start in grad school, but we do have what scholar Tara Yosso terms **community cultural wealth**: other forms of wealth—linguistic, familial, aspirational, and more—that contribute to our persistence and success.[11]

As a new grad student, your job is to find a way forward that honors the wisdom you have received from your home culture and from academic training. Combining these in careful ways is not selling out but rather preparing you for a long-term profession as an engaged scholar who uses your academic credentials to widen the path for those who follow. Historian Yuridia Ramírez captures this sentiment when she asserts, "By being yourself, you empower others around you to do the same. . . . The best academic identity you can develop is one that stands poised in your intellectual capacity without sacrificing all of the other complex identities that make you the person you are."[12] We revisit this idea in the conclusion of this book, where we lay out mandamientos for Latinxs in the academy.

Reflection Questions

1 When did I last enter a new stage of my education or career? What feelings emerged during that time? Were there things I was nervous about that later seemed like not such a big deal?

2 What are the biggest changes graduate school will bring to my current way of life? How can I anticipate and prepare for these changes?

3 What can I do to ground myself when impostor syndrome rears its ugly head? Who or what can help me stay focused on my existing skills and experience, which I am here to expand?

4 How can I begin to view living in a state of nepantla as a source of strength? How can I use this skill to my advantage? When have I code-switched in the past to adapt to multiple contexts?

Preparándome para Grad School: A Checklist

- Visit campus:

    Take a campus tour and learn where the key offices are located, including your department's main office, the registrar and bursar, and student health center.

Check in with your program's graduate advisor to connect with current students and faculty for advice on getting started.

- Figure out your living situation:

    If you are relocating, make sure you have a few months' rent and security deposit, and know how you will get to and from campus.

    If you are not relocating, reflect on what changes, if any, you may need in your current space to create physical and mental room to focus on your studies.

- Preview your course schedule by mapping out courses you may take in the first semester and possibly obtaining syllabi (even from a previous term) to help you visualize the amount of work coming your way.

- Prepare your work schedule, if you are continuing to work while in your graduate program. Speak with your supervisor about possible changes to your schedule in advance of busy times of the semester.

- Gather the tools you will need, depending on your budget:

    A reliable laptop with long battery life; perhaps also a tablet and a printer

    Noise-canceling headphones

    Software, including a word processor, citation software, a note-taking app, PDF markup (ask about student discounts or institutional access to help defray the costs)

    A cloud-based backup system for your documents

    A sturdy backpack or messenger bag

    Work space: a desk, comfortable chair, adequate lighting, reliable internet

    Basic office supplies: pens, highlighters, sticky notes, planner, and notebooks

    Leakproof tumbler for water, coffee, or tea throughout the day; lightweight lunch bag

    Comfortable shoes to get you around campus

- Self-care:

  Medical and dental checkups, as well as medication refills

  Support for your mental health and stress

  A plan for physical activity

  Meditation app

  General financial plan and realistic monthly budget

  Meal-planning system

  A reliable form of transportation to and from campus

- Prepare your personal relationships: check in with family and friends to help them understand some of the demands on your time as a graduate student.

3 Essential Skills in Graduate School

A required introductory seminar in my doctoral program was called the Modern Tradition. Meeting twice weekly, this course had a particularly intense reading load, often consisting of two full books per week. (Decades later, I'm still annoyed that I had to race to complete Gabriel García Márquez's masterpiece *One Hundred Years of Solitude* solely for one day's worth of discussion.)[1] It was in this class that my first-ever grad school paper was due. Because I felt it would predict my long-term academic success, I worked very hard on it alone in my room in the few days before it was due. I even included an epigraph, a brief quote that sets the theme of an essay, by Néstor García Canclini, a "famous" (by academic standards) Latin American anthropologist. Truth be told, I had never actually read any of García Canclini's work; I had only heard someone else talking about it. Nevertheless, there I was, sprinkling Important Quotes throughout my paper like I was seasoning a pot of frijoles.

Two weeks later, the paper was returned to me with a B+ at the top. Although it was not an A, it seemed like a decent start to my graduate writing career, so I felt rather pleased with myself. Talking with my friend Marisol, a first-generation Latina who was in her third year of a PhD program, I mentioned my relief to have earned a B+ on my first essay. She looked at me apologetically and asked, "Has anyone told you how grades work here?" When I shook my head, she gently explained that in most doctoral programs, an A means solid work; an A- says that you were close but missed the mark; a B+ indicates that you were off-track; and a B was more or less a failing grade. To earn less than that was unthinkable. "I only know this," Marisol added, "because someone had to explain it to me when I got here."

I share this story not to make you panic about grades—in fact, how grades are assigned and what they mean can vary across programs and universities—but rather to demonstrate how the norms in grad school can be very different from what you knew as an undergraduate. For example, as an undergrad, missing class without alerting the professor can seem like no big deal; by contrast, in grad school, your absence is more conspicuous because you are responsible for being an active participant. As an undergrad, you may have routinely cranked out papers the night before they were due, without getting feedback ahead of time; doing so in grad school leads to stress and poorly developed work. Yet, as we reiterate throughout this book, it is not until we bump against the unspoken norms that we even become aware that they exist.

In chapter 2, you learned about the importance of having a strong sense of self as you enter a graduate program. While that identity is critical, it is not enough to get you to your advanced degree. There are a number of essential skills that you must practice to set yourself up for success. The good news is that none of these skills are innate; you don't have to be born with them, and, in fact, no one is—all are learned through repeated, concentrated practice.[2] The bad news is that rarely do folks openly talk about these core skills. Oftentimes, faculty focus on conveying course content and engaging students intellectually; they spend far less time discussing the actual nuts and bolts of how to get writing and research done. Some professors may assume that you already have these skills or at least understand that you should be working on them. There's also the distinct possibility that your professors may themselves still be struggling in these areas because their advisors did not directly guide them—perpetuating the silence around these foundational tools.

When I set out to write this chapter, I brainstormed a list of core skills that graduate students should cultivate. They came to me in a flash; I quickly filled several pages with my ideas. When I was done, I was struck by the realization that I am familiar with these core skills now because I began practicing them in earnest when I was an assistant professor. In fact, I have picked them up from reading some of the resources listed at the end of this chapter and by doing them as part of my job. That fact seems remarkable to me: How is it that while I was training to be a professional writer and researcher, no one openly addressed the skills I would need to do that work day in and day out?

What I also realize now is that there are multiple axes of learning in graduate school. Most of the attention goes to the specialized knowledge gained through coursework and research. At the same time—but no less importantly—you are learning the technical processes by which professional scholars do what they do, that is, the daily grind of intellectual engagement, the less glamorous side of things. Do not underestimate the importance of this learning: as a graduate student, you have the opportunity to establish the strong habits and workflow that will help you maintain your energy and focus and do your best work during each stage of your later career. The bottom line is that aside from the technological tools and apps that enable you to complete projects, and beyond the fellowships or stipends that enable you to dedicate yourself to your studies, you yourself are your most precious resource. So you must learn to manage yourself by constantly building up the techniques and community of support that allow you to endure on this journey, as well as by redefining your relationship to time, reading, and writing.

A too-brief note on ableism and graduate school: the academy is marked with a latent assumption that all students are neurotypical and not living with a disability. Most universities are woefully inadequate at meeting the needs of students with disabilities, let alone enacting policies, procedures, and supports to ensure that students with disabilities can excel. The academy, like virtually all institutions, places the responsibility of accessibility on the student, rather than on the institution itself. Many scholars have done important work in this area, which includes a critical reworking of the very frameworks we use to consider disability and education (if you have not read up on DisCrit, please do).[3] Work on universal design for learning also offers a helpful starting point for all of us in the academy to truly consider what it would mean to (re)envision our institutions to remove ableism from the center, and the potential impact that effort would have for the learning of all students.[4] All this to say that if you are a Latinx student living with a disability, some of these essential skills may require a different approach, and we want to encourage you to (a) seek out the support you need, and (b) push your institution when it falls short of providing the support you need. Most of us faculty members are still learning what it means to truly support students living with disabilities, and we appreciate your efforts to collectively help us envision how the academy can do better on this question.

Cómo Vuela el Tiempo: Managing Time

The farther you advance in your educational journey, the more autonomy you have over your time. Think about it: from kindergarten through high school, school days are highly structured, with specific class times, bells that release us or call us back into a classroom, and adults who track attendance. In college, that rigid structure falls away: suddenly your courses may meet only twice a week, with large gaps between classes. Your faculty may not even know your name, let alone note your presence. You have to learn to take advantage of different pockets of time to visit the library, attend office hours, or put in volunteer or work hours. Whether living at home or on campus, you have to learn to be more accountable to yourself so that you can meet important deadlines and benchmarks on the way to completing a bachelor's degree.

Graduate school is even more fluid. Courses may meet twice a week, once a week, or even every other weekend in some programs. Once you enter the thesis/dissertation stage, your time is completely your own; there is a rhythm to the term that is very predictable, and sometimes it is hard to adjust when that structure disappears. No matter what your particular situation is, learning how to structure days and weeks that likely will have very little intrinsic structure and accountability is critical to successfully completing your program.

Learn to Visualize Your Time

The first thing to understand is that as a graduate student, you are working with multiple timelines: course/term dates, usually set by the professor and outlined in the syllabus; academic-year deadlines established by the university that determine when you can add or drop a class, pay fees, apply for graduation, and so on; program/department-specific timelines, which may span multiple academic years, with important benchmarks for your degree progress; and finally your own personal or family timelines. Your primary goal is to develop a system that helps you visualize the time that you have and learn to prioritize the most critical tasks that keep you on track. It is imperative that you use a planner or calendar app to map the semester, not only marking but also providing yourself with alerts about important due dates and deadlines. Note these critical dates at the start of each term and academic year, especially as the university typically publishes each academic year schedule at least one year in advance. A planner or calendar system gives you an overview of these multiple timelines and integrates them into your conceptualization of time. If you don't write them down, you can easily lose track of where you are in the overall scheme of things and what tasks are most urgent.

Let us make this very clear: calendaring is not a question of personality or inclination. You may be thinking, "Nah, I don't need that. I can keep everything clear in my head," or "That sounds nice, but I'm not the type of person who can keep a calendar. I just don't remember to write stuff down." The reality is that if you are not someone who is inclined to keep a calendar or feel like you do not need a calendar, it is because you have decided you don't need to. We are here to tell you that you are wrong. Sure, for some of us, this comes more naturally, but this is not about an innate trait or inclination; you are not born a calendar person—you become one. So make the decision to become one. Doing so is not just about being on top of deadlines; it is also about creating a mechanism that allows you peace of mind because you are clear on what you need to do and when, rather than constantly worrying about missing or forgetting something. Like the other essential skills in this chapter, time management gets easier with practice. Most universities offer educational counseling services, either one-on-one counseling or group workshops on issues like time management, and there is no shame in taking advantage of free resources and advice.

It is best if your system has both weekly and monthly views of your time so that you can engage in backward planning. Backward planning basically means that rather than planning forward, as we tend to do, we begin at the end. As an example, let's use the due date for a term paper. In backward planning, we map out the smaller steps that go into a bigger project and plot them in reverse. For a term paper, the plan might look like this:

- Week 16/finals: paper due on X date, target submission on X − 1 (to allow for any tech glitches)
- Week 15: make final microedits on the paper
- Weeks 13–14: work on organizational macroedits to the paper
- Week 12: discuss your preliminary draft with the professor during office hours
- Weeks 9–11: assemble rough draft, engage with background readings, and so on
- Week 8: visit office hours to discuss preliminary approach for the paper

- Weeks 6–7: collect notes, review current readings, map out loose outline for the paper
- Week 5: brainstorm ideas for the paper, drawing on class topics already covered and looking ahead to upcoming readings

If your school is on the quarter system (terms of ten weeks instead of fourteen to sixteen weeks), this timeline will be even more compressed; in fact, time management and advance scheduling are even more critical when there are only ten weeks in the term and less time to play catch-up when you start to fall behind in your work.

Maybe you are looking at the plan outlined above and laughing to yourself because it seems unrealistic: we're suggesting that you start working on a final paper only a third of the way into the semester or soon after the quarter starts? I will readily admit that I never worked on major assignments this way. My basic approach was to suddenly realize that a major assignment was due in only two weeks; freak out and complain to my friends for a week; then write feverishly and with very little sleep in the two days before the essay was due, with zero discussion about my ideas with the professor or other students—only to repeat the process for the next two days to meet a deadline for another class. Did I get assignments done and pass my classes? Yes. Was that an ideal approach? No. Now that I am a more experienced writer, I understand that writing is a process (more on that below) and that writing three different twenty-page term papers using my old method is both stressful and unsustainable. I look back and wonder what was I doing with all of my time.

One excellent time-management technique for short-term planning is the Sunday meeting.[5] The idea is that before a new week starts, you carve out thirty minutes to plan the week ahead. The first step is to do a brain dump, a list of all the readings, project tasks, errands, and so on that need to get done. The next step is to block out times in your schedule when you are in classes or meetings, commuting, having meals, working out, and such. An important element of this step is to include time for rest and relaxation. Though it is easy to regard rest as a low priority—and it is quite possible that you credit the hustle for getting you this far—you need to recast rest as nonnegotiable; you need to recharge in order to be healthy as well as to have the energy to get things done. Rest is critical to our mental, physical, and emotional health—and we have more to say on that below. The final step in the Sunday meeting is to map the items in the brain dump onto the remaining open windows in your calendar. The reality is that not everything will fit—which means that you must determine what is most important. Are there things you can take care of next week? Delegate to someone else or get help to complete? Or simply let go of? The result of this system is that you can empower yourself and reduce stress in the knowledge that the most important things will get done if you are able to stick to the plan.

This approach to envisioning time is critical because it helps you understand how limited your time is. Imagine you do not use a planner, and the department graduate advisor invites you to table at an upcoming graduate recruitment fair. Perhaps you are inclined to say yes because you want to help recruit more diverse students, and when you think ahead to your coming week it seems reasonable to squeeze that in. However, if you completed your Sunday meeting, then you would realize that your time is not as expandable as you thought. What needs to shift to accommodate the three hours that you'll be at the fair? Perhaps you can commit to showing up for the first half of the event, rather than the entire thing; maybe you cut out something you deem less important; or maybe you will determine that you cannot attend at all, and commit instead to the next one.

In addition to not overestimating your available time, you also want to avoid overestimating how long you can sustain your focus. A dissertation coach once told me that we can focus for about forty-five minutes at a time before our attention begins to fade.[6] It is important not to set unrealistic goals: "I'll spend all day Saturday and Sunday getting caught up on the readings." First of all, it is physiologically impossible to focus on anything for eight hours straight. Second, is that how you want to spend your weekend? No. So instead, chunk your time into hour-long segments that consist of forty-five minutes of focused work, followed by fifteen minutes of rest: get a cup of tea, step outside for fresh air, stand and stretch, and so on. Notice that examples of rest do not include checking email or your social media accounts. Ideally, the rest break should not involve a screen. When the break is over, settle back in for another period of focus. If you can do three or four of these sessions in one day, well done! Pat yourself on the back, and then go do something else that takes less concentration. It takes practice, but you'll find that you are getting more done even though you are spending less time sitting in your office chair, precisely because this approach is about building in breaks, which in turn allow you to be more focused and productive during designated worktimes.

Time management must also include time for rest. We are not machines who can work around the clock. In fact, without designated, preplanned time off, we risk burning out. How are you going to make your academic pursuits sustainable for the long term? You also may fall into the common trap of being too hard on yourself and never enjoying the time you spend doing other things. For example, when you are procrastinating on work by binge-watching your favorite show, you are neither enjoying the time spent watching because the back of your mind is consumed by guilt and the thought, "I should be writing"—nor are you doing the actual work that you feel you should be doing. It's a no-win situation. Careful time management will enable you to block out rest time and then truly take advantage of the opportunity to rest or pursue the interests and hobbies that make you who you are.

CONSEJO #2 One thing that made me successful in grad school was keeping a strict 8:00 a.m. start time at the office so that I could have afternoons to eat properly, go outside for exercise, and then come back refreshed to read for another two to three hours before bed (doing about ten hours of focused work most days). Since I am not a morning person, I also left myself an explicit to-do list with the first three to five tasks I needed to do in the first hour at my desk the next morning (this freed up my brain to sleep and relax at night and helped me do things on autopilot while my brain woke up in the mornings). Also, keep track of how much time you are actively working so that when you get to X hours per week (or whatever your limit is), you can tell yourself you have done enough and give yourself permission to take a day or a couple of half days off from the all-consuming grad school.

Esther Díaz Martín, Latin American and Latino Studies and Gender and Women's Studies, University of Illinois at Chicago

---

In addition to short-term/semester planning, it is also critical to create a five-year plan to visualize bigger benchmarks toward degree completion, dates, and timelines that span multiple years. As explained by academic coach Karen Kelsky, such a plan lets you map out over many months major writing projects or thesis chapters, notable program deadlines (scheduling an oral exam or thesis defense), yearly conferences you plan to attend, annual fellowship and grant deadlines, and more.[7] The benefit of this approach is that it can help you create more specific goals—so that instead of a vague idea of "finish my dissertation," you can instead say, "In January of [three years from now], I plan to have four dissertation chapters close to completion, and a draft of the final chapter that I will submit to the American Studies Association meeting in January. Then, if it is accepted, I will present it in October when I will be on the job market so that I can network with other scholars."

One last note on keeping a calendar: it is very difficult to keep more than one calendar successfully. Sometimes graduate students will take the recommendation to keep a calendar to heart and then go overboard. Keeping more than one calendar is not wise, simply because it is very easy to write something down in one place that conflicts with something in another place. Decide what system will work for you—be it Google Calendar, another calendar app, a bullet journal, or an old-fashioned paper calendar (for those of you into paper planners, check out Quo Vadis, which Genevieve has been using since 1998, or Uncalendar, which I have used since 2007)—and stick with it.[8] Record everything in that one place so you can make sure you always have it at the ready.

CONSEJO #3   Grad school is like undergraduate finals week, except every week is finals week. The feeling of urgency is nonstop. Endless deadlines, reading for your classes, reading for your own research, dreaming up and designing your research project, papers to write, going to the graduate writing center, networking, finding mentors, applying to fellowships and grants, applying to conferences, preparing presentations, scripts for said presentations, TAing, grading, trying to keep a roof over your head and your belly full on a very low income (if you're entering academia for the money, turn around now), socializing, nurturing your friendships and relationships, oh, and self-care??? The list is endless (and if you're a parent or caretaker, that list is even longer).

Jack Cáraves, UC Chancellor's Postdoctoral Fellow, Department of Gender and Sexuality Studies, University of California, Riverside

---

Bolster Time Management with Accountability

Once you have begun to redefine your relationship with time, you have set a foundation for short- and long-term goal setting, which you can then communicate to others as an accountability mechanism that keeps you on track amid so much unstructured time. Learning to cultivate accountability is an essential skill for academic researchers because we are expected to work independently, setting our own internal deadlines for every long-term writing project. This issue greatly challenged me in graduate school. I was productive while I was still engaged in coursework because there was a clear schedule set by the professor, and I enjoyed the social aspects of being in class. Once I moved out of courses and into thesis writing, however, I began to struggle with time management. I had goals ("finish chapter 2 of my dissertation") but did not know what a reasonable timeline was or how to break down that goal into specific steps. My advisors were supportive but hands-off, having confidence in me and, assuming that no news is good news, that I was making adequate progress. Unfortunately, I wasn't making any progress at all. In addition, I was lonely and missed seeing my friends in class, as some of them were also in the dissertation-writing stage, either no longer coming to campus regularly or traveling for their research.

Having greater accountability would have helped me significantly. Accountability can take many forms: a writing partnership or group of friends who meet regularly to share progress updates, set new goals, and/or write together; biweekly or monthly check-ins with faculty advisors to discuss the research and writing process; or even just having specific benchmarks mapped onto a calendar. It is a valuable exercise to reflect on what kinds of accountability you can begin to build and to practice it early in your program. Accountability groups also take different forms depending on where you are in the program: they can be class-based or for a limited time, such as a circle of classmates that meets to compare notes on the reading before class or a peer who agrees to meet at a café to crank out drafts of an assignment for class. Once you are in the thesis-writing stage, accountability becomes even more critical. If you work full-time or live off campus, you can seek out online writing and accountability groups, or take advantage of writing retreats and boot camps to help you make progress on your work between academic terms (examples are listed at the end of this chapter).

It's also important to consider what you find most distracting. We will talk about this a bit later in more detail, but a part of accountability is building internal accountability. Once you determine what is most distracting to you (Organizing your home and housecleaning? Social media? Netflix?), you can develop techniques to manage and minimize these distractions.

Before we move on to our next essential skill, we want to revisit a conversation that began in chapter 2: time management is even more critical for students who work part- or full-time in addition to going to grad school—especially if your job is unrelated to academics, which mentally can take you farther afield from your primary focus as a scholar. Your options for managing work depend in part on what kind of program you are enrolled in. Some master's programs offer courses in the evenings or on weekends specifically to accommodate the schedules of students who work full-time. Yet, even while the program may schedule courses in such a way, keep in mind that you are still responsible for setting aside the time to do the work for your classes. Consider the changes you may have to make throughout the day to sustain your energy and focus for tackling coursework on the days—or week—you don't have class. In a similar vein, if your classes fall on the weekend, then you should plan ahead earlier in the week if you are used to using Saturdays for running errands. Of course, managing time between school and work is all the more complicated if you have caregiving responsibilities—and we have much more to say about navigating family relationships in chapter 6.

Most doctoral programs have the unspoken expectation that you will be a full-time student. To make this manageable in social sciences and humanities fields, many PhD programs offer tuition benefits, modest fellowship stipends, assignment as a teaching assistant, and/or small research or conference travel stipends. Yet, as discussed in chapter 1, grad school is expensive, and even in the best of these scenarios, you may need loans or another job to supplement your income. If you can, see what part-time employment opportunities exist on campus, such as working at the library or affinity-group centers, as these are jobs that can help you expand your social network on campus and make it easier to manage your time because you will already be on campus.

A personal anecdote that goes a bit against the grain: Genevieve worked thirty hours a week throughout her time in graduate school, in a program in which it was assumed (though not explicitly stated) that everyone should attend school full-time and not have other substantial work. Though many worked on campus in various graduate student employment opportunities, she worked for a nonprofit organization that funded a scholarship program on campus for students of color. So, while her work was largely (but not entirely) on campus, she was not doing the typical sort of graduate student work, and she was working much more than her peers. It was a personally fulfilling job and also was necessary because the graduate student stipend she was offered as a part of her fellowship was not enough to survive on in the Bay Area. Time management was key, and truthfully, it is not a model she would necessarily recommend (largely because she slept too little, drank too much coffee, and had way too much going on), but she shares the example to acknowledge that it can be done. Work is something personal that we need to make decisions about, like every other part of balancing life along with graduate school.

Read Like an Academic

No matter how well or poorly you plan your time, there is always a honeymoon period at the start of each term when you are excited to dig into new readings and topics. Then, a few weeks in, the readings do turn out to be really great—but they are also incredibly dense, so it takes you twice or even three times as long to understand them. Even though you have carefully mapped out your time, the readings start piling up, and now you are reading faster or even showing up to class having barely read even one of the readings, let alone the four that were assigned, hoping and praying that the professor does not ask you something you feel ill-equipped to answer because you definitely don't want to look like the Latino who didn't do the homework.

Okay, let's take a pause—and acknowledge that what differentiates graduate-level study from the undergraduate experience is that there are more readings, they are more complicated, you are expected to engage with them on a deeper level, and they come at a faster pace. The key to staying on top of things is to learn to read like an academic, which means reading strategically. So, what does that look like?

To start with, academics rarely pick up a book, open to page one, and plow right through to the end. In grad school, there is too much for you to do to spend time treating each assigned text as a mystery novel where you must pay attention to every word. Rather, begin by reading the table of contents or, in the case of a journal article, flip through the pages, observing how the text is organized: What is the title? What are the chapter titles or headings within the article? How long is each chapter or section? Paying attention to these details will enable you to understand how the text is constructed so that you can identify particular sections that catch your interest. Spend time reading the abstract (found at the beginning and providing a brief summary of the piece) or introductory chapter, which will help you understand the aim and focus of the piece before you jump into the text. Armed with this overview, you can then read the sections or chapters that seem most interesting or relevant. Yes, you read that correctly: in graduate school, no one expects you to have read every word of every single assignment. What is expected is that you have read enough of it to be able to engage with it substantively, whether in preparation for discussion or to bring it into conversation in your research. You are expected to understand the argument and/or intervention that is being made in the text. Side note: there will be certain foundational texts you are expected to read carefully and know inside and out. These vary by field and discipline. Professors will identify these for you. So, yes, sometimes and with some texts, you need to do a very careful, very deep read. But most texts are not foundational texts.

As you read, do your best to stay intellectually curious and to read charitably. In every graduate course, there is at least one student who jumps into every reading ready to point out its flaws and shortcomings. This negative point of entry is the mainstay of students who mistakenly believe that they will impress the professor by tearing down another scholar's work to demonstrate their own superior thinking. Don't be intimidated by that student—or, worse, don't become that person. Set yourself apart by striving to show nuance in your thinking by acknowledging what the author was trying to do, pointing out some strengths in the piece, and then raise the objections or questions that occurred to you. This engagement is different than searching for ways to disregard, discredit, or debase every reading on principle. Read the work of others the way that you would like your own publications to be read in the future—pointing out some things that could have been done better but first acknowledging the valuable or innovative aspects of your contributions.

On the flip side, no text is pure perfection. Many readings will absolutely change the way you think about topics that are important to you, introducing concepts and methods that will rock your intellectual world. Hold on to those moments. These are some of the best parts of being in grad school. However, try to keep the same inclination toward nuance. Do not treat even your favorite writers as gods who should never face critique. I recently heard a colleague say, "Be loyal to ideas, not to people." So the advice shared above also works here: engage with texts the same way you want your readers to engage with you. While it would feel great to be in a room with colleagues who are fanatical about your work, you want to see your ideas applied, expanded, questioned. Superficial declarations that your work is "amazing" will not help you grow as a writer and thinker.

Keep the same open mind with works that do not obviously connect with the topics and methods you came to graduate school to explore. You will be assigned some readings that initially seem boring or unrelated to your broader interests. Yet even these texts can help you further your own projects if you consider not just the content but the writing: perhaps it is a book with a compelling introduction that draws you in, or is well organized and makes its arguments clear—in which case, make a note of how the author achieves this effect as a model for your own writing. If the piece is challenging to get through, the language is too dense, or the book is poorly organized, then make note of the experience you had as a reader and reflect on how you can avoid doing the same things to your readers. This approach is all the more important when you are reading theory, which at times can alternate between thrilling (discovering fascinating critical concepts) and frustrating (pulling out your hair because you read something three times and still do not understand it). Reflect on your reactions here, even when you are confused; there are likely instinctual threads where your scholarly self might do more digging.[9] Always remember that while theory may feel intimidating, it is a critical part of graduate education. If you need inspiration, check out "Theory as Liberatory Practice" by bell hooks, which opens with a powerful message: "Let me begin by saying that I came to theory because I was hurting—the pain within me was so intense that I could not go on living. I came to theory desperate, wanting to comprehend—to grasp what was happening around and within me. Most importantly, I wanted to make the hurt go away. I saw in theory then a location for healing."[10] Consider what you might heal through an engagement with a tough and thought-provoking theoretical piece.

Con la Pluma en la Mano

It is important to interact with the text as you read—which may sound odd, since reading is generally a solitary activity, though all this interaction requires is that you read with a (physical or digital) pen or highlighter in your hand. You need a tool so you can mark up the text, underlining passages and marking important points, questions, or reactions that you can return

to later or add to class discussions. If parts of the reading moved you, underline or bracket those and write a note about why each is significant. If
you are confused or feeling lost, mark that too, with the question that is
going through your mind. An important aspect of this work is to always
leave a note about your mark or highlight—otherwise you will return to the
reading, see something highlighted, but not recall why it was notable. You
will have to waste time reviewing the piece to try to remember: "Wait, why
did that quote seem so great the other day?"

In a text that is broken down into chapters, it is a good habit to jot down
key takeaways on the first or last page of a chapter, again as a way of leaving yourself a trail that enables you to find your way back into the text and
recall what you read. In this deep work of reading, always rephrase core
insights and takeaways in your own words, which also will aid your ability
to recall and write about these ideas in your own voice.

Over time, you can turn these highlighted passages into strong reading
notes. As I once learned, you should aim to take notes along three different
levels:[11]

1   Summary: here you seek to answer the basic questions: What is
    this reading about? What is the author's core argument, and what
    evidence do they provide to support it? The answers are usually
    embedded in the introduction to the piece and underscored in the
    conclusion.
2   Dialogue: at this level, you want to understand the broader con-
    text and reasoning behind the author's argument. What other
    scholars is this author in dialogue with? What are the larger ques-
    tions and academic fields they are responding to? Where and why
    are they entering the conversation? In a well-organized text, this
    information is provided in the literature review.
3   Application: this final level is most critical to your intellectual de-
    velopment, as it is where you engage with the text in a more active
    way. The most important question is: How can you use this text to
    develop something that you want to say? Is it a piece that supports
    an argument that you intend to make? Is it one that you will have
    to provide a counterargument for? How do you want to respond as
    a scholarly colleague?

Essentially, by recording these notes you are developing an annotated bibliography, which is a list of the books and articles you have read, each of

which is accompanied not only by a short summary but also—more help-fully—a personal record of your thoughts on how it relates to the overall field and contributes to your thinking on a given topic.

Keeping Track of Your Readings

Now that you are prepared to read in a substantive way, the final thing to consider is how to keep track of the numerous readings you will encounter through your coursework and research. The earlier you develop a system for tracking (a) citations and (b) your reading notes, the easier it will be to develop literature reviews, prepare for oral exams (if your program has them), and recommend readings to others.

Many scholars use citation or reference-tracking software. There are a wide range of programs available; some are free, some may be available through your university library, and others are fee-based (but often have student discounts); a few are listed at the end of this chapter. Though each has its own particular set of features, they generally do the same thing: record citation information, help you generate a list of works cited in the correct format, and allow you to enter tags and notes that help you organize and search through the entries for easier recall. While you can survive grad school without using such a tool, it can be very useful to have this information all in one place rather than spread across different documents and handwritten notes—especially the night before an essay is due and you cannot recall the author and page number of the perfect quote that will help you underscore a key point. Save yourself the stress and panic by investing the time to explore and make regular use of reference software.

Another benefit to tracking your readings is that, over time, you will be able to look through your reading notes and begin to identify topics and questions you repeatedly explore. Sometimes we get so busy in the day-to-day grind of the semester that we do not pause to reflect on what we have been learning or how it relates to the broader intellectual questions that drive us. However, reviewing your reading notes will illuminate impor-tant themes in what you are processing and issues you find exciting. These notes will lead you to the bigger questions that you may not even realize are guiding your intellectual journey. Once you tune in to those, then each class provides you with the opportunity to explore different facets of that larger problem or issue. As a result, when it comes time to identify a topic for a writing project, you will have a strong starting point to home in on your focused research questions.

A reference-tracking system also enables you to connect different readings and create a map of the scholarly dialogue you want to engage in through your own original research. The ability to envision this conversation comes from your notes that you took on dialogue, recording who each author was responding to and why. You may discover that readings you did in two vastly different courses are in fact grappling with the same questions. And once you can see that connection, then you are less likely to think, "Well, for my paper on sugarcane workers in the Dominican Republic, the readings in my Twentieth-Century Caribbean History class are probably the only ones I can use." Rather, you will be able to take a more expansive view of different ways scholars have explored the larger question, drawing interesting connections to readings from different areas of your studies.

Become a Thoughtful Contributor

In my first quarter of graduate school, I took an introductory seminar that was taught by an anthropology professor. The class was a mix of students in and outside of my program. My mom had given me the impression that, because I had taken one year off between undergrad and grad school, I would be the oldest person to ever enroll in a PhD program. On the first day of this class, I realized that, at age twenty-three, I was one of the two youngest people in the room. Many of my peers had earned master's degrees and were a few years older than me. As I mentioned previously, they spoke and acted with confidence.

Our first assignment was to read Baudelaire's "The Dandy" and "write a response to it"—that was it, no further instructions about format, length, or a guiding question to use as a starting point. I read the piece. Despite feeling lost, I literally penned some thoughts on a sheet of loose-leaf paper. I stopped at my program's computer lab to walk over to class with the people in my cohort—one of whom saw my handwritten response and gasped, "You didn't even *type* it?!" It had never occurred to me to do so—again, the professor had not given any specific instructions—and, embarrassed, I quickly typed and printed my response before we headed to class. The professor asked us to take out our reflection and pass it to the person to our right, who would read it, pass it to the next person, and so on. He said we would do this for the first fifteen minutes of every class to kick-start discussion. I slid my paper to the right and took the one handed to me. What brilliance seemed to emanate from that page! And the next, and the next. Reading the words of my peers made me realize that I had completely misunderstood the point of "The Dandy." I watched helplessly as my reflection made its way around the room, exposing my inadequacies to everyone whose eyes scanned that sad little sheet of paper.

It took me a long time to get over that feeling of incompetence and to see myself as an equal contributor in the classroom. I felt terror as I would read challenging texts and understand very little, yet had to show up to class and act as if I knew what was going on. Now, nearly twenty-five years later, I wish I could go back in time and tell myself, "It's okay. You don't have to already know what you came here to learn."[12]

I share this memory as a way to illustrate that one of the most essential skills in graduate school is to learn to see yourself as an interlocutor, a term for someone who contributes to a conversation by sharing their thoughts and asking interesting questions. Ultimately that is what academia is: an ongoing conversation among people who are dedicated to reading, analyzing, and asking new questions to cultivate deeper individual and collective understandings of important issues and debates.

Being an Interlocutor in Class

One of the primary differences between undergraduate and graduate education is that faculty expect graduate students to take significantly more ownership of the class—meaning they expect you to be fully prepared by having completed the readings, identified key points, and developed your own insights or questions about the materials. Speaking from my experience as a professor, when I teach a graduate seminar, I come to class with my own key points and reasons why I assigned the reading, yet when it is material that I have taught for many years, the exciting part for me is engaging in a dialogue with a new set of students who, individually and collectively, bring new perspectives on and questions about the reading that keep me learning. Nothing is more frustrating than trying to get a conversation started and realizing that few, if any, students are prepared for meaningful engagement. It makes for a very long class session and puts all the responsibility on the professor to keep the conversation afloat.

As a graduate student, your role is to push yourself to participate in academic debates and to propose new ideas and questions to help other scholars see new angles of a problem you are exploring together. Aim to contribute at least one solid question or response in each class meeting. Of course, this aim is easier said than done when you are encountering new and complex concepts and trying to connect them to what you learned as an undergraduate (not to mention also harder to do if you have not made much progress in the assigned reading). It takes practice and courage to be willing to risk thinking aloud, but if you show a willingness to do so, you can keep yourself in the conversation and get support from others in the class to help you focus your ideas.

Sometimes you may feel put on the spot or get called on directly, only to find that your mind has totally blanked or you have no idea where the conversation is because your attention was elsewhere. In those situations, the best answer is "I don't know" or "I'm not sure," both of which are hard to say aloud. But here is a critical move: learn the pivot—that is, admit that you are not sure and then add a *but* that connects to something you do know. Here are some examples: "I'm not sure what Baudelaire is getting at in this essay, but his focus on style reminds me of what I learned about zoot suits and the ways that young people of color used that style of dress to flout societal expectations during World War II." Or, "I am not familiar with the concept of liminality, but it sounds similar to what Gloria Anzaldúa calls 'mestiza consciousness.'" Pivoting with "I don't know, but" can offer you some breathing room when the fear of not knowing strikes. You will get others in the room to pause while also keeping the conversation moving by contributing connections to other ideas that you have encountered previously.

A key strategy for figuring out places where you can jump into the conversation is to bring your reading notes with you to class and to take notes actively during class discussion. Again, easier said than done: if you're sitting in a three-hour seminar that is based on discussion or with a professor who rarely lectures, does not use presentation slides, and does not write on the board, it can be challenging to know what to write down. Some things to note during class include core concepts from the readings; important definitions and examples that emerge during discussion; insights offered by other students; references to other ideas or texts shared by others; and your own emerging questions or ideas. Making an effort to take class notes can help you maintain your focus during a long seminar. Some classes may meet once a week for three hours, and, depending on the time of day the class meets, it can be challenging to sustain your energy for that long. Active note-taking can help you stay fully present. As you take notes for class, do not attempt to capture every comment word for word; you'll get overly caught up in the act of note-taking and be less engaged in the discussion (you are not a court reporter). For this and other reasons, taking notes on paper is often encouraged rather than on a tablet or laptop.

One final important point about engaging in class: listen carefully and respond thoughtfully to what the other students are saying. Also, when you speak, remember to make eye contact with others, not just the instructor. When I facilitated class as a professor, I often noted that whenever I posed a discussion question, the respondent typically looked directly back at me, forgetting to turn toward their peers who were also participating in the conversation. Or I would see essays where I recognized a great insight that had been shared by another student during class discussion, yet went uncited. Your peers are other emerging scholars who will have interesting perspectives, so when they say something amazing, aim to respond to their comments by acknowledging (verbally and later, as you are writing) how their words added to your own understanding.

Contributing Outside of Class

In addition to making yourself visible by participating in class, you have the opportunity and responsibility of being an interlocutor outside of class in two key locations. The first is during office hours. Perhaps, as an undergraduate, you visited office hours rarely, if at all. Yet, when done right, these visits are an effective tool for talking through your ideas and connecting class readings and discussions to the core questions you came to grad school to explore. These visits also help you gain a sense of the different advising styles and strengths of the faculty in your program.

If you are having difficulty in a class, then you must push yourself to visit office hours to enlist the professor's support in finding a way forward. But you do not need to have a challenge to visit office hours—in fact, you should go precisely to discuss a reading that has galvanized you or an idea raised in the class that has sparked your interest. You can ask for further readings on a topic that is important to you. You could also talk about graduate school by asking your faculty about their graduate school experience and the techniques and tools that they use in their work. Develop the habit of regularly checking in with faculty, even after your time in their course has ended. The more advocates you develop, the better. There is a longer conversation about office hours in chapter 5.

The second key place to cultivate visibility as an interlocutor is at campus talks and events. It is a good idea to attend them whenever your schedule allows because oftentimes these are important academic social occasions where you get to know who's who around campus. You will get to see different presentation styles—again, picking up ideas for techniques you would like to emulate or avoid when you present your work—and learn about emerging scholarship in your field. You also may get to meet well-known or cutting-edge scholars. Take notes at these talks, just as you would during a class, always noting the speaker, date, and title of their talk. Consider participating in the question-and-answer session after the presentation with a thoughtful follow-up question. It can be intimidating at first, no doubt, but remember that your goal is to practice cultivating your professional scholarly persona and to help others see the kinds of interests and questions you bring to the table as a colleague. You never know what kind of generative intellectual and social connections may develop from attending these kinds of campus events.

CONSEJO #4   An immense shift needs to happen between undergraduate and PhD studies: undergrads are mostly expected to consume knowledge produced by others; doctoral students are training to be knowledge producers. Reframe your role as a "student." A PhD not only requires you to read and retain more information, but you must now also understand the genealogy of ideas to figure out how you want to position yourself and what interventions you want to make in which scholarly conversations. More than just studying for tests, you are learning that everything in academia—every research method, methodology, theoretical framework, citational practice, organizational approach, academic journal—is a marker and a tool. Besides developing expertise on your topic, you are learning to wield these tools to create the knowledge and the change you want to see in the world—within a system that communicates on many levels. Stop thinking about writing progress based solely on how close you are to meeting a word requirement; instead, practice developing robust arguments and engaging meaningfully with existing research to help you produce the necessary building blocks to move fields in new directions. Most importantly, take on these challenges by grounding yourself in the ideas and communities that inspired you to pursue this journey in the first place.

Leisy Abrego, Department of Chicana/Chicano and Central American Studies, University of California, Los Angeles

---

Envision Yourself as a Professional Writer

Did you do a double take when you read the title of this section? Did you gulp, "Who, me? A professional writer?" That would have been my reaction back in the day—because I went into grad school thinking I would become a professor, not a professional writer, little suspecting that successful professors are professional writers.[13] So, guess what? I have some good news: writing is not an innate ability, something you are born to do. Far from it! As stated earlier in this chapter, writing is a learned skill developed through intentional practice. Consider the star tennis player who is able to deliver a decisive serve as if by instinct—because they spent years doing mundane drills of each stroke until they perfected it.[14] The same is true for academics: we practice writing over and over again, get feedback, make revisions, get more feedback, and so on.

Many of us do not realize the depth and intensity of this process, however, and we often do not even know where to begin. Writing can feel overwhelming and can even strike fear into us to the point where we get stuck, staring despondently at the blinking cursor on a blank page. The stakes can feel high when what you are writing has a deep connection to your life and your identity. Genevieve and Leisy Abrego talk about this effect, as it relates to undocumented students writing about the realities of navigating undocumented status, in the introduction to their book *We Are Not Dreamers: Undocumented Scholars Theorize Undocumented Life in the United States*.[15] The reality is that most writers have anxieties, doubts, and insecurities; in fact, these feelings are part of the writing process. The good news is that it is possible to recognize them as anxieties and thus learn to manage and work around them.[16]

Writing anxieties often manifest in some variation of the following three phenomena. First is perfectionism: submitting assignments late or not making progress in your writing because you get so wrapped up in perfecting each word and sentence, or continuously looking over what you have written because you cannot let it go. At the root of perfectionism is a fear of judgment. Second is procrastination: avoiding your writing by instead focusing on endless unrelated tasks, such as cleaning the house, rearranging your books, or scrolling through social media. Sometimes procrastination masquerades as scholarly engagement by falling into a research rabbit hole: "I should read more on the origins of the Spanish-American War before I begin my essay on Puerto Rican migration to the

US in the 1950s." A third way writing anxieties manifest is through writer's block: staring at a blank screen or page, unable to commit to a single word. Reflecting on her experience as a writing teacher, Sandra Cisneros notably observes, "I'm convinced that writer's block doesn't mean that you don't have anything to say. Writer's block means that you're *afraid* to say what you really have to say."[17]

Understanding that anxieties are just anxieties that can be contained enables you to reframe your views about yourself as a writer. You can begin the work of seeing writing as a personally meaningful act that is worth the pain and effort. This reframing is significant for first-generation Latinx scholars, who may enter the academy feeling as if we are trespassing or only conditionally accepted. It is important to view writing as a privilege, a gift that we give to ourselves—we deserve the right to write. And though it may be hard to imagine this right now, there are folks coming behind you who will read your writing and who may find a home in your words.

So let's reflect on this question: Why do you write? There are many different ways you might respond, the most obvious of which is, "Well, I have to for school." That is true: throughout your education, your instructors have required you to submit written assignments, which you pushed yourself to do to complete a series of classes in pursuit of a degree. You might reply, "It's a practical skill to have." Indeed, there are very few white-collar career paths that will not expect you to be able to communicate clearly, concisely, and effectively, whether through reports, presentations, memos, or even basic email. Yet another, bigger response is, "I have something to say"—and many of us strive to disrupt the dominant narratives about our home communities held in mainstream scholarship and media. In other words, writing is powerful. Author Teju Cole captures this sentiment when he describes "writing as writing. Writing as rioting. Writing as righting. On the best days, all three."[18]

That is what it comes down to: we write because writing moves us. Think back on something you read that changed your life. All of us have that one piece of writing that sparked a flame within us. For me, it was bell hooks's *Black Looks: Race and Representation*, a collection of essays on race and pop culture. I read it during the summer after my first year of college, on a friend's recommendation. *Black Looks* was the first academic book I read by a Black woman scholar that openly addressed race and helped me put words to things I had noticed but did not yet have the language to describe. What a revelation! hooks's writing showed me that there is a way in academia to explore race (which was not clear in the assigned curriculum, which was pretty much all white dudes) and that scholarly work can be engaging and highly readable (and not boring, like so much of the work of the aforementioned dudes).

Take the time to reflect: What essay or book would you identify as having galvanized you? One that made you exclaim "Yes!" and underline whole passages? Hold on to that memory, that feeling of being transformed by the words on the page—because your words can one day play that same role for someone else. Sean Thomas Dougherty expresses this sentiment in his poem, "Why Bother?": "Because right now, there is / someone / out there with / a wound / in the exact shape / of your words." In other words, you have insights and perspectives that only you can put into the world where they can reach someone else who needs to hear them.

It is through our writing that we contribute to the conversations that matter. Far beyond anything else, the ability to develop a strong writing practice is the most important tool of academic success because "to write is to think."[19] Forget about the thousands of tools, calendars and planners, apps, coaching sessions, and whatnot that seem like keys to scholarly productivity and success. None of them will help if you do not embrace this core truth: writing is the most important tool because as an aspiring academic, you must learn to see yourself as a professional writer.[20]

Yet, for many Latinxs, embracing the identity of professional writer does not come easily because it requires us to radically redefine our relationship to writing and to question long-held narratives we have about ourselves as writers. Perhaps English is not your first language and there is a voice in your head that, as you write, whispers doubt about your word choices and syntax. Maybe that voice echoes the actual words of past teachers or school officials who shared negative feedback about your writing or doubted your potential. That voice could be rooted in experiences of being the only Latinx-identified student in your courses, so you felt little community as you learned to develop your writing. Again, we want to emphasize the main takeaway here: you are not alone. You are not the only student with writing anxieties and self-doubt—in fact, Professor Wendy Belcher, former editor at UCLA's Chicano Studies Research Center Press, identifies (and offers solutions for) twenty-eight common writing obstacles, many of which will feel familiar to you.[21] If you can find ways to work around those issues, just imagine what will be possible once you are ready and able to claim your identity as a professional writer.

Ways to Create Positive Writing Experiences

So how do we do the actual writing? There are several approaches that can help.

COMMIT TO A DAILY WRITING PRACTICE · If you engage in the act of writing only when an important assignment is due, then this activity will inevitably feel high-stakes. However, the more frequently you do anything, the more routine and less threatening it becomes. In *Becoming an Academic Writer*, Patricia Goodson recommends establishing a daily writing practice by setting a timer for fifteen minutes and writing until the timer goes off. Each day, add one more minute to your timer, until you work up to blocks of forty-five minutes to an hour.[22]

CONSCIOUSLY WORK TO CHANGE YOUR MINDSET TOWARD WRITING · How can you turn writing from a foot-dragging experience to one that puts a spring in your step, even when it is so challenging? Rather than viewing writing as something you *have* to do, try to see it as something you *get* to do. Think about how rare it is for people from our backgrounds, who are resilient, fierce, and brilliant in so many different ways, to actually have the time, energy, and invitation to record their thoughts in writing. Moreover, you came to graduate school in part because you wanted the opportunity to expand your knowledge and skills, so now is the time to engage. This type of reframing can make the work more enjoyable.

MAKE WRITING A CEREMONY · Approaching writing as a ritual may help you view it as a sacred element of your day. Create a small ceremony that helps you mark writing blocks as special. I recall one former student who explained that he began each writing session by preparing a cup of coffee, lighting a candle on his desk, burning sage to cleanse the space, and placing his favorite affirmation near his laptop. This ritual mentally prepared him to focus on each day's writing goals and to situate writing as a mindful exercise.

OR, HEY, MAYBE DON'T MAKE WRITING A PRECIOUS CEREMONY · Take inspiration from writing groups like Shut Up & Write!, which do exactly what the name implies: show up, sit down, and get to work. The more you approach writing head-on and matter-of-factly, the sooner it will become as mundane as brushing your teeth. Sometimes, elaborate writing practices impede writing, because they train us to think that we cannot write unless everything is perfectly aligned and in place, and often we do not have that luxury.

SET SPECIFIC GOALS FOR YOUR WRITING SESSIONS · Identify manageable tasks within your broader writing project that you can focus on when you sit down to write. If you start with a vague goal like "work on my essay," you will likely be unable to gain much traction. By contrast, if your goal is "integrate the three articles I read yesterday into the literature review" or "draft the introduction to my essay," then you have something concrete to keep you focused during your writing time. Another way to concretize your writing goals for the day is through setting a target word count: "I am going to draft five hundred words for my methods section today."

HELP YOURSELF FOCUS ONLY ON THE WRITING · To the extent that you can, eliminate the distractions that lure your attention away from writing. There are myriad apps that can assist you—and though exploring and testing them can become a rabbit hole, if you find some that help, then it is worth seeking them out. For example, there are internet blockers, bare-bones writing apps, word count targets, soundscapes, and more (samples are listed at the end of this chapter). There is even Write or Die, which commits you to a time or word count goal, with unpleasant (virtual) consequences if you do not reach your goal.

CREATE A MISSION STATEMENT FOR YOUR PROJECT · When writing becomes painful, it is easy to become dejected and wonder why you signed up for this. Writing a clear mission or statement at the start of your project can help you maintain a sense of purpose and envision the connection between what you want to say and the community you want to represent. In two or three sentences, explain what you want your essay to do, the scholarly intervention you want to make, and why. Hold on to this mission statement and revisit it when you have lost your way in the process.[23]

MAKE WRITING SOCIAL · So often we work on our writing alone, miserably hunched over a laptop, squirreled away in our bedrooms. Yet, as Belcher reminds us, "Without community, writing is inconceivable."[24] Join a writing group or enlist a friend for a weekly writing date. This group or partnership can be for accountability (weekly progress updates and support for working around the challenges), actual in-person writing for companionship or to exchange feedback, or a combination of these purposes as needed. Having trusted partners in the writing process also enables you to talk out your ideas and get quick feedback that pushes your project along.

KNOW WHEN YOU NEED TO SET BOUNDARIES AND/OR WRITE ALONE · Okay, I know we literally just advised you to make writing social, but the reality is that sometimes the writing can get a little too social, meaning folks meet up to write in community but end up chatting more than writing. Find a core group of folks who are willing to commit to a brief check-in, then set a timer for focused work, followed by a round of writing updates, and then hunker down for another writing block. If your cohort or near-peers are not into the Shut Up & Write! model, you can always locate a local or online meetup with that name.

KNOW THAT WRITING IS NOT A LINEAR PROCESS · Maybe you imagine a real writer as someone who has a fully formed, brilliant argument, sits down, opens up a new document on their computer, and proceeds to type all the words, perfectly ordered from start to finish. Release that fantasy. As a writer, you must push yourself to corral your rambling ideas into a "shitty first draft," actively shape it into something readable to others, then get feedback that points out everything that is still wrong about it and sends you back to the drawing board.[25] On some days, your topic—especially when it has personal meaning—may feel too painful to write about, so instead of generating new text you have to switch to working on the bibliography or fixing the formatting, and you may feel like you lost a day of writing. The writing process is full of fits and starts, dead ends, surprise twists, and more. When it does not go smoothly, it does not mean something is wrong with you—it just means you are in the struggle alongside all other writers.

UNDERSTAND THE DIFFERENCE BETWEEN WRITING AND EDITING · What we refer to as "writing" is composed of different activities, from generating raw text, to macroediting (organizational editing) and microediting (proofreading spelling and grammar). Do not try to engage in these distinct activities all at once, because they work at cross-purposes. Generating raw text is akin to a brain dump; it requires you to turn off your inner editor to meet your goal. By contrast, macro- and microediting take a different kind of focus and require input from other people. In fact, you may want to do each type of writing in a different location to enforce the separation in

your mind—for example, generating text at your favorite café, then working on macro- or microedits at the library.

A final bonus tip: TAKE CARE OF YOURSELF PHYSICALLY AND GET REST ·
Writing is one of the hardest activities we engage in as scholars. It takes
tremendous brain power, and it taxes us not only intellectually but also
physically. Squinting at a bright screen can be tough on your eyes; meanwhile, hunching over the table while reading and typing can wreak havoc
on your neck and shoulders. Remember to take breaks, get some fresh air,
engage in whatever types of physical activity bring you joy (which also helps
the ideas flow), and do your best to establish a wind-down routine that enables you to get a full night's rest.

CONSEJO #5   I advise everyone to figure out their own writing process, which
may include physical, emotional, and spiritual dimensions (Do
you have to clean the house or make some tea first? Do you need
to write in your journal beforehand or talk through your ideas?
Do you need to offer a prayer or light a candle?). My own process
is: I write in a journal to confront emotional roadblocks, then I
print out an outline (that often changes) and an abstract with
my argument and intervention. I brainstorm write, then revise
endlessly, sometimes reading aloud, before sharing it with my
writing group, and then revise again. When I'm in writing mode,
I know insights will come first thing in the morning, so I keep a
notepad by my bed. I have learned to trust that I will get through
writing blocks by putting culo a la silla, that writing always
takes longer than you think, that regular exercise is critical for
clearing my head, and that I actually like writing despite the
challenges.

Pat Zavella, Department of Latin American and Latino Studies, University of California, Santa Cruz

---

What to Do When the Writing Is Not Happening

It is critical to develop a writing community because during the times
when you are truly stuck and unable to make any progress, you need to
have folks to turn to for help. The key, however, is to make sure that you are

turning to the right people at the right time. Here are some scenarios and steps to consider.

TROUBLE GETTING STARTED

- Move away from the screen. Set a ten-minute timer and freewrite with pen and paper, even if it means starting with "I'm having such a hard time getting started."
- Talk out your ideas using dictation software or a voice recorder.
- Start by writing what you know about your topic. Summarizing what you have already read or class notes that relate to your topic can help you generate momentum.

TROUBLE ARTICULATING YOUR IDEAS

- Take a friend out for a coffee or beer, ask them to hear out your ideas, repeat them back to you, and ask follow-up questions to help you see how to connect the strands of what you want to say.
- Imagine you are talking to a younger sibling or cousin who has asked what you are writing about. How would you explain the core points of your argument and its significance? Sometimes it helps to reflect on how to explain your topic to someone who is brand-new to the conversation.
- Make an office hour appointment with your professor to talk about the topic you are exploring and what you have developed so far.

TROUBLE ORGANIZING YOUR WORK

- Start off with a solid, argument-driven outline (thanks, Ananya Roy, for teaching Genevieve this one!). Craft an argument statement (check out *The Craft of Research*)[26] and then develop the headings for each section. Attach a word count (your best estimate) for each section heading. Then jump in one section at a time. That way, you are not tackling the entire paper or journal article each time you sit down; you are just sitting down to work on that six-hundred-word introduction today or that four-hundred-word methodology section.
- Look for a journal article that you can use as a model: examine the overall organization of the piece, how the sections are divided, how long they are in proportion to each other, and so on. This

process can help you break down your larger essay into more digestible components, turning them into building blocks that are easier to maneuver.[27]

TROUBLE MAINTAINING MOTIVATION

- Pull out your project mission statement (described above) to help you remember the core question and sense of purpose you identified when you started the essay.
- Keep a notebook next to you to capture your interrupting and/or resistant thoughts. Sometimes the act of moving these thoughts from your head to the page helps you to literally set them aside. As a bonus, you can then track them over time to identify the themes within your negative self-talk.
- Consider what is at stake by not writing this piece. Presumably, you are working on this because the topic or intervention it makes is meaningful to you, right? Spend some time reflecting on what would be lost if this piece were not out in the world.
- Remove the distractions and build in rewards. Identify what is distracting you (Netflix? Instagram? family issues?) and think through ways to minimize those distractions (Ask a friend to change your account password and not give it back until you write five thousand words? Put your phone on "do not disturb" and let your family know you'll be unreachable until 8 p.m.?). Take action—distractions will not go away unless you are intentional about putting them away. Also, build in the celebrations. What will you treat yourself to once you finish that article or submit that final paper? Identify it on the front end to serve as motivation.

CONSEJO #6 When working on a piece is so overwhelmingly painful, I just tell myself I am only going to write for five minutes. Inevitably, five minutes turns into twenty-five, and I feel super accomplished. I remember that I actually like to do this.

Esther Díaz Martín, Latin American and Latino Studies and Gender and Women's Studies, University of Illinois at Chicago

---

Ready for an Argument? Asserting Your Voice as a Scholar

Sometimes it is hard to make progress on a piece of writing because you did not start with a clear argument, which is the foundation of everything we write. As scholars, we are always arguing—not in the dramatic, yelling sense of the word but rather to take a clear stand on a certain topic, even if that stand is not a clear "I agree" or "I disagree," but instead "it's complicated." Even when you are assigned to write a brief reading reflection or discussion board post, you should think of yourself as forwarding at least one idea or viewpoint, however tentative, on the topic at hand.

However, as a graduate student, it is easy to wonder, "Who am I to take issue with this famous author?" While that sentiment is real, at some point you have to learn to see yourself as an interlocutor who thoughtfully questions what an author says, the evidence they bring, and how they present it. In fact, a large part of your journey as a graduate student is to learn not just to repeat the arguments of others but to build the courage to enter the debate in pursuit of new perspectives. In fact, that is one of the most important differences between being an undergraduate student and being a grad student, that is, someone developing into a professional writer. Moreover, as explained earlier, just because something is published does not mean that it is infallible. (If the challenge of engaging with a particular work is that you did not yet complete the readings, then that's a separate issue. The solution, in that situation, is to do enough strategic skimming to gain an overall understanding of the work so that you can begin a dialogue.)

The first step to crafting a strong argument is to understand where and why you are entering into an ongoing dialogue. Belcher draws a powerful comparison between writing a literature review and entering a room where people are already engaged in conversation: "It makes perfect sense that you wouldn't just walk into a room and start talking about your own ideas. If there were people already in the room, you would listen to them for a while first. If you decided to speak, you would do so because you agreed or disagreed with something someone else said. If the conversation went on for a long time without addressing some topic dear to you, you might say, 'I notice that we haven't talked about such and such yet.' In all cases, you would acknowledge the conversation and then make your point."[28] In other words, you want to contextualize your thoughts within the readings and class discussions that have informed your thinking to this point.

Oftentimes, you do not know where you are going with an argument until you reach the end—which underscores the truth of the statement "to write is to think." In case you missed it in the previous section: writing is not at all a linear process. No academic sits down with a fully formed argument, writes an opening sentence, then produces a sound and clear argument in gorgeous prose all the way to the end. That literally never happens! Writing is incredibly messy work, and usually it is not until you reach the end of your essay, when you have completely worked through your ideas, that you can finally articulate a clear version of what you wanted to say all along. For this reason, you must go back to the beginning to ensure that your introduction reflects your actual argument (not the one you thought you were making way back when you started). In fact, it is probably best to wait to write the introduction until the very end of the process.

I would like to share a great technique that I learned from Genevieve, who in turn learned it from one of her faculty mentors, Ananya Roy. Before you begin to write your essay, map out a full-sentence outline of the main points. The full-sentence part is critical—this is not the vague topic outline that I used to write before I learned this method (which explains why I used to feel that creating an outline was not much help). In the full-sentence outline, you do the advance work of making sure that your argument is structurally sound and that each section of your essay is connected to and builds upon the one that came before it. In this way, a full-sentence outline challenges you to think through each step of your argument. Once that is done, it is much easier to make progress on your essay when you have created a map that identifies the way. We provide an example at the end of this chapter.

Not only is a full-sentence outline a powerful tool, but so is its cousin, the reverse outline. You can use this technique to check your draft once it is complete. Begin by copying and pasting the first sentence of each paragraph into a new blank document, which will allow you to see the construction of your essay more clearly. Does each point pave the way for the next? Does the development of your argument represent a strong chain, or are there some gaps between your main points? If there are notable leaps from one point to the next, then those are places where you may need more evidence to support your argument.

Finally, just as when you are reading, remember to argue charitably with other scholars. Do not replicate that in-class dynamic of tearing down others' work to prove your own acumen. Adopting a snarky tone in your writing may feel witty and satisfying in the moment but will read as immature and unnecessary. Again, think about yourself long-term, cultivating a reputation as a thoughtful interlocutor from an early point.

Getting Feedback on Your Writing

One of the most challenging aspects of the writing process is receiving feedback. Many of us have been deeply scarred by painful feedback over the years—getting your essay back only to find that the instructor's red pen has torn it to shreds, followed by a hurtful critique. Nevertheless, we must learn to accept that feedback is an important part of the writing process. It is critical to seek out honest feedback on your writing so that you strengthen your skills and assert your findings clearly and persuasively. Understand that there are different aspects of feedback: sometimes you need macrofeedback, such as help organizing the elements of your argument or placing it more clearly within academic conversations; other times you need microfeedback, like proofreading grammar and spelling or word-smithing for more effective style. Not all faculty advisors are adept at or have the time for providing both types of feedback, so make sure to seek out different readers and editors. In fact, do not assume that your primary advisor(s) will provide microediting; instead, check out the writing center on your campus for that level of support. It is better to use your advisors' time working on the broader macroediting concerns. There is a broader and deeper conversation about critique in chapter 5.

When it comes to critique, it is also critical to distinguish between critique that is intended to strengthen your work and that which is meant to tear you down. Meaningful critique should not simply point out the flaws in your writing but should explain how and why the feedback would strengthen your overall argumentation in your essay or chapter. Poet Carmen Giménez Smith frames revision as helping someone find the heart of a piece of writing, underscoring the gift of pointed, constructive criticism that helps you identify and build on what is good and already strong within your work.[29] By contrast, critique meant to tear you down will highlight what's wrong and just leave it at that, without offering suggestions about what you can do in response. Such feedback achieves its aim by leaving you feeling at a loss about how to salvage what's good in your writing and carry it forward.

So, what about when the feedback is great? Well, be cautious here, too: beware of empty praise. We all dream of being told, "I really enjoyed reading your work—great job!" Such a response feels great in the moment; there is tremendous relief in seeing a short, positive statement, followed by a high grade. Whew! But let's be real: Is your essay actually perfect? Is there nothing you could have done to improve your writing? Highly unlikely. Sometimes, empty praise is a manifestation of a professor's discomfort working with historically underserved students: they are either afraid of providing critique across lines of ethnicity and race or not invested enough in you to give substantive feedback; instead, they take the easy route with a pat on the back. Yet they are doing you a great disservice because you will proceed farther into your education thinking that you are doing well, only to find a professor down the line who is able and willing to provide the tough love that you need, which will then come as a shock. You may look back and ask, "But I've always written that way—why didn't anyone tell me this before?" In other words, praise is helpful and can give you a boost of confidence, but always push to get critique as well.

Another downside of empty praise is that it makes receiving meaningful critique feel even more painful. Part of the issue here is to practice separating yourself from your writing: although you may have put your heart into an essay on a topic that is important to you, the reality is that your writing is not you. Critique of your work is not (in most cases) critique of you as a person. A helpful way to think about feedback comes from writer Tara Mohr, who encourages "unhooking from praise and criticism" so that we are not paralyzed by feedback that we take too personally. She explains, "Feedback doesn't tell you about you; it tells you about the person giving the feedback."[30] Through this lens, critique can be seen as a meter of how well you reached your intended audience. Taken to heart, this perspective can be liberating, because it helps you focus on your project's aim rather than on your personal worth as a writer.

Know When to Stop Writing

Part of the process of growing into your identity as a writer is to fully embrace all the stages of the process, from brainstorming and drafting to seeking feedback, revising, and editing. Again, the more you practice, the easier it is to understand where you are in the process, make revisions without feeling personally attacked, and genuinely look forward to getting developmental feedback that improves your work. However, this process cannot go on forever: there comes a point at which we need to let the project go. This can be hard to do when you know it's still not perfect and does not reach the heights you originally envisioned. That's okay. Writing is just writing—yes, it can be a powerful force, but the reality is that a single class essay or chapter of your thesis will not solve society's problems overnight.

Sometimes an external deadline (set by the professor) provides that stopping point: the paper is due, turn it in, and move on. But for longer projects, where we often set our own deadlines, we have to listen to the internal cues that may be pointing to the end of the project. At some point, you will find your mind wandering into other tangents and trails established by the current project. You may begin dreaming of the next project or study that has begun to capture your intellectual imagination. Let your current project begin coming to a close. Know that you may not have achieved perfection or established the final word on the topic at hand—but that your voice entered the conversation in an earnest effort to further the dialogue, and that is as good as it gets. Time to begin nurturing new ideas and writings.

If Essays Are Sprints, Then a Thesis Is a Marathon

Much of the advice shared up to this point has been general writing guidance centered on essays, that is, short, stand-alone pieces that summarize your learning on a topic specifically related to the course in which it was assigned. We would like to share some thoughts that are specifically focused on writing a thesis. There are two kinds of theses: a master's thesis, which is a long, independent research project, and a dissertation, which is a book-length research project required to complete a doctoral program. Both types of theses require you to engage with existing research on a specific topic and to contribute original insights to your academic field. Both are broken into distinct chapters, typically including an introduction, literature review, methods, findings, and conclusion, at least in social science fields. In the humanities, instead of a distinct lit review or methods section, there may be more of a historical background of your topic followed by thematic chapters. No matter which type of thesis you are working toward, it is a major scholarly accomplishment and something to be proud of.

Another defining characteristic of both master's theses and doctoral dissertations is that they do not happen overnight, in a week, or even in a month. In fact, as the heading above declares, an essay is to a sprint what a thesis is to a marathon. Think about it: If you had a goal of running a marathon, would you slap on some sneakers and run for more than twenty-six miles right out the door? Well, technically you could, but you would basically be asking for an injury, and it is highly unlikely you would complete the run unless you already were an experienced and fit athlete. The better way to undertake a marathon is to sign up for a running group, get guidance from experienced runners, and slowly build up to running more than twenty miles at a time over several months. Similarly, when you are preparing to write a thesis, you will engage in months of planning with your faculty advisors and create long-term structures of support with your peers. There are five important considerations when it comes to writing these longer projects.

The first challenge is how to make the idea of a thesis concrete, when the task seems so monumental—talk about the fear of a blank page. If it feels tough to get started on a fifteen-page essay, then try to imagine an eighty-page master's thesis or 250-page dissertation. Remember that when you begin working on the thesis, you are not starting from scratch, even though it feels like you are. You have selected a topic that has been shaped by your prior coursework, research, and ideas you have already explored. As an example, toward the end of my first year of grad school, I took an anthropology class called Postwar Jazz and Cultural Studies, where I wrote a research proposal on pre-1950s Mexican American music. A year later, that proposal formed the basis of my qualifying paper (a longer research project that demonstrated my preparation to take on a dissertation) on representations of women in corridos, a popular Mexican style of music, of the 1930s and '40s. That qualifying paper, in turn, became a chapter of my dissertation on early twentieth-century Mexican American cultural expression—and, years later, when I was a tenure-track professor, it was published as a journal article.[31] This example demonstrates why you should keep an open mind in all your studies, viewing both required courses and electives as fertile ground for great insights. I had enrolled in Postwar Jazz because I needed more units and someone assured me it was an easy course, but it inspired me to change the time period I wanted to focus on from the 1960s–70s to the 1910s–40s.

To bring together your existing work as well as make the thesis less abstract, try the following technique: buy a three-ring binder and 250 sheets of paper. Then review papers you have already written; copy and paste any sections, paragraphs, or even single sentences that are relevant for your thesis topic; and print them on the blank binder paper or take scissors and tape to literally cut and fix them onto the blank pages in the binder. You can also print out any daily freewriting you have done and place it in the binder. The key idea is that this binder makes an intangible thing (the thesis) into something you can literally hold in your hands as the elements come together.[32] This technique can be especially crucial when so many of our files live in the internet cloud; when you only see your work on the screen, it can be hard to appreciate the totality of what you have drafted.

Second, practice all the good writing habits we walked you through above so that you become more adept at simultaneously juggling the different phases of writing: freewriting and putting fresh thoughts on paper, macroediting those early drafts, and then microediting and polishing the nearly complete versions of your work. I say this because far from working on a thesis, you are actually working on a specific section within a much larger work: you are not simply writing but instead compiling the literature review, preparing the historical background, generating the introduction to chapter 2, and so on. Your goal is to move sections of your thesis through the pipeline in different stages: when you give your faculty advisors a draft of your first chapter, you can begin freewriting and mapping out the next chapter while you await feedback. Once you get that feedback, you will edit the first chapter while continuing to chip away at the first draft of the second, working on different parts of the thesis at the same time.

For that reason, it is critical to stay organized on a couple of levels. You should keep a thesis journal (physical or electronic, whatever works for you). This is a place where you record recommended readings, ideas that occur to you while listening to someone present their work, notes about the status of your work—even logging those resistant or negative thoughts as you write to get them out of your head, as mentioned earlier. You may want to use a bullet journal (if you are unfamiliar with a BuJo, an internet search for this term will yield examples and inspiration) or use organizational software such as OneNote or Keep It, which keeps your notes organized and searchable.

Another aspect of staying organized is developing a clear file-naming convention, such as "Title-Status-Date" (e.g., Introduction-Final-2022-06-17 or Chapter1-Draft-2022-08). Nothing is worse than editing part of your work, only to realize that you deleted a paragraph or section that can still be used after all. If you don't separate and back up your files, you risk losing earlier iterations of your work that may be helpful. You can always archive the old drafts later. Also, please don't try to keep your entire thesis in a single Word or Google document. It is better to organize your work into more manageable files, one per chapter or major section of your thesis. Moreover, you may be interested in investing in a specialized app for managing large writing projects, such as Scrivener or Dabble, programs that enable you to organize drafts, research notes, and related files all in one place.

A third consideration is to make a sustainable work plan. I cannot say this enough: the writing process is incredibly challenging. Remember all the time-management talk at the start of this chapter? Reflect on what time of day you are most focused and save the most challenging writing tasks—integrating new reading and insights, fleshing out your thoughts, and macroediting—for that time of day. Use the times when you are less focused on the easier writing tasks, such as updating your bibliography, tracking down upcoming readings, and formatting and proofreading your work. Establish regular and reasonable working hours—because you are not a writing machine. Schedule time for breaks, meals, exercise, sleep, and so on. One of my most productive periods in grad school was in my final year, when I made a commitment to my overall health, which had gone neglected in earlier years. Funded by dissertation-writing grants internal to my institution, one of which included a grad student office/study space at El Centro Chicano, I set the following schedule:

8:00 a.m.–12:00 p.m.:	Four focused forty-five-minute writing blocks
12:00–12:50 p.m.:	Daily workout on campus
1:00–1:45 p.m.:	Freshen up and eat a healthy lunch
2:00–3:30 p.m.:	Tackle the less-challenging tasks and prepare work for the next day
3:30–5:30 p.m.:	Mentor undergraduate researchers in feminist studies (a part-time campus job)
5:30 p.m. onward:	Commute home and personal time

This year was one of the most rewarding of my graduate career, as I felt in the zone with my writing, had more energy because I was taking care of myself physically, and finally felt like there was a light at the end of the dissertation tunnel. To be real, my example is predicated on the fact that I was fully funded, had a campus work space, and had no outside work or familial obligations. But whatever your circumstances, I hope you take away the reminder to not lose sight of the simple things—like meals, self-care, and downtime—that are essential to your ability to engage in your work over the long term and to manage your overall stress in the process.

The fourth consideration is to know that while it is your research project, that does not mean that you are writing it alone. You will have a team that sees you through, composed of the faculty who serve on your thesis committee and your peers who are also in the thesis-writing stage. While there are times when you may need some isolation to focus or avoid distractions, there are an equal number of times when you need community, commiseration, and feedback.

We have more to say about communicating effectively with faculty in chapter 5, but for now I will emphasize the following point: be in regular communication with your thesis committee, keeping them apprised of your work. When you are ready to share a draft with them, include a brief memo/email that (a) outlines what you have added, changed, or developed in this chapter since your last check-in and (b) identifies your current questions about your work and where you need feedback. Providing this memo will go a long way toward helping them focus their comments and zoom in on the new areas of your work. Do not be afraid to ask for their help as you tackle a major research project. While you want to be proactive in identifying next steps, you should also check in to make sure you are on the right track. There is a difference between asking, "What should I do now?" and saying, "Now that I've completed the methods section, I plan to complete the transcription of my interviews and begin a preliminary coding of the responses. Please tell me if there is a step I might be missing before I proceed."

When it comes to your peers who are also in the thesis-writing stage, consider meeting regularly to share upcoming writing goals, read early drafts of each other's work, and provide real talk and encouragement. If you are in a program that schedules public thesis defenses—a culminating event where a graduate student briefly presents their completed thesis, then engages in a scholarly discussion with their committee members—attend these. They will provide you with the opportunity to see how people who have completed their thesis speak about their work and help you visualize the day when you will present your own finished work.

The fifth and final thing we want to share is the following: your thesis is just that—a thesis. It is an intellectual exercise and stepping-stone toward degree completion (which itself is a stepping-stone toward a longer-term career plan). Your thesis is not your life-defining work or your greatest achievement. Now, this is not to say you shouldn't be exceptionally proud to have undertaken the work—you should be. But keep it in perspective: it is but one of many major achievements you will have in your lifetime.

You may feel tremendous pressure about its significance in the moment, but do not let that pressure keep you from completing it. Many students reach the **ABD** stage and then get stuck because they are so freaked out about writing the thesis. Don't let this happen to you. You can finish your thesis—and life will go on. Part of the pressure stems from feeling like a dissertation is a book, but here's a news flash: the dissertation is a book-length project, not an actual book manuscript. If you are preparing for an academic career, know that you have more work and editing ahead to turn the dissertation into a real book.[33] Recognize the thesis for what it is: a tool that gives you the experience of taking a big idea, breaking it into parts, and assembling it bit by bit over a very long stretch of time. In other words, it forces you to practice becoming a professional writer.

On Beginning Again (and Again)

Perhaps you are an advanced graduate student who has just read this chapter and is slightly panicked, thinking, "I'm at the dissertation proposal stage, but I have never used a citation app!" or "I'm entering my second year of the master's program but I haven't attended any office hours." Have you been doing grad school all wrong? No, you are fine—look, you have made it this far, and that already is a great accomplishment. Or perhaps you are about to start your first semester of a graduate program and are worrying, "How will I remember to do all of these things?" The reality is you won't—but you can return to this chapter as often as you need and practice a new skill each term.

Our evolution as writers and thinkers is ongoing, and one of the best things we can do for ourselves is to develop a long-term perspective about our scholarly development. The skills that get you through one stage of your journey may not work in a later stage—or you may encounter new tools and techniques that take your skills to the next level. As writers and thinkers, we are always works in progress. It is never too late to try out or begin incorporating in a sustained way the practices outlined here. As explained earlier, I did not learn many of these techniques and strategies until I was a professor. The purpose of this chapter is to gather a sampling of approaches that can be tailored for your existing skills and current needs, as well as make the work of producing scholarship sustainable and enjoyable for the long term.

Reflection Questions

1   What did you see as your strongest skills as an undergraduate? How would your professors and peers answer that question? How would your family answer it?
2   What tools and techniques were part of your workflow prior to graduate school? Were there any gaps?

3   What kind of system and tools will enable you to keep track of your ideas, readings, and goals, and why? Are you a classic pen-and-paper person? Do you prefer all-digital tools? A combination of these?

4   Think back on your best paper as an undergraduate—either an essay that earned high marks or one that you felt proud to submit. Why did working on that paper feel good? What was your approach to putting it together? What did you do that enabled you to do such good work?

5   What was a text that deeply moved you as a reader? What made it powerful: the topic, the style of writing, and/or the questions it evoked from you? What might your response reveal about what motivates you to continue your education?

6   How do your writing anxieties tend to manifest themselves? Are there strategies you have used in the past to combat negative feelings about writing?

Suggested Readings, Resources, and Tools

Writing Guides

Complete citations are provided in the bibliography.

Wendy Belcher, *Writing Your Journal Article in 12 Weeks* and "Solutions to Common Academic Writing Obstacles"
Patricia Goodson, *Becoming an Academic Writer*
Gerald Graff and Cathy Berkenstein, *They Say, I Say*
Paul Silvia, *How to Write a Lot*

Reference-Tracking Programs

EndNote
Mendeley
RefWorks
Zotero

Programs That Support Focused Writing

Internet blocker: SelfControl
Soundscapes: Noisli, myNoise, BrainWave

No-frills writing apps: Ommwriter, Ulysses, WriteRoom
Daily word count: 750Words, Write or Die
Specialized software for lengthy writing projects: Scrivener, Dabble

Writing Resources, Blogs, and Retreats

Academic Ladder (https://academicladder.com)

Shut Up & Write! (https://shutupwrite.com)

InkWell Academic Writing Retreats (https://www.inkwellretreats
.org)

Cathy Mazak: Academic Writing Coaching for Womxn (https://www
.cathymazak.com)

National Center for Faculty Development and Diversity (https://www
.facultydiversity.org)

Ideas on Fire Writing Resources (https://ideasonfire.net/category
/writing) and *Imagine Otherwise* podcast featuring scholars and
creators discussing their craft (https://ideasonfire.net/imagine
-otherwise-podcast)

Example of a Topical versus Argument-Driven Outline

In this chapter, I encourage you to develop an argument-driven outline to help you progress in your writing. Let's use a part of this chapter as an example. After we received the suggestion from an early set of reviewers to include advice specific to thesis writing, I brainstormed the topics I knew I wanted to include. A topical outline of that section would look like this:

I. Types of theses
II. Longer writing projects versus shorter writing projects
III. Making a thesis less abstract
IV. Being organized
V. Setting a schedule
VI. Support team
VII. Thesis as stepping-stone

If you review that section, you will see that is basically the structure of what I drafted. However, put yourself in my shoes as a writer: Do these general topics provide enough of a guide for how I can guide a reader through these points? What will be the connection between them?

A more helpful approach is to develop an argument-driven outline. In this type of outline, you map out how you will get from one part of your argument to the next. An initial argument-driven version of that same section might look like this:

I. Building on our previous general writing advice, there are some pointers that are specific to writing both master's and doctoral theses.
   a. Similar to a marathon, writing a thesis takes time and requires significant preparation.

II. One of the biggest challenges is how to make a thesis more concrete and tangible when you have never written one before.
   a. You can get a running start by incorporating pieces of previous writings.
   b. Using a binder can help make a thesis feel more real.

III. A thesis requires strong organizational skills to keep the major sections moving through each stage of development and to keep track of many files.
   a. A thesis can be broken into sections and your work on them will have to overlap at times.
   b. There are systems and apps that can help you keep track of multiple files and notes.

IV. You also will need to use time-management skills to make the work sustainable over time.

V. Try to develop and adhere to a daily schedule that builds in time for rest, physical activity, and relaxation.

VI. Luckily, you do not have to figure out how to write a thesis alone, because you have a set of faculty advisors and peers whom you should rely on for support throughout the process.
   a. Communicate regularly with faculty and help them provide you with the feedback you need to continue making progress.
   b. Build community with other thesis writers.

VII. Don't imagine the thesis to be more than it needs to be; while it is a major accomplishment, it also is simply a stepping-stone along the way to a graduate degree.

You will note that both outlines have seven parts—but the second outline provides significantly more detail, putting you in the position to connect the dots as you move from one part of your argument to the next. Developing an argument-driven outline takes more time, but it forces you to think more carefully about how you are organizing your thoughts. When you sit down to write, you will then have a clearer map of where you want to go and how you intend to get there.

4 Unwritten Rules of the Academy

NAVIGATING THE GRAY AREA

I will always remember the moment when a professor I liked and respected tugged on my elbow at a campus event, pulling me close with a whisper.[1] It was the kind of touch that might come from a friend so she could tell you that your fly is down or you have a piece of lettuce stuck in your teeth; not quite intimate, but close, and inviting you to listen to something that couldn't or shouldn't be shared loudly. I leaned in, and she said, "It gives people the wrong impression of you when you bring your son to events like this." What? My kid, four years old at the time, was sitting in a chair, eating berries and flipping through the pages of his favorite book about construction vehicles. He had not been disruptive or loud. I must have stared at her with a look of total confusion because she clarified, "If you plan to go on the job market, your kids shouldn't be on campus." My stomach sank— not because the weight of her words had struck me (truthfully, that did not happen until I was home that night) but because, though gently stated, her admonishment was clear, and I had run afoul of a rule I did not know existed. (Side note: once I fully understood the meaning of her intervention, little changed about the decisions I made to bring my kid along. But the difference is that I knew I was breaking convention in doing so, and I was comfortable with—and proud of—that.)

There is a way to talk about demystifying unwritten rules that reifies them, making them more sacred and mysterious. It can be a performative inclusivity that nevertheless remains exclusive: "We can pull back the cover and expose these unwritten rules, but only *some* people get to see the truth." What we are trying to do in this book as a whole, and this chapter in particular, is to push back against that kind of faux inclusivity and talk in explicit ways not only to illuminate unwritten rules but also to explore why they exist in the first place and how to develop an orientation to them. Our intent is to place this conversation within the context of the exclusionary practices that sideline people like us in the academy. We are not inviting you into the secret but rather encouraging an academy—and academic practice—where there are no secrets to be uncovered.

The starting point for any conversation about navigating the gray area of the academy is acknowledging that the culture of the academy is white and middle class. Many people learn this culture before they ever set foot in a graduate program because it is also their home culture and community culture. Moreover, it is at the root of how educational access and inequality are generationally transferred. Understanding this process is fundamental to understanding the essential nature of the institution of higher education. You can't ask about what you don't know to ask about. And here's the real kicker: we already feel like outsiders in the institution, so when we catch a little glimmer of something we do not know—we hear someone talk about a **predoctoral fellowship** or catch a reference to **normative time** and have no idea what those things are—because we already feel marginalized in the academy, it becomes even more difficult to speak up and ask for clarification, which then, of course, predictably disadvantages us even more. You see the cycle here?

Moreover, if higher education is laden with unwritten rules that all of us must navigate carefully, much like a landmine, you often do not know about these rules until you have violated them, a profoundly unfair occurrence. Imagine if you went in for your annual review at your job and were told, "You will not get a raise this year because you have been parking your car a little too close to the painted parking slot lines." You'd be like, "What? I had no idea my parking would be scrutinized as part of how well I do my job." That would be bananas, right? The unwritten rules in academia function similarly: you do not know they exist until you have violated them, at which point, depending on the particulars, the damage might already be done.

Learning these unwritten rules is essential in learning how to navigate the academy, not simply so you can uncritically follow them but so that you can knowingly develop an orientation to them (this is an important distinction). In this chapter, we start off by talking a bit more about racism and unwritten rules as a way to set the context for this discussion. We then move on to talking about an orientation to navigating the unwritten rules of the academy, before delving into a discussion of four key areas we have identified in the academy that are particularly high stakes and rife with unwritten rules: professional dress/attire/appearance; justifying yourself, your methods, and your positionality; conferences and networking; and social media. Our hope is that you will not only understand these unwritten rules on a microlevel to manage the particular kinds of scenarios we outline here but also understand the terrain of unwritten rules more broadly, so that you will know how to deal with contexts and scenarios we have not talked through explicitly.

Racism and Unwritten Rules

Before we go into the nuts and bolts of navigating the unwritten rules of the academy, we will provide some context to ensure we are all on the same page when we talk about these rules. When you are on the outside and don't understand the rules of the game, it can feel like it is either your fault or an accidental omission. Certainly, there are many places in the academy that will reinforce the idea that if you do not know something that you should, that is on you. It is an example of a kind of culture that is really problematic as it reinforces preexisting lines of privilege while also blaming the people who are left out for their own exclusion.

Let me be very clear and state simply that the academy is a tool and reflection of white supremacy. We cannot understand the history nor the contemporary context of higher education without understanding this fact. The historical roots of the university are clear: higher education was not only designed as a training ground for society's elite, it was designed within and through the tools and mechanisms of white supremacy.[2] Margaret Nash talks about the dispossession of Native peoples from public lands to build land-grant universities, and Craig Wilder does an incredible job of tracing and tracking the deeply interconnected threads between higher education and slavery.[3] Of course, it is not simply a historical fact; this legacy of racism and elitism is rooted in the institution and manifests through many university policies, practices, and terminology that we see today as normal, logical, and just part of university life.[4] If you have never delved into this body of literature or are unaware of what I am talking about, my brief explanation here does not even begin to do it justice. If this is an institution that you are planning on spending from two to ten more years in, you should know this history.

The central point here is that the university is an institution steeped in a legacy of racism, white supremacy, and elitism. Simply stated, people like us were never meant to be here. There is power in our presence here; we have literally fought our way into institutions that intentionally locked us out. When I say that we fought our way in, I am not exaggerating. The entry of our people into the halls of academia was the result of social movements led by marginalized people.[5] That history is equally important to know. And because an intersectional analysis is critical to all of our liberation, we would be remiss if we did not mention that gender and sexuality are also axes upon which the unwritten rules are unequally enforced.

So why harp on this historical legacy of exclusion as an entry point into talking about the academy's unwritten rules? Because they are part of the same story. That there are unwritten rules and truths that people are expected to understand and abide by, alerted to them only once they have broken them, is part of the system that maintains elitism and exclusion. If the culture, practices, and processes of higher education have felt foreign to you, you may have thought that they feel foreign to everyone. Guess what? It is not true. It still trips me out to hear people say, "When my mom was in college" or "My grandma graduated from XYZ university." I feel like those people may as well be saying, "When my grandma traveled to the moon." It's like, "What? Your *grandma* went to college?" So yeah, what I am trying to say is that there is a whole sector of society for whom university culture and everything that goes into it are not only *not* foreign but rather very familiar territory. Those are the people who do not stumble over the invisible rocks that are made up of unspoken rules and expectations because they already know them, whether they realize it or not.

This exclusionary legacy manifests on college campuses in different ways that may shape your graduate school experiences. There is of course, blatant racism: the exclusion of people of color from certain spaces, low expectations by professors and other faculty, the everyday racism that we are so used to ("Wow, you speak English so well!"), and hostile campus culture. This type of explicit, in-your-face racism is easy to spot. I lived in a Chicano/a co-op on fraternity row when I was in college, and some memories of those years are deeply seared into my brain: being called "Mexican cunt" by drunk frat boys when walking past their houses on a Saturday night, as well as the "cross the border"–themed party that was held every year in the frat next door to us, where people would don stereotypical "border-crossing" gear, like sombreros.

Importantly, however, there is also the other kind of insidious racism that permeates university life that is much less overt than drunk frat boys in sombreros. Liberal racism is a real thing, and one way it manifests in the academy is relevant to the conversation about unwritten rules.[6] (We will return to the conversation about white supremacy and academia in chapter 5, when we talk about navigating professional relationships in graduate school.) Something I have seen over and over again is that people who consider themselves to be aware and cognizant of the racism of the academy practice something that I can only describe as a liberal racist reduction of expectations and hopes, under the guise of understanding the difficulties of being an underrepresented student of color navigating graduate school.

Here is what it looks like: a student of color produces something—a dissertation chapter, a paper for a class—that needs improvement. The professor or classmate, understanding the ways that racism keeps us out of the academy and that getting even this far is an accomplishment, then withholds, denies, or otherwise avoids giving feedback that can be construed as negative. Their motivations are probably mostly good—they think they are being supportive—but these actions have a detrimental, and at times disastrous, impact. I have seen, many times over, a student who is not given solid, constructive critique but rather passed on through with many pats on the back and a half-hearted "good job!" Those students did not get jobs, did not get fellowships, and did not get published. Many of them had been planning and hoping for an opportunity to enter the academy as a professor and ended up finding a dead end on that path. These outcomes are rooted in racism, and I raise it here because it is one way that these unwritten rules require our vigilance. Don't ever let them get away with not giving you critique.

An Orientation to Unwritten Rules

Here's the deal: Knowledge is power, and the intent of this chapter is to make these implicit rules concrete so that you can be empowered with that knowledge. Let us be very clear, though, that we do not encourage you to understand these unwritten rules simply to acquiesce to them; rather, we uncover them so that you can navigate them more adeptly. The starting point for that process is figuring out your orientation to them. As you encounter the sorts of decisions that arise as you navigate these unwritten rules, ask yourself: What do I stand to gain? What do I stand to lose? How do I make these choices? All of this will become clearer in the sections that follow.

Presenting Yourself Professionally

There is no shortage of information about presenting yourself professionally in the academy. There are blog posts, book chapters, instructional videos, and online resources that talk about professional attire, makeup, and other norms for academic job interviews, conferences, and other professional contexts within academia. Yet even though most of those resources do not say explicitly, "The information contained here is for white people and assumes you have money to spend on a new outfit," this is another place in which dominant culture subsumes the conversation. In advice on how to present oneself professionally, the default tends to be to white, middle-class culture, which (again) is the culture of the academy.

Let me sidetrack here: saying that "white middle-class culture is the culture of the academy" is not to say that every graduate program is steeped in that culture (I have had the opportunity to teach in two graduate programs that fall outside of that). It is also not to say that every corner of the university defaults to that culture. Rather, it is saying that academia as a whole—Academia with a capital A, if you will—is steeped in a culture that is part of a historical legacy that has current concrete ramifications. So, in this section I want to talk about professional norms around clothing and presenting oneself in the academy, reinterpreting those norms for different contexts (because although the academy is spoken about as if it is one thing, norms are different if you are going to a job interview, a professional conference, or your graduate seminar). I then continue on to explore the issue of developing your own professional style by having a conversation about race, class, gender, and performance in the context of professionalism.

It is important to start out by saying that professionalism and professional presentation are deeply raced and gendered. I had white male professors in college who came to class each day with rumpled untucked shirts and bedhead, and who noisily ate soup while we were taking a final exam. No joke. Now ask me if I would ever dream of being that professor, and the answer is hell no, because there is no way that I would be taken seriously if I showed up looking like I had just rolled out of bed. Chicana professors are not given that kind of flexibility. Thus, there is a longer conversation to be had here about the leeway given to certain people in academia, but given that you are reading this book, we will assume that you are not that professor and the leeway is not yours. So, don't look like you just rolled out of bed. That's step one. Step two is that you want to dress for professional settings in academia like you would dress to go to church on Sunday morning. Did you catch that? Sunday morning. So, not Saturday 5 p.m. mass and not Easter Sunday. Got it? Professional attire in the academy is what is referred to in the world as "business casual." To paint a broad brush, except in a few circumstances, you are not required or expected to be in a full suit but rather in nice bottoms, a business-appropriate top, and professional shoes (not tennis shoes or sandals, but flats are fine). If you are going to go by some general rule, that is it.

Not all of academia is the same. In most places, you are not expected to dress up for class. Now, the specifics of what that means differs in different contexts. While it may be fine to show up in sweats and a hoodie for class in some places, in other places that would be seen as a bit too sloppy. Until you learn the culture and norms in your particular program as a new graduate student, it's best to go middle of the road: jeans or decent pants and a top that is not sloppy. It does not need to be a dress shirt or a blouse, but it should be nice enough. Then, when you see what the culture of the department is, you can adapt accordingly—keeping in mind that none of us will ever be given the leeway of an old white guy tenured professor. It is also helpful to note that professional dress can vary by discipline. A general approach is to ask others who are farther along than you, and take time to observe so you can orient yourself accordingly.

Let's expand on that a bit, and also bring gender into the conversation. You may notice that I am taking care not to split up recommendations by gender, as is often done. That is because, you know, gender is a construct, and fuck anyone who says otherwise. Also, we should consciously try to undermine gendered expectations and constructs in this area—work all of us can take part in, whether you see yourself as gender-nonconforming or not. As I explained in the introduction to this chapter, you should understand unwritten rules so that you can determine how you are going to relate to them, how you are going to navigate them, and, yes, how and when you will subvert them. Let me be clear: we are not saying you need to learn the rules so you can follow them. Rather, if you are going to resist, to subvert, to challenge, to push back, do so with intention, not accidentally; be informed and thoughtfully aware of the possible risks and with an intentional and conscious assumption of those risks. Reread that if you need to, because the distinction is really important.

That leads us to a conversation about developing your personal style. I want to root that conversation in the idea that some of these rules—especially the ones that police gender, femininity, and race—should be challenged. If you go with the mainstream advice on this, you will find that the general recommendation is to be muted. Don't wear really loud colors; stick with blues and blacks and grays, save a pop of color for a pocket square or a tasteful scarf. You will see that the advice is to go mellow with your jewelry, to be subdued with your accessories, to look as much like a Banana Republic or J.Crew catalog spread as possible.

Now, there may be some disagreement here, but I want to share my alternate advice. There is one piece of this traditional advice I agree you should abide by, and that is that you should look neat and put-together. This is possible for everyone. It does not matter your body size, your income, or your skin color. Your clothes should fit you well, your hair should be intentional, and you should not be disheveled. Now, you may wonder why I am drawing such a stark line there, one that puts me squarely in agreement with the traditional advice on this. It goes along with my earlier comments about intentionality, and the idea presented in chapter 5 about having your shit together and looking like you have your shit together. You want people to know when they look at you that how you appear is intentional and that the image you project is deliberate. You want to make sure that it is nowhere in their heads that you threw this together on your way out the door, that you didn't think too much about what people would see when they look at you. And why do you want people to think that about you? Because you want them to know that you have your shit together.

Now comes the place where I depart from the traditional advice. It is important to say that in some places, and in some academic contexts, formality is expected, and you will stand out if you are not in the blue-gray-black-muted-accessories category. It is up to you to decide how important it is to you to blend in, and, yes, it is important to think about the fact that on many campuses and in many academic spaces, we are already marked as different or other by our skin color alone. On my campus and in my department, a job candidate who showed up for her daylong interview wearing big hoop earrings and bright blue pants would not stand out because many of the faculty members in the interview audience would be breaking similar traditions in their own dress. If a job candidate showed up that way to interview for a physics job at Princeton, she would likely be making a statement with her attire. Many folks I know in academia have actually used the breaking of certain rules related to professional appearance and attire to feel out the environment for a person of color. When a friend went for a job interview in the traditionally more-buttoned-up New England region, she intentionally went with a more masculine presentation (her general day-to-day gender presentation is pretty fluid, some days more traditionally masculine, some days more traditionally feminine). She wanted to make clear that her genderqueer and sexual identities would not be hidden; she was not trying to blend into the all-white, heterosexual department. Could it potentially cost her the job? I mean, yeah, it could. We all know how racism and homophobia work in hiring. But she decided that being out and proud was more important than securing the offer because she did not want to work in a hostile place. (She got the offer, by the way, and, yeah, she turned it down.)

What it comes down to is that you may, for various reasons, decide to take a risk with how you present yourself professionally. Feel free. Make sure you look put together, but then be yourself. Wear your Jordans instead of loafers. Wear a blazer or don't. Your pants do not need to be black or blue or gray. Go for the red ones! If you are a woman, you do not need to wear a skirt. Be put together, and then figure out what will make you feel good for your presentation or job talk or interview or conference mixer.

For some of us, there is great power and pride in breaking these sorts of rules. In my case, I often wear a Mexican huipil to prospective-student events. Why? Because it is a nonverbal signal to Latinx students and, hopefully, other students of color about who I am and what our program stands for. One time, my Latina colleague and I were standing to the side at an orientation event for new students. One of the newly admitted students, a Latina in her early twenties, approached us to say, "I just wanted to say how excited I am that I will have two Latina professors. Honestly, it is why I chose this program. To look over and see my professors, both wearing big huge gold hoops, it's just more than I could have ever imagined or hoped for." I have a friend who used to say, "Show up and show out—you never know who might be looking for you."

Justifying Your Work, Methods, Research, and/or Positionality

Students of color, Latinx students, and students with other marginalized identities (queer, disabled, undocumented, first generation) will frequently decide to focus their graduate research, master's thesis or capstone project, or dissertation topic on an issue that is connected to this marginalized identity. Why? There are generally three reasons a student may choose to do this: (1) the topic is an area of personal and political passion, often fueled by personal experience; (2) there is not enough research on the identified topic; and/or (3) there is research on this topic, but it is problematic, limited, or written by outsiders to the community. To many professors, including the two who are writing this book, that choice is logical and even to be encouraged. There are many esteemed scholars who write and talk about the importance of oppressed and marginalized people researching and writing about our own experiences and expand on the ways that "insiderness" can produce meaningful and critical scholarship.[7] Still, one of the gray areas of navigating academia is that in many corners—sometimes hidden, sometimes in plain sight—there is a distrust of or even disdain for researching one's own community or identity group.

Students of color and students of other marginalized identities are often made to justify their work when it focuses on or relates to their own community or identity group. Even stating this fact does not happen nearly enough in academia. We want to say it specifically, talk about what it means when this critique is levied, and how to respond—because, frankly, it is often rooted in problematic conceptions of research and marginalized communities.

So why does this happen? Why the distrust or disdain? There are two answers to this, one that is a more optimistic view and one that is a realistic/pessimistic view. On the optimistic end, sometimes this critique comes from a place of concern about the rigors of research. For example, when a doctoral student of mine wanted to conduct her dissertation research as a case study of the youth program where she worked as a way to explore how race and class shape young people's experience of international immersion experiences,[8] I really pushed her to seriously consider potential complications. What if, through the course of her interviews, there were things that did not paint the organization or its staff in the best light? How would she relate to that? How would she navigate conducting interviews with young people with whom she had preexisting relationships rooted in this programmatic work? How would those relationships shape the interviews, possibly in ways that could skew the data? I asked her to think through those questions as she developed her study, because as an insider you need to be very thoughtful about how your insiderness can shape—or obscure—certain aspects of the research process. At the same time, I encouraged her to take up this study because I could see the incredible benefit to an insider engaging in this work. I felt confident that her findings would immediately benefit the young people in this program, and there was a clear way these findings could translate into concrete changes on the ground because my student was the person empowered to make those changes. Still, as her dissertation chair, I knew that special care must be taken when an insider plans to research her own organization. In the best light, folks who are concerned about, say, a researcher from El Paso conducting an ethnography at his high school to look at sexuality and race in a border community are concerned about how the researcher will navigate insiderness in that context in a way that preserves the integrity and rigor of the research process. As you can see, there are valid methodological questions that arise in this sort of situation.

Now, it is important to explain that oftentimes when this critique is levied, it may be masked as the above when in actuality it is about something else. There is a set of ideas shared by some in the academy, which is basically a messy tangle of the following:

- Insiders cannot be objective.
- Research should always be objective.
- If you are too close to a research subject, you are incapable of conducting the research in an unbiased manner.

Now, is there a kernel of truth here? Yeah, there is, as you can see in the above example. So let me tackle the rest of it with a simple 1-2-3 takedown:

1 There is no such thing as objective research.
2 Objectivity in research is not only impossible, it is undesirable.
3 The perils of insider research are policed unequally.

Let's walk that out a little bit more. On objectivity: there is no such thing as objective research because research is conducted by real people with real biases, interests, and positionality; it would be disingenuous to pretend that those do not impact the research process. While there is no such thing as truly objective research (and you should be wary anytime someone makes this claim), good researchers take steps to acknowledge their subjectivity and implement research practices that help to mitigate the impact of bias. To tackle the second point: there are great benefits to insiders conducting research in their communities. They include an ability to access and build connections with research subjects; insights and familiarity that may be nuanced and harder for an outsider to grasp; and greater ability to establish a reciprocal relationship with the research site or context. Pushing for research to be conducted in ways that involve an outsider being introduced into a foreign community or context ignores all of the benefits of insider research. Finally, and most importantly, on the third point, let me repeat: the perils of insider research are policed unequally. Does anyone express concern about the middle-class researcher who conducts an ethnographic study of corporate America? Is there any worry about a white person doing a study of a white community in the Midwest? Of course not. Because whiteness is the normative category, and the rest of us are expected to orient around it, in the way that the earth orbits the sun. And that's some bullshit.

So, what should you do if you have to defend yourself and your research? First, if you need resources on how to defend this sort of insider research, look at the work of scholars who theorize it.[9] There are scholarly sources that do a fantastic job of discussing what it means to do this sort of research and how to do it well. Second, work with trusted mentors and faculty to figure out how you can build elements into your research plan that enable you to mitigate the challenges endemic to insider research and account for your bias. Third, practice talking about your research in ways that position your insiderness as an asset rather than a liability. How you frame your research is important, and it matters when you are put in the position to defend yourself, your research, and your choices. Fourth, assess the context in which you are being expected to defend yourself and respond appropriately. How you will respond when your dissertation advisor raises concerns is different from how you will respond to someone who raises this question in a Q&A after you present your research at a scholarly conference. Finally, surround yourself with people who understand the importance of your research, who understand the benefits of insider research, and who will be supportive and also push you forward in doing this work. For example, if your advisor is not supportive of this fundamental aspect of your research and directs you to find another topic, that relationship may be worth reconsidering. Additionally, there are many spaces in academia—perhaps outside of your discipline—where this sort of research is respected and valued. Ethnic Studies is, by and large, one of those spaces. Explore those spaces, even if outside your field, find ways to be connected, and do the important work you feel called to do.

Conferences and Professional Networking

If you are like me, networking makes you want to run to bed and pull the covers over your head. But in academia, having a network is really, really important, and these networks must be built. Anyone who knows me will say that I am a pretty talkative, outgoing person. Still, not only does the idea of networking make me feel a bit queasy, but I still have to talk myself into attending a conference reception rather than, say, hiding out in my hotel room. What has helped me—and, clearly, I am still very much a work in progress on this question—is to reframe *networking* as *connecting*. See? Doesn't that feel a little better already? This reframe has helped me because I realized that when I was thinking about networking, I associated it with self-promotion, superficiality, and awkwardness. Truthfully, sometimes networking is those things. But it does not have to be. In this section, we are going to talk about conferences in particular, and professional networking more broadly, in hopes of giving you a way to think about building a network that is not daunting and is actually maybe even a little bit enticing. (We can hope, right?)

Academic conferences have long been a fixture of academic life. We are judged in our tenure files by what we present, at what conferences, and how often. Many of the awards in our professions are granted by these professional associations and connected to annual conferences. Numerous journals and academic publication venues are attached to these same professional associations. On the more social end, conferences are one of the few times you can catch up with people in your field despite being in far-flung institutions across the country. On an intellectual and professional level, conferences can be where you meet your intellectual crushes, hear giants in your field talk about ideas, connect with others who are doing similar work, practice talking and presenting your work, try out new ideas on others who are grounded in the same set of conversations you are, and get feedback on your work.

Conferences may be fixtures of academic life but have to be navigated thoughtfully. And—you get a dos por uno on this one—here is another unwritten rule to keep in mind: sometimes the optional stuff is not really optional. It is unlikely you will ever be formally required to attend a professional conference as a graduate student. However, if you apply for an academic job and you have never attended a conference in your field, you will face questions about that. So, sometimes optional isn't optional. Academic conferences definitely fall into that category, with some caveats, detailed in the following paragraphs.

As was made clear in chapter 3, there are numerous benefits to getting feedback on your work. Beyond circulating a written draft, another way scholars seek out such feedback is by presenting their work at academic conferences and campus talks. In fact, that is the true purpose of such events: an opportunity to preview work in progress or to promote recently completed work. As a graduate student, you will benefit from attending as many conferences and talks as you can; as an audience member, you will begin to understand the conventions and wide range of behaviors modeled by other scholars. It is also a way to cultivate a visible scholarly presence, practice asking focused questions, and develop your networking skills. Be aware that academic talks can be pretty lively events, especially within conference settings, because these occasions are often long-awaited reunions of longtime academic friends. There is often a party atmosphere, with hors d'oeuvres circulating and cocktails flowing. We have a lot more to say about navigating the social aspect of conferencing in chapter 5. For now, let's focus on the skill-based side with the following list of do's and don'ts of attending or giving talks:

When you are attending

- Attend with an open mind and try to focus on what the presenter is actually saying versus what you wish they would say.
- Do your best to be fully present; put away your phone and other distractions.
- Take notes, writing down the speaker's name, institutional affiliation, title of the talk, and the date, in case you want to reference it later or follow up with the speaker.
- Ask a question or share a follow-up comment—and make sure that it is focused.
- If you know that you will have to leave early, sit near the end of a row and toward the back.

When you are presenting

- Complete your presentation ahead of time. Nothing is worse than seeing a speaker work through their ideas in the moment—cutting down from a longer work by flipping through pages or slides, saying, "Let me skip this," and trying to find their place again.

- Time your talk so that it does not go over the allotted time. This reflects positively on you, indicating both that you prepared for the specific parameters of this context and also that you won't cut into the time allotted to others as a professional courtesy.
- In some fields, it is customary to talk through ideas with slides as a guide, and in other fields (looking at you, humanities!) it is customary to read through your paper word for word, with minimal extemporaneous commentary. Figure out the norms in your field and plan accordingly.
- If you are in an academic field where speakers commonly read their conference paper, practice reading it aloud ahead of your actual presentation. Long sentences that a reader can easily follow often do not translate well for a listening audience.
- Be fully present: while other panelists are speaking, listen and/or take notes on their talk. Don't visibly edit your own talk or presentation while they are sharing theirs.
- Employ the pivot: audience members usually ask questions that relate to their own work, so respond to questions that seem unrelated to your topic with a gracious "Thanks for that question. I'm so glad you raised [X] issue because it relates to a point I'd like to expand."

We lay out these suggestions because "every time you present your research, you have an opportunity to convey not only your interesting findings and the sophistication of your analysis but also your collegiality and ability to convey material effectively."[10] In other words, you are shaping the ways current and future colleagues see you as professional, polished, and prepared to engage in discussions that matter.

How to Make the Most of Conferences

If you have decided to attend an academic conference, or you are at the part of your academic journey where you need to start attending them (generally important in the second half of your graduate school career), here are some tips to help you get the most out of the conference.

BEFORE YOU DECIDE ON A CONFERENCE, ASK OTHER FOLKS FOR INSIGHTS ON WHICH CONFERENCES MAY BE A GOOD FIT FOR YOU · Some conferences are really large. That may be good if what works best for you is to be relatively anonymous and see some of the giants in your field. For example, in my field, the American Educational Research Association (AERA) annual conference regularly pulls upward of twelve thousand attendees. On the other hand, there are smaller conferences that are known to be quite friendly to graduate students. The Sociology of Education Conference is like this, with just a few hundred people in attendance and lots of focus on presenting works in progress. Talking to others in your field, including other graduate students, is the best way to find out about different venues.

LOOK THROUGH THE PROGRAM AND HIGHLIGHT THE PANELS AND PLENARY EVENTS THAT INTEREST YOU · Identify presentations that relate to your area of interest. Ask questions. If you find a meaningful scholarly connection—for example, a graduate student at a different institution who is researching something similar to you—go up to them after the panel, introduce yourself, exchange business cards, ask a question, and/or share a bit about your work. This is how genuine collegial connections are made.

PRESENT A PAPER OR A POSTER · Not only is it a good experience to push yourself to talk about your work, it looks good on your CV and can help you forge connections with others doing similar work because they may see your presentation title on the program and attend your session. A poster session can be a lower-stakes way to get this experience in a slightly less formal way that still counts on your CV and also gives you good experience in sharing your work. You may not feel ready to present your work; we all feel that way when we start. Push yourself at first to present something you feel confident about or want to get feedback on. Be clear that it is a work in progress. People are generally generous, and if they aren't, brush it off.

CONVENE A PANEL, IF POSSIBLE · This not the best idea if you are not yet familiar with the academic conference scene, but after you have attended a couple conferences, consider convening a panel. This pushes you one step beyond simply presenting a paper to play a facilitative role. It is also a great excuse to reach out to other scholars—some senior, potentially—to make those sorts of connections. In addition, panels almost universally have a higher acceptance rate than individual papers, because it saves conference organizers the work of assembling disconnected presentations into a coherent panel.

LOOK FOR WAYS TO GET INVOLVED AS A PARTICIPANT · Some larger conferences have info sessions for first-timers or open meetings that are organized around interest or area of focus. These sessions are a low-stakes way to learn the lay of the land and sit in on sessions where there is no pressure on you. Push yourself to say hello to the person sitting next to you.

TAKE ADVANTAGE OF ANY IDENTITY SPACES THAT EXIST · Some conferences will have ethnic caucuses or special interest groups. Sometimes there will be events geared toward a particular subsection of attendees—a reception for LGBTQ scholars, for example. We all know it is easier to strike up a conversation with people like us; even if you need to work up the nerve to attend a big conference reception, these smaller gatherings are a great way to meet folks.

ASK FOR BRIEF MEETINGS WITH OTHER SCHOLARS · Different fields have different practices around this, but in my field, it is not uncommon for a junior scholar or advanced graduate student to email faculty members who they see are going to be presenting at the conference and ask for a brief meeting. If you do this, do it with a specific intention and request in mind, such as wanting to meet with them to ask some methodological questions about their study because you are attempting to do something similar. You want the scholar to feel that you are making good use of their time. Make clear that your intention is a short (fifteen to twenty minutes) meeting, making them more likely to say yes while keeping the pressure off you. This can be a great way to intentionally foster connections that otherwise may be hard to come by.

CONSIDER YOUR STAMINA, PERSONALITY, AND PREFERENCES WHEN THINKING ABOUT HOW TO STRUCTURE YOUR TIME AT THE CONFERENCE · It may be worth it to stay an extra day to build in some downtime. This is particularly true for introverts. Being at an academic conference means that you will be around lots of people, perhaps thousands, for twelve or more hours a day. Consider what you need to do and build in downtime so that you can bring your best self to the conference.

The Cost of Conferences

So, I guess it's time to admit that despite the important components outlined above, I think the whole conference thing is also honestly kind of irresponsible. When I am in a hotel banquet hall, surrounded by overpriced food and a bar, I cannot help but think what it would have meant if we could have used that money instead for student scholarships. When I am paying a conference registration fee, I think about the graduate students who are paying those fees, often out of pocket and with little to no financial support, because they have been told that they should go to these conferences for the professional experience. Conferences can be costly (there are student discounts, so make sure you always look for those), and when you add in the other costs of travel, transportation, lodging, food, and childcare, you could be spending a couple thousand dollars. Always consider if it is worth the cost. You can make it more worth the cost if you are (a) presenting and (b) finding ways to save on the costs, like sharing a room and bringing some of your own food. What I mean is that if you are paying a couple thousand dollars to attend a conference, make sure that what you get out of it is worth what you are putting into it. Presenting your work is important and is a respected form of professional development. If you are going to pay to go to a conference, you really should make sure you get a line on your CV out of it.

Additionally, it is always smart to think about conferences in general and not just specific ones. Set aside the time to develop a conference strategy for the year—do not take it conference by conference. Before you plunk down the big bucks for a plane ticket, find out if there are any conferences within driving distance that you may want to attend instead. Are there any bigger conferences that are a better fit for your work? If so, you may want to save up for it and skip the smaller ones. It is easy for a faculty member who knows nothing about your bank account to tell you, "Sure, you should go!" It is another thing for you to make peace with it and make it work for said bank account. Don't stumble into it. There is no right or wrong about how to approach this decision; just make sure it suits your goals and your budget, do what you can to reduce those costs, and do whatever is possible to make sure you are getting something out of it professionally (ideally, a line on your CV).

Finally, explore all possible options to help fund your conference travel. Professional associations often have reduced rates for graduate students or community members. The sponsoring organization or association may also have fellowships or scholarships specifically for graduate students, which may require advance planning and an application of some sort. Explore these options early to ensure you do not miss any deadlines and can apply for anything you are eligible for. Also keep in mind that your own institution may have sources of financial support for conference travel. Check in with your mentor about offices on campus that provide this sort of support, including the dean's office of your college, your department, diversity and inclusion offices, and identity-specific offices (like the Queer Student Resource Center, the Undocumented Student Center, etc.). As we mentioned in chapter 1, when you are researching programs it is a good idea to ask how students fund conference travel. Finally, some associations offer a discount to participants who volunteer at the conference. Check the conference website for this information; if you cannot find it, do not hesitate to reach out and ask.

Conference Socializing

Conferences have official and unofficial gatherings, and are generally pretty notorious as social gatherings for academics. It is cool to embrace that part of academic culture, but it is also important to do so thoughtfully. While conference receptions and parties are common, know that your professional reputation can hinge on the people in those rooms. If you drink, do so in moderation. Remember that you are not at a grad student party; you are in a room that is likely filled with people in your field who may be asked about you or may be put in a position to pass judgment on you at some point. You are an adult, so we will not belabor this point, but we do urge you to think consciously about navigating alcohol and partying in the context of academic conference social spaces and suggest you keep the following in mind: you are also building your professional reputation in spaces like these, not just when you are wearing a blazer and presenting your work on a panel the next day. Additionally, though it goes without saying, just as neither you nor I could ever get away with showing up to teach class in a rumpled shirt and bedhead like the tenured white professor, the same holds true for this context. Just because you see other scholars drinking too much does not mean you would be given the same latitude or grace. Not fair, rooted in racism, but the truth. Act, and drink, accordingly.

Last Thoughts about Networking

Let's return to what I said at the beginning of this section. It can be helpful to think about networking as connecting because it helps rip away some of the negative connotations associated with networking. There is a way to approach networking that is about connecting and building relationships in authentic ways that are not about self-promotion and trying to get something from the other person. Academia can feel highly transactional; try to approach networking in a way that is consciously stepping away from that. Maybe that's how we build a different kind of hegemonic academic culture, no?

Social Media and Managing Your Online Presence

In cautionary tales about what they should and should not do online, I have told my kids many times how grateful I am that social media and the internet did not exist when I was a teenager doing dumb shit. And while I did have a MySpace (ha! Remember MySpace?) and Facebook account while I was in graduate school, the sheer scope and volume of social media and other ways to connect online today make this moment distinct. Someone could probably write a whole book on this topic alone, and truly there are many parts of this conversation that raise bigger and deeper ethical implications like information tracking, digital citizenship, and the limits and possibilities of online activism. However, for the purposes of this book, we are going to touch on only a small slice of this much bigger conversation: the double-edged sword of social media and connection, social media and your professional profile, and social media as a time suck and mental health liability.

The Double-Edged Sword of Social Media and Connection

Social media—whether it's Facebook or Instagram or Twitter or whatever cool new site is out by the time this book is published—is truly a double-edged sword. It is both a tool that keeps you in the loop personally, professionally, politically, and culturally and a pitfall that can keep you stuck in a loop.[11] What do we mean by that? Everything that is great about social media is *great* about social media. You can easily keep up with your cousin in Panama and stay connected to family and friends throughout the globe; you can get a quick daily injection of what is important in both pop culture and world politics in the time it takes to have your morning cup of coffee; and you can keep up with current debates in your field by perusing your feed while in line at the bank. For real! Social media is amazing! It keeps us in the loop like no other force has been able to, merging our professional, familial, cultural, and personal circles and identities in one easy, handy place.

And that is also what is hard about social media: it can easily become a pitfall that keeps us stuck in the loop. That loop is different for everyone. Maybe it is the loop of your family drama that, thanks to social media, means you get updated fourteen times a day on who is beefing with whom and who is on whose side. Maybe it is the loop of competition with your peers in your program and feeling discouraged when they post about finishing chapters of their dissertations or getting accepted to PhD programs or interviewing for great jobs, fueling your own insecurities. Maybe it is the loop of the continual news cycle and the difficulty of escaping the daily horrors committed against our people, which, thanks to social media, we know about within minutes of them happening. Social media is connection, and connection brings both joy and difficulty.

Social Media and Your Professional Profile

There is a lot written about this elsewhere, so we are not going to belabor the obvious points: nothing you write online is private, everything can live forever via screenshot, and you should be prepared to stand by anything you have put online. I once saw a hilarious tweet that said, "Dance like no one is watching, and email like it will be read aloud at a deposition." All of that is true, and if you don't believe it or think it is overblown, we urge you to do some reading and deep consideration about what sloppiness on social media can get you.

We want to make a few additional points related specifically to academics, aspiring academics, and graduate students. First, you may find some protection in the idea that you can keep a personal profile and a distinct professional profile, so that you keep your questionable stuff on your personal profile and reserve the professional one for the professional stuff. Maybe—but it is important to know that avoiding any spillover between those profiles is very difficult and should not be relied upon as a strategy. Second, do not have confidence in your friends. Ha! I mean, in this context, do not assume that saying something to your friends online creates any sort of safety because they know who you are and the context for your commentary. All it takes is someone to stay logged in accidentally on a public computer or sharing a screenshot (not even out of malice, but possibly), and your rant or complaint or commentary flies out of your connected sphere and beyond your control.

Listen to me when I say this: assume that anything you have shared on social media can be shared with the hiring committee of the job you really want or the admissions committee of the graduate program you are trying to get into. I'll be honest and give a concrete example: I have social media acquaintances who post a constant stream of complaints about their students. I teach at a teaching-focused university. If I were on the search committee, I would have to think twice about their fit if one of them applied for a job, because they seem to not enjoy teaching. I share this example because, although advice about how you present yourself online may seem glib or outdated, you should assume that everyone you connect with in that space has a connection to work you would want to do or opportunities you'd like to access. And for however real and authentic we try to be, remember that social media is ultimately a performance—so perform accordingly.

Before we move on, I should also acknowledge that, increasingly, many scholars use social media to advance their professional visibility, amplify their work and their politics, and build a public persona as a public intellectual. Doing so can be beneficial in making you known among a broader audience, providing a space to intellectually connect with others, and expand the scope of your reach, which can undoubtedly be helpful to your own scholarship as well as when and if you apply for jobs, fellowships, and awards. We will not delve deeply into the how-to's of this here (largely because we are ill equipped to do so). Keep in mind that this approach can be beneficial as long as everything is going well, but ensuring that things are going well requires a lot of management. There are many examples of scholars whose work and words are used against them, including in completely unfair ways, because social media makes it easy to do so. So, while we cannot and will not tell you that it is always a bad idea to use social media to build your professional visibility, know that this must be done very carefully and does come with risks. Our best advice is to seek out a trusted mentor who is skilled and experienced in this area to help advise you.

Social Media as a Time Suck and Mental Health Liability

Aside from what we have already covered, there are two reasons it is important for graduate students to be on guard as they (hopefully, continually) assess and reassess their relationship with social media. The first is obvious but needs to be said: social media can be a huge time suck. Anybody who has ever mindlessly scrolled Facebook or gone down the TikTok rabbit hole of babies getting knocked over by their big friendly dogs and then realized, bleary-eyed, that they have been watching the loop of those videos for an hour knows the danger of social media as time suck. But for real, especially when you reach the part of your program where your time is less structured (like the thesis-writing stage), it can be really easy to spend time mindlessly scrolling. If you do not keep a close count of this, it can negatively impact not only your productivity but also your focus. Second, it is important to note that there is a lot of research about the negative impact of social media on our mental health.[12] Much of this focuses on the "highlight reel" nature of social media and performativity, namely that we are not seeing the anxiety or stress or difficulty that people are navigating, only the picture of their beautiful hike or a smiling picture with their partner. And, yes, social media can be addictive (by design), and it is up to us to make sure that, like alcohol, we are consuming it responsibly and in moderation.

Last Thoughts on Unwritten Rules

In some ways, this chapter is sort of a catchall to address different aspects of academic life that did not fit neatly into other chapters. Part of why we wanted to cover these topics is to highlight the larger point about the fact that these topics do not fit neatly into other chapters. Academia can be a place where the rules are not clear until you've broken them, and sometimes not even then. This is particularly true for Latinx first-generation students and scholars. We do not, for the most part, have family members who have navigated this terrain before us. Many of us do not even have friends who have walked this path. While we cannot know what we don't know we are supposed to know, we can take steps to demystify the academy for everyone. Keep in mind that other graduate students who are farther along than you are an invaluable resource in helping you navigate these unwritten rules. Remember that your professional reputation is being formed from the time you start graduate school. I am not asking you to remember this in a way that is stifling but in a way that is open and inviting. You have the opportunity to build your professional identity, and you do not need to wait until you get that tenure-track job to do so. In other words, act right as soon as you show up to the party, but also enjoy being there.

Reflection Questions

1 Which topics from this chapter stuck with you the most? Those may be the topics you should reflect on more in terms of your own practice.

2　How do you feel about presenting yourself in a professional setting? What are your concerns and insecurities about this aspect of professional life? What do you want to project in terms of your personal style and identity? What is the best way to do that?

3　If you are going to research a topic that is close to you, why is doing this work important? How does being an insider benefit the work? How are you uniquely positioned to do this research?

4　When you think about networking, what is your first reaction? If it is not entirely positive, or if the idea brings up some anxieties or insecurities, how can you work on this? What are ways that you can connect with others in your field or discipline that feel genuine and beneficial?

5　Which of your social media practices are nourishing to you? Which are detrimental? How can you set some goals and limitations around social media to maximize the benefits and minimize the harmful effects?

5 Navigating Professional Relationships in Graduate School

As a senior in college, I had the great fortune of taking a class with Ruth Wilson Gilmore that changed the way I thought about the world.[1] When I was ready to apply to graduate school, I emailed Ruthie to ask if she would be willing to write me a letter of recommendation, and she said yes but also invited me to have a conversation about my research interests and professional plans, which was a pivotal point in my decision to pursue a doctoral degree.

As a graduate student, I signed up for a class with Ananya Roy, not recognizing at the time that she would become one of the most influential mentors in my career. That was nearly two decades ago, and over the intervening years she continues to step in when I need her—to talk through ideas, to advise me on professional quandaries, to be a sounding board and a helpful critic. (I also credit her with saving my life two years ago when she insisted I go to the hospital in a series of events that led to my diagnosis with a congenital heart condition I had never known about, but that is a story for another day.)

As a new professor, I met Leisy Abrego and Arely Zimmerman. We were brought together by overlap in our work and research interests, but my relationships with these women soon became some of the most cherished in my adult life. I delight in the overlap between our professional and personal lives—a fifteen-minute text thread can move from a citation question to a deep pondering about the future of the discipline to a funny story about one of our kids to a Netflix show recommendation and back to a pedagogical question. My relationships with them have anchored me through difficult professional moments and health scares and provided a deep joy in the possibilities of academic sisterhood.

The professional relationships I have forged in and through the academy have kept me afloat and have given me a reason to be hopeful in even the hardest moments. In this book, we talk about the two main categories of relationships you will navigate—professional and personal—as well as the messy and glorious place they sometimes overlap. This chapter focuses specifically on professional relationships: with professors, advisors, dissertation chairs, and colleagues in the field and in your discipline, as well as your graduate school peers. This conversation is rooted in a broader framing about how white supremacy structures and mediates all kinds of relationships for students of color, and how being clear about white supremacy and the academy is critical for thinking in a nuanced way about building and sustaining healthy and useful relationships of all types in graduate school. The focus in this chapter is not only how to take care of professional relationships in graduate school but also how to understand them and navigate some of the daily practices through which these relationships are forged and maintained.

White Supremacy and Grad School Relationships

In chapter 4, we talked about how the unwritten rules of the academy are enforced along racialized lines. That reality is rooted in a deeper and broader reality about higher education, something we mentioned in the introduction but want to reiterate at the outset of this chapter: higher education is an institution steeped in white supremacy—not just racism as an act but white supremacy as a system. Therefore, professional relationships are forged, performed, mediated, and negotiated within and through white supremacy as well. (Here is a reminder that you are not reading some normal "guide to graduate school" handbook because in the culture of graduate education, "normal" equals white.) We say this for a few reasons. First, you should be prepared. Anybody who has ever been in a fight knows that a punch in the gut hurts more if you are not braced for it. Second, you should know you are not imagining things. Some of the incidents of racism that are hardest to deal with are the ones where you are caught in a roundabout battle with yourself, thinking, "That wasn't cool, right? There was something there—I am not imagining that, right?" Third, we say this to acknowledge it as reality and to give you permission to see it, name it, and decide not to fight every battle—and to begin the very personal process of determining when and how you stick around to fight.

So, what does white supremacy in relation to professional relationships in graduate school look like? You may come into contact with racist professors. Just as in K–12 education, they come in all varieties, including the low-key racists ("You speak English so well! You are so articulate!"), the discipline-specific racists (the anthropologist who speaks about Indigenous people as less than human, often disguised as paying respect to their culture), the overt racists (the professor who only picks the white guys as his graduate research assistants, fondly saying he likes to work with people who remind him of his son), and the old racists (the ones everyone make excuses for because they are so old, so set in their ways, and "didn't even realize saying 'Oriental' is racist because that was just a normal word back in the day!"). Except in a few cases, being Latinx on a college campus means that you are an underrepresented group. That is true for undergraduate students; for graduate students, you are likely even more underrepresented. (This is not true, of course, for every campus and every discipline and every program. I am proud to teach in an MA program that brings in cohorts that are generally about 90 to 95 percent people of color, which is a rarity in the field of education.) However, it is important to note that being a Latinx student on campus means that you are likely one of few, and connecting with the others can be a lifeline.

It is also important to go back to the old adage that "not all skinfolk are kinfolk."[2] Finding Latinx/a/o faculty on campus can be instrumental in building a network of support and mentorship. At the same time, it is important to be honest and say that, in my experience, while the overwhelming majority of Latinx/a/o faculty members are very invested in supporting Latinx/a/o students, some resent being put in the position to do so. The same can be said for your peers; while you may seek connection with other students from Latinx/a/o backgrounds, it will not always be reciprocated. Not all skinfolk are kinfolk. We devote a whole section to navigating the development of relationships with peers as a Latinx graduate student, but it bears mentioning here as well: you may come into contact with racist peers, either of the overt variety or of the clueless, privileged variety. Graduate education is steeped in elitism, and the gatekeeping, as you well know, is fierce. The students who make it to graduate school are often from more privileged backgrounds, and this frequently shows up in the politics of race and class among peers.

The last thing we want to mention here, before we jump into a longer conversation about the kinds of relationships you are likely to navigate in the context of graduate school, is the divide between the academy and the community. Is there a difference, practically and culturally? Of course. But this distinction is also often trotted out as a way to exalt what is happening within the boundaries of the academy and belittle the work that is happening in the community. Or the bridging of the two is talked about as a move for inclusion but is actually approached in a unidirectional manner, such as "let's figure out how we can get 'community people' to participate in this thing that we are doing on campus" (likely crafted with no actual community input because we do not seek true collaboration but rather tokenistic representation). I bring this up here because these approaches, too, are rooted in white supremacy and class politics—and, as we know, class often falls along racial lines in our society. You'll see a clear bias: we do not believe that the academy is somehow inherently better than the community. We also do not think that this entrenched division is real for Latinx graduate students because we are boundary and border crossers in so many ways. We come from and return to the community daily; we are made from and trained in the community as much as the academy. The dichotomy is a component of white supremacy at work in the academy, and something we should call into question every chance we get.

Caretaking Professional Relationships

As general practice, it is important to gain clarity on what each person's responsibility is in each of your professional relationships. We want to make two concrete points here. First, your professor/faculty advisor is there to support your learning process. They will put in work to ensure that the professional points of connection are fruitful to you, and they will in many cases guide these interactions. However, your responsibility in the relationship is to steer and take responsibility for your own learning. You are the person who should make sure you are on track, completing what needs to be completed, reaching out for support when you need it. Taking ownership of your learning process is critical as a graduate student. Wrap your head around this and figure out what you need to do to be ready to take that on (this is where the time and priority management addressed in chapter 3 come into play).

CONSEJO #7   I always tell my students that they are in charge of their education. With so much hidden curriculum in the academy, we can lose sight of the fact that we have some agency in this process. We lose sight of all of the skills we are learning that are marketable inside and outside higher education. For me, thinking about your dissertation or thesis as project management is a way to take back some of the power we can lose in this process. A thesis or dissertation requires you to be in control of managing your time, securing skills and resources, and expertise. These different components help you complete the best version of your project with *your* timeline in mind. Suppose you think of your thesis or dissertation as project management. In that case, you can also put all suggestions from your committee members (comments, funding goals, completion goals, publishing goals, etc.) into a larger context of the overall project goals. This reframing can be especially powerful if you feel lost or powerless in the process, and if you need to remind yourself of your strength and power.

Katy M. Pinto, Department of Sociology, California State University, Dominguez Hills

---

Second, at the start of every new professional relationship, it is helpful to take some time to get clarity about who is responsible for what. You may be able to accomplish this by doing some reflection, consulting the syllabus, and laying things out for yourself; these steps may be sufficient for a class you are taking with a professor. For a relationship you are developing with a longer-term advisor, perhaps a more explicit conversation may be helpful. Some faculty advisors and mentors will initiate this sort of conversation with you, and others will assume that you will figure it out. What is fundamentally important is that you have the clarity you need to know how to engage in the relationship in a professional way. Keep this in mind as we move through this section.

Communicating with Professors

You will have several professors during your graduate student career because you will take classes with different faculty members. It is important to see each of them as a professional in the field with whom you will likely interact in the future. As such, it is important to keep relationships professional and courteous. Later in this chapter, we discuss how to navigate a situation when it is difficult to stay professional. Communication with professors should be considered carefully, especially now that so much communication is done electronically.

In my experience, Latinx graduate students handle communication fairly well; I assume this is rooted in the way many Latinx families regard teachers. In many Latino households, teachers are revered, and our interaction with them is deferential by nature. Whatever the teacher says is right; whatever the teacher thinks should be respected. While in general a respectful approach to your teachers and respect for their profession is helpful, graduate school is a bit different, and simply being deferential is not enough—and often not appropriate. It is important to navigate communication and relationship building with professors in graduate school as a professional, which can be difficult because you may not yet feel like a professional. However, the best way to think about communicating with your graduate school professors is as you would with a professional colleague who is your senior.

Here are a few tips for communicating with professors with whom you are taking classes. (These principles also work for communicating with professors regarding department business, professional opportunities, or other general matters related to your graduate education.)

COMMUNICATE WELL, BUT DO NOT OVERCOMMUNICATE · You should be in regular communication with your professors, but remember to communicate only what is necessary: "Professor Sánchez, my train is delayed and it is possible I will be a few minutes late to class. I will enter as quietly as possible and I apologize in advance for any disruption this may cause." That is an appropriate way to communicate an unexpected delay. Writing, "OMG I am so sorry I am running late! My brother took the car this morning, which left me to take public transit, and I thought I had checked the schedule but just realized I was looking at the Saturday schedule, not the weekday schedule. Argh! So sorry! I will be there as soon as I can! I hope I don't miss too much!" is quite different. Es demasiado. A good rule to live by is to communicate only what you need to so that you come across as a professional. Do not communicate more than necessary or make your professor read a three-paragraph email that only needed to be two sentences. Similarly, do not include extraneous details that are unnecessary for professional communication ("I am sorry I am so scattered, I had a big fight with my girlfriend"). Be courteous and concise, but also do not hesitate to reach out to communicate when you need to.

COMMUNICATING VIA EMAIL · Err on the side of formality when communicating via email with a professor or a faculty advisor. Take the extra two minutes to write in full sentences, include a correct salutation, use correct punctuation, and formally sign off. The question of how to address your professors deserves particular attention, because it is a point of contention for some faculty members and a point of confusion for many students. Address your professors formally, particularly when you are still developing a relationship with them. They may give explicit or implicit instructions signaling that you can drop the formality, but it is always a good idea to err on the side of formality, especially at first.

Now let me be clear: Are there egotistical professors who insist on being called "Dr." because it allows them to feel superior? Sure. Don't waste your time worrying about those professors; address them how they want to be addressed as a matter of collegiality and keep it moving. However, we also know that race and gender shape how students see professors, and that often is illuminated in the way that students address professors. Virtually every woman of color academic I know has had the experience of getting an email that is addressed to "Dr. Roberts and Valerie" or something similar, referring to the male colleague by his full name and title and the female professor by her first name. Compounding this trend is the fact that we are addressed this way not only by students who may still be in the process of learning their own biases and have never learned the correct way to address faculty, but also when we are being publicly introduced in professional settings. All this is to say that when you are addressing a faculty member verbally or in writing, opt for formality, addressing them as "Dr. FulanitodeTal" or "Professor FulanitodeTal." (Note: Do not ever actually say "Dr. FulanitodeTal," but you know what I mean, right? If you are not bilingual, Fulano/Fulanito de Tal is like saying "So-and-So," but with the right inflection it can be dismissive, akin to "What'sHisFace." It is a useful phrase—both as an innocuous one and as a dismissive one.)

CHECK TO SEE IF YOU HAVE THE ANSWER TO SOMETHING BEFORE ASKING IT · I know, I know. You are like, "No shit." But, honestly, you would be surprised at how many times professors get questions from students about things that are in the syllabus, on the Canvas or Blackboard site, or have been stated repeatedly in class. If you need to ask a question—particularly about specifications for an assignment, the professor's office hours, and so on—do yourself a favor and check first to see if you have that information. If you are seeking information that has not been captured anywhere but that you know has been said in class—for example, say your professor recommended the Purdue OWL website for help with learning citation systems—don't let shyness preclude you from asking her to repeat it. Personally, I appreciate when a student simply acknowledges, "I know you mentioned in class a website for citation help, but I can't seem to find it in my notes. Can you please tell me what it was again?"

DO YOUR BEST TO MEET DEADLINES · You may be tempted to skip over this point because you think it gets filed in the category of Captain Obvious, but trust me when I say it's worth repeating. Things happen; sometimes you are going to miss a deadline or need an extension. When that happens, make sure that your professor can read that email and think, "This student is always on time and has their act together. This request is out of the ordinary and must really be necessary." I guarantee the professor is more amenable to granting an extension to a student who is not habitually late than to the student who is. Things happen in life, which means that things happen in graduate school as well—especially true for people like us who may be navigating graduate school alongside other responsibilities like community work, caring for extended family, social activism, or family responsibilities. Keep yourself organized and meet the deadlines you are given. Communicate early and clearly when you cannot. Ask for grace respectfully and do not demand it; an extension is ultimately your professor's prerogative and not something you will automatically be granted or deserve.

STAY ONE STEP AHEAD ON ASSIGNMENTS · Most professors will not have a problem with walking you through an assignment. Maybe you have specific questions about how to approach it, have questions about the requirements, or need to talk out your ideas. Here is the important part: your professor will likely be willing to entertain that conversation with you, but not the night before the assignment is due. Do not send an email the day before that asks for feedback on the topic you have chosen for your paper. In fact, even if you have a fairly easy-to-answer question, and you send it the day before the assignment is due, you should not expect to get an email reply. So how do you avoid this situation? Set aside time (perhaps in your weekly meeting with yourself—go back to chapter 3 if you need a refresher on this concept) to review upcoming assignments and see if you have any questions. This will allow you the time and space to gain clarity without coming across as a last-minute Nelly sending a midnight email about something you should have been working on a week ago.

CONSIDER WHAT FORMAT IS BEST BASED ON YOUR QUESTION · Email is often the easiest way to communicate with professors, both because it takes away the stress of a face-to-face interaction and because it is easy to fire off an email while you are commuting home from work or sitting on your couch at midnight reading for class. However, keep in mind that email is not ideal for all types of communication, and it can be helpful to explicitly mention that you realize that when reaching out to faculty via email. For example, if you are asking a professor for feedback on your writing, to expand on a theory that she covered in class, or for a list of supplementary readings on a topic you are interested in, it may be easier to engage in a face-to-face conversation. Sometimes a student shoots off an email request like this in fifteen seconds, oblivious to the fact that the professor might need to sink an hour into crafting an appropriate and thorough response. Some professors might simply say, "Please come to office hours to discuss this," but it is a good idea to offer that up front. Consider adding a line to your email that says, "Thank you in advance for your time, and if you prefer to discuss this in person, I am happy to make an appointment during office hours to do so."

BE COGNIZANT OF YOUR REQUEST FOR TIME · Students do not always realize that there are many demands on professors' time. Faculty are assessed on the quality of our teaching, research, and service to the department, the university unit we belong to, the university as a whole, the community, our field, and our profession. Teaching is only one part of our responsibilities, and though this work is most visible to students because it directly involves you, your professors appreciate your keeping in mind these other dimensions of their work. It may take a couple of days for a professor to reply to your email because she is collecting data at her research site, planning a big event as a part of her committee work on campus, or traveling to a conference.[3]

It is doubly important to think about how power, hierarchy, privilege, race, and gender play into this consideration as well. If your professor is an adjunct professor, they are likely poorly compensated for their time and may be teaching at multiple universities per semester. Depending on the institution, they may not even be compensated for time they spend in office hours. Meanwhile, assistant professors working toward tenure are on a strict timeline to prove themselves in all three areas of teaching, research, and service; their time may be tight, and they may be struggling to fit everything in. It is well documented that faculty of color and women (imagine the women of color!) do the lion's share of diversity work on campus, including mentoring marginalized students who seek us out. This takes up an incredible amount of time, and often it is not compensated or formally recognized by the university. We lay this all out not so you can feel bad for us or stay away from office hours, but so that you can be cognizant of the load your professor may be carrying.

Last, remember that while your advisor will be an important person in your graduate school journey, don't make the mistake of putting all your eggs in one basket. Your advisor is critical, but not the only person who can be central to your journey. Build many relationships across and outside of campus, surround yourself with folks who believe in you and your work, and seek out connections with scholars from different areas on campus. This will be important in your development as a well-rounded scholar, as you will benefit from having multiple perspectives on your work. Moreover, it will also help your relationship with your advisor because they will not be the only person from whom you seek advice, mentorship, and guidance.

The Purpose of Office Hours

Office hours are time that your professor has set aside specifically to meet with students—often in person but sometimes via videoconference. If you are one of those students who completed your undergraduate degree without ever visiting office hours, wow! Also, don't get too excited—that actually was not the best, and it needs to change. There is no way that you can or should get through graduate school without going to office hours. Students frequently avoid office hours because they are nervous about meeting professors one-on-one, feel that they should only go if they have a problem they need help resolving, and/or feel guilty about taking up a faculty member's time. Here is the deal: professors are contractually obligated to offer time for students to stop by. Most of us enjoy these visits; office hours give us the opportunity to connect with students, clarify course material, and answer questions in a more leisurely way than in the five-minute break during the graduate seminar, which is also the only time we have to use the bathroom or refill our water bottles. We would rather you stop by for office hours.

For graduate students, office hours are a time to (a) build a relationship with your professor, (b) get clarity on coursework and course content, (c) check in on concrete work or abstract ideas either directly or indirectly related to the class, and (d) demonstrate that you are on top of your work. While some of these aims may feel more or less pressing at any given time depending on the class, the professor, and where you are as a student, keep them in mind and frequently ask yourself if you should go to office hours even if you do not want to. Minimally, you should go to office hours at least once per semester for each class.

Not every professor is going to be warm, inviting, and personable in office hours. Some will be, some will not. Try not to let that matter. (Magdalena remembers a professor who set a fifteen-minute timer as soon as she walked through the door for office hours and said, "Go." Predictably, Magdalena visited that professor in office hours only once.) Go in prepared for possible scenarios. In the first scenario, you walk into office hours, and the professor, sitting at their desk, invites you in, asks how you are doing, how your semester is going, how you are finding the class so far, and then asks, "What can I help you with?" Now picture the second scenario: you walk in, and the professor is on their computer, seemingly deep into work, and then looks up when you knock and says, "Yes?" Of course, the first situation will make you feel much more comfortable, because the professor is carrying the conversation. In the second scenario, the responsibility is on you to carry the conversation. The trick is that even if you are greeted with the second scene, approach the encounter with the same confidence as you would the first. If it truly seems like you are interrupting, you may want to double-check: "I am here for office hours. Is it okay for me to come in?". When sitting down with a professor who is less open, read their body language: if this professor seems more about business and none of the small talk, then jump right in. Move the conversation along, be clear in your agenda, and get done what needs to get done. If you are greeted with the first scenario, take the professor's lead (it's like dancing salsa!): answer the questions that are posed to you, and then when the professor invites your questions, you can pull out your list.

Yes, you should have a list. Writing a brief agenda is a simple trick that allows you to be prepared for either scenario. Go in clear about what you want to talk about, what your questions are, or where you need clarification. Write these things down in case you get nervous, overwhelmed, or sidetracked once you are in there. Your agenda should not be overly ambitious, but it should be enough so that if you are in the position to steer the meeting, you have sufficient material to do so. Be as clear as possible—this is why it helps to have this written down—so that you do not meander or get lost.

It helps your professor to know exactly why you are there. You may be asking about something specific: "I have a question about the final paper"; "I wanted to clarify a point you made in class yesterday"; or "I was hoping you could provide some feedback on my assignment so I can improve next time." Depending on how far along you are in your graduate program, you may go in for something less specific: "I am starting to think about my thesis project and wanted to hear your thoughts"; "I am considering applying for this dissertation fellowship and wanted to see if you have any feedback for me"; or even "I am working through this theoretical framework and would like your insights on what I should be reading to deepen my understanding."

Most professors—even the grumpy ones who are tight on time and short on goodwill—will respond positively to a student who comes in organized, clear, and with specific questions. It not only shows that you are organized and together but also demonstrates respect for the professor's time and that you are engaged in the class (which is what we want). Having your list of topics is good because, whether it is paper or electronic, you are now in a position to take notes during the conversation. From the professor's perspective, it can be disconcerting to share suggested readings, ideas, and strategies, but not see you write anything down. Are you sure you will remember all the insights gleaned from the conversation? Better record them somewhere.

There are a few more logistics on office hours to briefly mention because professors often assume students understand these details, and also because not understanding how something works can be the reason why some students don't do it. Sometimes students wonder if they should sign up for an office hours time slot or just stop by. Most professors will make this clear either in class or in class materials (make sure you check the syllabus). If a professor has a sign-up sheet (on their door or online), you should sign up for a slot. If there is no sign-up, you can assume that you can just drop by. If you have a tight time frame (say office hours are from 3 to 5 p.m. and you have a class that starts at 3:30), it is best to be up-front with the professor. Send a brief and polite email that simply states your time limitations and your desire to go to office hours, and ask if your professor can see you right at 3:00 p.m.

I remember as a student never being sure how to deal with approaching the door to my professors' offices during office hours. It may sound silly, but these are the things that can make an anxious student just decide to avoid the whole thing, which is counterproductive. Unless a professor has made clear that they have different preferences (like a sign outside their door that says, "Have a seat, I will see you next"), it is polite to knock (if the door is closed) or politely and quickly wave from the doorway (if the door is open), saying, "I just wanted to let you know I am here for office hours. I am happy to wait."

One last thing to be aware of: if your professor has crafted office hour time slots, be respectful of them. Some professors only teach small graduate seminars and have no problem chatting with a student for forty-five minutes; in general, it is fine to take the professor's lead. If they keep the conversation going, you should feel free to stay and keep chatting. However, it is possible that the same professor who teaches your eleven-person graduate seminar also teaches a two-hundred-student undergraduate class, and for crowd-control purposes that professor may have their office hours split into ten- or fifteen-minute blocks. Be aware and respectful if that is the case. Get in, get out, and allow your professor to keep it moving.

When Difficulties Arise in Your Life

When something arises that will impact your performance in a class, assume that your professor will want to know about it. Use the above advice about how to communicate well without overcommunicating, but give your professor the benefit of the doubt in assuming they are human and want to support you. The trick, of course, is to do so without sounding like you are making excuses. When I was in college, my then boyfriend/now husband was commuting back and forth from his family home forty-five minutes away, caring for his dying mother. He understandably began to fall behind and missed a few assignments. When I asked him if he had communicated with his English professor, he admitted he had not and that she had no idea what was going on with him. I pushed him to tell her, and of course, she was generous in granting extensions.

Building on the previous point, we want to say a few things about due dates and deadlines. While this advice relates most centrally to the relationship with a faculty advisor or chair for a thesis or dissertation, there are three principles to keep in mind when you approach due dates and deadlines.

First, do everything in your power to honor these dates. Keep in mind that while things happen, most of the time, if you had completed things ahead of time, you would have been able to weather whatever comes up at the last minute (computer crash, sick kid, etc.)—and your advisor knows that. So be organized, be on top of things, and treat deadlines as real benchmarks, not just suggestions. Do whatever you can—including taking the advice in chapter 3 about organizing and planning your time—to ensure that you are one step ahead and meet the deadlines that are set. Assume that your advisor is the person who will be writing your letters of recommendation for the postgraduate job of your dreams. What do you want them to say about you? That you are on top of things, reliable, and get shit done. Think about it in those terms. And Handle. Your. Shit.

Second, when you are in a position to set your own deadlines (for example, for a draft of your dissertation as opposed to a deadline imposed by your professor for submitting your final paper), do so with a balance of ambition and reality. It is easy to overpromise and underperform, and it sets you up for failure. When you are asked to set a deadline for yourself (for example, deciding when you will send your advisor your first three chapters of your dissertation), don't give an arbitrary date and then stress about it. Look at your calendar, figure out how many words you can write each day, and calculate a reasonable deadline for yourself. Be ambitious but grounded in reality.

Third, communicate clearly when you need a deadline extension. When things happen and you cannot meet the deadline you set, be professional, communicate clearly without giving a long-winded explanation that sounds like you are making excuses, and—this part is really important—give a concrete plan about how you are going to move forward and meet your goal on a new, specific timeline. You do not want your advisor to have to solve the problem for you or to notice that you missed a deadline but did not acknowledge it. This move is a part of professional comportment: take responsibility when you have misstepped, and then lay out a plan for how you will make it right.

Getting Critique

The joke among my graduate school friends about my dissertation chair was that going in to see her was like sitting down for a game of *Duck Hunt*, the 1980s Nintendo game where you used a little plastic gun to shoot the flying ducks on-screen. The analogy went like this: No matter how much you had gotten done ("I wrote 150 pages!"), no matter how sharp your analysis ("I think I have developed a new conceptual frame!"), no matter how good you felt the writing was ("I have revised it five times and feel really good about the state of this chapter!"), Professor Roy would nod politely and hear you out, then slowly pull out her little plastic gun and start to shoot your ducks out of the air. Splat—you need to make more progress. Splat—this conceptual frame is not sound. Splat—this chapter still needs a lot of work. She was a hard-ass and expected greatness; regardless of how well you had done, she knew there was room for improvement, and she would push you to get there. Jokes aside, though, I knew people in graduate school who decided not to work with her because of her fierce reputation. This was true for other professors, as well, though it was certainly relevant that Professor Roy was young, brown, and a woman.

Let me be very clear that critique is different from hazing or academic abuse. There are professors who will try to cut you down and treat you poorly because they suffered as graduate students under their advisors, and they think academic hazing is necessary to produce good scholars. Or something. I don't actually know how they justify it, but the point is that there are professors who will break you down rather than build you up. That is not acceptable. My general outlook is that you should not endure abuse from anyone, not someone you are dating, not toxic family members, not "friends." Graduate school advisors and dissertation chairs are not exempt from that principle. Of course, we know that there are ways that certain kinds of abuse find a home in these lopsided power dynamics very easily; the #AcademicMeToo movement, for instance, has put this on full display.[4] The point here is that staying in an abusive dynamic is harmful in myriad ways, and although in some moments and in some spaces there can be an accepted practice within the academy that justifies problematic and even abusive behaviors, we need to denounce it at every turn.

There is a critical difference between a professor who critiques your work because they are trying to belittle you and one who critiques your work because they are trying to push you to be a better scholar. Read that again if you need to, because this is a crucial distinction. I watched friends in graduate school walk away from working with certain professors because they could not cope with harsh feedback on their work. They saw this sort of critique as inherently negative and could not help but take it personally. As a result, they consciously or unconsciously searched for an advisor who would mostly praise them. What was difficult to see at the time, of course, because we were all so steeped in it, is that what they had actually walked away from was an opportunity to sharpen their analysis, tighten their writing, and make their work better.

My advisor was harsh. The *Duck Hunt* analogy was partially true; no matter what you went in with, you left feeling like you could do better and knew you had a lot of work ahead of you. What I realized, though, was that Dr. Roy was doing this because she respected me. She was doing this because she saw my promise and wanted me to produce the best possible dissertation. She was doing this because she knew I aspired to be a professor and that I wanted to stay in the Bay Area; because that combination of a geographically bound tenure-track job search in an area people often want to live in could be impossible, she wanted me to have the best possible odds on the academic job market. Her critique was not an insult; it was a compliment. She cared enough about my work, and believed enough in me, to carefully read every draft I submitted and to give me thoughtful critiques that pushed me further. I am better because of it; in fact, I am the scholar and mentor I am today because of her time and investment. The way I thought about it was this: if there is a hole in my argument, a piece that I am not executing well because of sloppy writing, or an example I am giving that does not land, I would rather hear about it in my advisor's office, knowing that she is trying to help me become a better scholar, than from some dude who stands up in Q&A at a conference after I have presented with a smirk on his face because he has a sound gripe about my work. Punto. Final. When the critique felt hard to take because I was trying so hard—oh man, I was trying so hard!—I conjured up that image and was able to set aside my feelings of being critiqued so I could focus on the substance of her feedback.

It is important to add that Latinx junior scholars and graduate students are used to interfacing with teachers who do not believe in us and communicate in both direct and indirect ways that we are not good enough and not smart enough. I imagine almost every one of us can pull up a story and mental image of that teacher just by reading those words, whether she was your second grade teacher who never called on you or your high school history teacher who told you there was no way you would cut it in college. I say this because it is important to recognize that taking criticism as an insult rather than a compliment has its roots in a very logical place, but at the same time, it is crucial that we do not confuse the two.

So, on a very practical level, here it is: critique can be hard to hear, but it is crucial to your professional and intellectual development. I have talked mostly about critique from a dissertation advisor or professor in this section, but it is important to note that in academia there is no shortage of critique to go around. You will get critique (or rejection) on campus from professors, but you will also apply for grants you do not get, submit papers that do not get chosen for publication, apply to present at conferences that you are not accepted to. Here are best practices around getting critique that you can hold in your pocket and pull out when necessary:

1 Disentangle the hurt feeling you may have from the substance of the critique. Remind yourself, "It does not feel good to get critique, but it does feel good to make my work stronger."

2 Sit with the critique. Don't rush to adopt it or ignore it. Set it aside for a day or two and then come back to it once the sting has subsided.

3 Bring in a trusted colleague—not to assure you that the critique is not founded (yes, it is an impulse to complain about the hard meeting with your advisor to the friend who will reply, "Ugh, he's such an asshole!") but so that the trusted colleague can help you make sense of the critique.

One last story: I once got a harsh letter from a leading journal in one of my fields following my submission of an empirical article. Technically, it was a "revise and resubmit" or R&R, which means that the invitation to resubmit it to the same journal was there, provided I attended to the major revisions flagged by the reviewers. Now, an R&R is perfectly normal; in fact, it is the most common outcome when it comes to publication submission, as incredibly few papers are accepted as is. I know this now, but at the time I was so bummed. I had worked really hard on the submission and felt like it was strong. I read the reviewer's comments and felt super overwhelmed by them. It was by someone outside of my field, I suspected, and they were coming with all kinds of specific references and issues that I had no grounding in and could not make sense of. I read the feedback a couple times and then set it aside, overwhelmed by the idea of tackling the revisions. It sat there for nine months.

A scholar friend in my accountability group, Sylvia Nam, kept gently nudging me: "Hey, girl, did you get around to that revise and resubmit yet?" I would sigh and assure her that I would get back to it. Finally, Sylvia said, "Send it to me." I demurred, "No, it's terrible. I can't." I had internalized the harsh review and felt like I couldn't let anyone see it—though I had not realized that was what I was doing. She insisted, "Do it right now while I am on the phone with you. Email me both the manuscript as well as the review." She's a good friend, and I knew she would not think less of me for this awful paper, plus I knew she wouldn't take my bullshit putting off the revisions for much longer, so I sent it. She called me back the next day and said, "You are a fool for having sat on this for almost a year. This is a good paper, and the revisions are totally doable. Get a pen and let's talk this through." She reviewed the reviewer's critiques sentence by sentence, talking through how I could address them.

Doing this exercise with her not only broke me out of my immobility and shame, it also cut through the bullshit. She saw what I couldn't: the negative review was long and complicated, but the fixes were actually easy. We made a bulleted list of what I needed to do. I sat down that weekend and handled the revision in less than four hours. The revised version was undoubtedly stronger. I resubmitted, the article was accepted, and it has become my most-cited journal article. A couple years later, it was selected for inclusion in a print anthology for that journal that is published once a decade. It is the article that almost wasn't. The moral of the story is: don't sit on something for nine months, and know that a trusted colleague can help you break through the shit you aren't even aware that you are hanging on to.

As a professor, and a mentor and advisor to both MA and doctoral students, I can tell you with 100 percent certainty that what is most difficult for me to deal with is not a student who is struggling with writing or who is not quite where they need to be in their analysis. It is a student who is defensive when you offer feedback or who acts like they are open but then does not do anything differently the next time or try to incorporate the feedback. A coachable student is a student I love working with, no matter how much coaching they need. So, don't be worried about not having it all figured it out or not being smart enough or not being a good enough writer. We can work with that. What you should worry about is if you cannot take feedback, if you get defensive with criticism. Be honest with yourself. Do you need to work on this? If so, make it a priority. Graduate school—and your academic life—will be so much more enjoyable and easier to navigate if you do.

Letters of Recommendation

We talked through the nuts and bolts of requesting letters of recommendation in chapter 1 but would like to add a couple points on these letters as they relate to professional relationships. You may need letters of recommendation to apply to graduate school, to apply for fellowships or scholarships, and to apply for jobs as you head toward graduation. Remember that your advisor is the principal person who will write letters of recommendation for you, and they will be pulling from their full body of experiences with you to do so. While we are not trying to increase the stress or make you feel like you need to perform at all times in front of your advisor, it is worth thinking about who you are and how you are with them, and what they will be able to say about you when asked to write a letter of reference on your behalf. It is okay, for example, for them to know about hardships that you have encountered, but you want them to be able to say that you met those challenges head-on. It is okay for them to know about moments in your research process when you hit bumps in the road, but you want them to be able to tell a story about how you were able to get past this. You do not need to hide any difficulty or hardship from your advisor—in fact, they are there to help you through the inevitable challenges—but keep in mind that your response tells them a lot about who you are. You owe it to yourself to demonstrate a good, strong response when difficulties arise (because they will).

On the more logistical end of things, professors will get prickly if you ask them for a letter of recommendation with a tight turnaround time (one month is standard; some professors will need more—it is always good to ask). As we alluded to in chapter 1, professors also get prickly if you enter their name in a portal to offer a letter of recommendation before you have asked their permission to do so. Let me restate that differently: do not ever put the name and email of a reference writer before they have agreed to write a letter for you. It is presumptuous and disrespectful. Many times, those sites send out a prompt automatically, which means that they may get the request from the system before you reach out. Avoid this at all costs! Last point on letters of recommendation: always ask the professor what information they need from you to write a strong letter, and also be prepared to share application elements like your personal statement or cover letter when you are requesting a letter. A thank-you note is always appreciated.

Dealing with a Difficult Professor
(for One Semester, Maybe Two)

It is likely you will have a professor who is not a great fit for you. Maybe they are disorganized or phoning it in because they dislike teaching, they are at an institution where teaching is not valued, or they are at the end of their career. Maybe you dislike their teaching style and feel it does not work for you. Or maybe there is something more serious going on: your professor is abusive, or racist, or flirting with you. While we cannot anticipate every particular scenario here to provide a blueprint for how to navigate it, we will provide some key steps to help deal with this sort of situation and figure out how to move forward.

1 Try your best to figure out what is going on. It is easier to develop a solution if you properly diagnose the problem.
2 Decide if this is something that is annoying and you can live with or if you need to take action. Some helpful questions to consider might be: Is this professor negatively impacting my educational experience in a lasting way? Is what this professor is doing illegal or unethical?
3 Consider if there is anything you can do, that is within your power, to mitigate the impact of the problem on you.
4 Discuss with a trusted mentor or advisor—preferably not a peer, and not someone like a friend who will feel compelled to take your side regardless of the specifics of the situation.
5 Take appropriate action as you see fit; seek out resources on and off campus to support you.

Three more suggestions. First, remember to keep records in case they become necessary; if no written records exist, keep a journal of incidents (with dates, specifics of what happened, who else was a witness). Second, be principled in your own actions, with the recognition that anything you do or say could be made public and undermine your ability to call out the misconduct of someone else; while it may be hard, refrain from shit-talking and gossiping. And third, make sure that you understand the chain of command, that is, the order of escalation for serious concerns, so you know exactly whom to go to and in what order if things do not resolve (for instance, don't go to the dean without first talking to the department chair).

While we recognize this is really broad, the reality is that there are so many specific scenarios that you would want to deal with in so many different ways that we feel it is best to focus on some broad steps: diagnose the issue, ascertain the level of importance, reflect on yourself, seek wise counsel, and then take action. Action may be doing nothing, depending on the situation, or it could be a serious and significant effort for you. There is no blueprint about how to do this correctly, but we hope these broad steps will give you a way to think about what to do in a strategic way that also holds central self-preservation and care for yourself.

Dealing with a Mismatch or Difficult Advisor

In most programs, you are assigned an advisor when you begin your graduate studies. There may be a place on the application where you identify someone you would like to work with, or an advisor may be assigned to you based on your research interests. In some doctoral programs, advisors take on a certain number of students each year and essentially choose those students during the admissions process; if a faculty member chooses to work with you, then you are admitted to the program; if no faculty member chooses you, then you are denied. Regardless of how your advisor is selected, remember that you should have the authority to change that assignment if it is not working for you.

It would be a lie to say that switching advisors or requesting a change is an easy and apolitical process. In some places it may be, and in other places—or with certain people—it is not. The reality is that your advisor may be upset or angry or have hurt feelings if you want to switch away from them, but that does not mean that you should shy away from doing so. If your advisor relationship is not working for you, a helpful first step is to figure out for yourself what exactly is not working and then speak to your advisor about trying to fix it. It may be that you feel you need more oversight and regular meetings, but your advisor has no way of knowing that unless you say it. Reflection is also helpful because it may be that you realize that what is not working for you is that your advisor is critiquing you (read the above section on critique), and that actually what you need to change is not your advisor but your orientation toward receiving challenging feedback. If you decide to change your advisor, communicate clearly with them, be professional, thank them for the support they have given you up to that point, and do all you can to retain a cordial, professional relationship with them.

Relationships between advisors and dissertation chairs will be different on each campus. Generally speaking, when you are assembling your dissertation committee, you should have developed a working relationship with your advisor, and it is common for that person to serve as your chair. If you were randomly assigned to someone, the point of choosing your dissertation chair can also provide a natural point at which to change your advisor if that is how things work on your campus. The takeaway here is that if you are dealing with a difficult advisor/chair, you should not just suffer in silence. You should do something about it, and when you do, you should take care in that process, take care of the relationship, and hold principled and professional interactions as central.

Last, make sure you have decided that a particular professor is not a good match based on your own personal experience—not that of anyone else. Building on the earlier conversation about critique, it is important to note that sometimes a professor will get a reputation as being "hard to work with" when in actuality this is a euphemism for "expects a lot." It is always okay to move on from a professional relationship that isn't working, but be sure you are figuring this out for yourself rather than relying on chisme or rumor.

Maintaining Relationships with Your Mentors over Time

Maintaining relationships with advisors and mentors while you are in graduate school is important, but oftentimes graduate students do not understand how to do it. A related, though distinct, topic is maintaining those relationships after you graduate. I will briefly discuss both. It may seem that there is no general maintenance for your relationship with advisors or mentors when you are in graduate school because you are both at the same institution. Maybe you see each other at campus events; maybe you run into each other in the hall a few times per semester. Even though that may be true, that is not a substitute for meaningfully reaching out to connect, updating them on how things are going on your academic journey, and seeking their advice. That is the *why* in terms of this question—now on to the *how*.

The best tools to employ here are either email or office hours. Your advisor is likely busy; try to not increase the demands on their time by asking to meet at a time that is not already set aside for meeting with students, or by grabbing them in the hallway when they may have other plans for their time. You can check in and update your advisor on your progress, either by visiting them during office hours or by sending a long email. If you are meeting during office hours, it is wise to let them know the purpose of your appointment beforehand. Some students find it easier to send a detailed email with an update, and then add a note that makes clear that if your advisor would like you to come in for a meeting, you are happy to sign up for office hours. If you feel confident you are going to get a substantive reply, if you know that they are easy to reach via email, then this can be a fine way to go, especially for students who feel a bit shy and find it easier to communicate details in writing.

When you email or meet with your advisor, you should prepare beforehand. Jot down the following items: what you have been working on and progress toward your degree ("I completed my methods class and now just have four more required courses"); any major accomplishments (like getting a grant); and your immediate plans for the future in terms of moving forward on your degree plan. Consider if you have any pressing questions or if you need any advice. If so, put some thought into the question and write it down so you will remember to ask it. Finally, in the meeting or in the email, make sure to ask the following questions: "Do you have any feedback for me? Given the stage I am at, is there anything you think I should be attending to? Do you have any advice for how I should navigate this next phase in my studies?" These questions indicate to your advisor that you are open to feedback, which is a good look in general, but also invite commentary on things that you may not be aware that you should be thinking about—for example, it is time to start thinking about your research question; you should consider applying for postdoctoral fellowships; you should take a class with this new faculty member because her research intersects with yours; and so on. Being in regular contact with your advisor allows you to check in and get advice, and it demonstrates you are on top of things and coachable.

If the relationship is a formal one, like the one with your dissertation advisor, you should have an explicit conversation at the beginning of the relationship and ask directly, "What works best for you in terms of how often we should check in, how often you want me to update you with my progress, etc.?" Getting clarity early on is helpful to you, to the advisor, and for the relationship. Once you hear their answers, schedule those check-in reminders on your calendar so you are not relying on your memory to keep track of it all.

The Cohort. Oh, Lord, the Cohort.

Not all graduate programs are cohort-based, but many are. A cohort is a group of students who are admitted at the same time and who more or less navigate the program on a similar timeline. In other words, the cohort is a group of people you enter graduate school with and who become your de facto crew. You'll hit milestones at the same time (like preparing for **qualifying exams**, choosing dissertation committee members, etc.) and are likely taking most or all of your classes together, particularly in the beginning of the program. The closeness of the cohort—the fact that you are all navigating the difficulties and triumphs of graduate school together—is both the delight and the difficulty of being a cohort member. In the best scenario, the cohort is a group of people you can lean on for support, collaborate with, and share camaraderie, especially when others outside academia do not understand or cannot relate to what you're going through. But the cohort also can be a source of strife. Being on a similar timeline means that you may be applying for dissertation or departmental fellowships simultaneously, so the competition is not abstract but rather someone you know—your direct peer was awarded the departmental grant you were denied.

It can be difficult to know how to navigate cohort dynamics when you find yourself outside of the group in some way. Maybe you are the only person in your cohort with kids, so while everyone else hangs out in the grad student lounge after class, you have to rush home to relieve the sitter. Maybe you are the only BIPOC student, and you don't feel welcomed by or at home with the other cohort members. Maybe you are in recovery, and your cohort's favorite social spot is the bar down the street. Maybe you are single and queer, and everyone else is coupled in heterosexual relationships. We lay out these examples because regardless of your cohort's dynamics, we want to acknowledge that, for many, it is not a big happy family.

The single most helpful advice we can offer about how to navigate cohort dynamics is for you to (a) assess what the cohort can be helpful for; (b) figure out how to orient yourself accordingly; and (c) not make the cohort your entire social support in graduate school. Let's take each of those things one by one. First, depending on the particular dynamics, you will need to determine what your cohort will be helpful for. Maybe information is difficult to track at your campus, and the cohort will help you get the scoop on when award applications are open, events on campus, or deadlines to turn in paperwork. Maybe your cohort is not a particularly welcoming space for you, but you can easily maintain cordial acquaintances in that space, which is also helpful. Maybe your cohort is not a social space but a great place to go to break down readings, share work and get feedback, or bounce ideas around. Assess your cohort in an ongoing way—not once in your first week in the program but continuously, so that you can figure out how to relate to it.

That brings us to our second point: once you figure out what the cohort is like and what it is good for, figure out how to orient yourself toward it. That may seem like a really obvious statement, but let me say it a bit differently. Let's say you observe that the cohort is not going to be a social space for you for whatever reason. Don't fret and lose sleep over seeing a social media post of three of your cohort mates going out to dinner when you did not get an invitation. If they are not your social group, don't get wrapped up in the social dynamics. Consider another example: if your cohort is a place for you to get and pass on information, relate to it as such. If a cool opportunity comes across your radar, don't hoard it; be a helpful member of the community and pasa la voz.

Now to the third point: even when you get along well, do not make the cohort your entire social support in graduate school. Graduate school can be insular and isolating in many respects. Particularly for first-gen and Latinx students, you may be the only person in your family and your friend group who is navigating oral comprehensive exams, **position papers, dissertation proposals**, and assembling a **dissertation committee**. What I really mean is that perhaps nobody in your friend group or in your family understands the deep levels of stress and anxiety that come along with those sorts of tasks and milestones because they do not understand the importance they hold. As a result, it can be easy to allow the insularity of graduate school to take over. You do not want that to happen. Even in the best case, when you have cohort mates who get you, are also students of color, are fun to have a beer with, and are even cool when your partner or your kid comes along to the picnic, you do not want your grad school crew to be your entire social crew.

It is really important to maintain, and nurture, your relationships with people outside of your graduate school world for many reasons. First, sometimes you just have to escape that grad school world for a bit. It is important for your mental and physical health to take a break from work that is as all-consuming as graduate school can be. Second, having connections with people outside of graduate school—especially people who do not understand the grad school hype—is helpful in keeping perspective. When I was in graduate school, most of my social circle were folks who were doing community organizing and nonprofit work full-time. We shared a political affinity, and they were generally supportive of my being in graduate school, but they only understood what that entailed in a cursory way. Some of them had college degrees, and some did not. They were supportive but did not truly get it. And you know what? That was really helpful. When I would show up for dinner at one of their houses stressed about a paper I was working on, they'd be like, "Dude, take a break—you have been writing all day!" And while it is not that simple, guess what? It also is that simple.

Another factor here is really important: although I kept one foot in activist work while I was working on my graduate degrees, it was not the same as doing that work on the ground and full-time as I had been doing before grad school. But my friends were still doing that work. My husband spent his days doing grassroots organizing with welfare recipients and workfare workers in San Francisco who were fighting the city for reasonable and safe working conditions. One of my closest friends was working with an Asian Pacific Islander community organization that was fighting against environmental racism. My sister, whom I have always been close to, was doing advocacy and support with homeless people in San Francisco. My friends are dope, right? Okay, but I am sharing it because honestly, when I would get a bit too steeped in the ivory tower and too caught up in the dramas of the cohort, I had these other folks who were fighting serious battles of real importance with people who were suffering—and that was crucial for me in keeping perspective on what was really important, what deserved to be fretted over and what did not, and what was really at stake.

Maintain connections with folks who are doing that sort of work, and also your folks who are working at Mi Pueblo Grocery Store and who are apprenticing to be electricians. Maintain the connections to your family. The ugliest part of academia is the elitism, and one of the ways that academic elitism is perpetuated is when grad students only hang out with grad students—and that is totally in our power to dismantle, not only because elitism is bullshit but because maintaining the connections to our folks on the ground is good for us, good for our mental health, and good for our communities.

It also bears mentioning that while I am talking about the cohort as a monolithic group, that does not need to be the case. In fact, one way to subvert difficult cohort dynamics can be to relate not to the cohort as a bound unit but rather to work on developing (professional and/or personal) relationships with just one or two or a handful of people that you decide to build with. When I was in my PhD program, I maintained cordial and friendly relationships with the cohort broadly and developed a close relationship with one other person in the program. She was another woman of color, and we just got each other. She was all I needed, to be honest.

Additional Considerations about Cohort Dynamics

Competition within the cohort is pretty much inevitable, because as a group of people in the same field and often the same subdiscipline reaching milestones simultaneously, you will literally be competing with each other at different points, whether for postdocs, jobs, fellowships, or teaching positions. At the same time, keep in mind that a competitive environment can be healthy or it can be toxic. Also remember that cohort relationships are not automatically or even naturally reciprocal—even if you have the intention of giving 100 percent to your cohort, there is no guarantee that others are relating in the same way. While institutional norms come into play in this dynamic, remember that these sorts of dynamics are made—and broken—by people. Consider what you can do to ensure that the competition in your cohort is a healthy environment that encourages everybody to do their best and to understand that collaboration, when done right, can help everyone achieve. Consider what you might be doing, intentionally or unintentionally, to contribute to unhealthy competitive dynamics. Of course, this is easier said than done, and first-generation Latinx students are often navigating very real dynamics in the context of graduate school that make things like postdocs and fellowships and jobs not something that theoretically would be nice to have but rather can mean the difference between our ability to enroll in school next semester or not. Still, or maybe because of this, we need to choose collaboration and healthy competition. It is good for us individually, in terms of navigating the dynamics in academia that can be toxic, unhealthy, and frankly detrimental to our happiness and well-being, and we need to do it because this is how institutions change. Let's remake them together.

On a related note, there may be times when your milestones are not aligned, when you see people moving ahead of you by weeks, months, or even entire semesters, taking their oral exams ahead of you, passing their dissertation proposal defense ahead of you, and so on. It is important to stay grounded and remember that everyone moves at their own pace based on many factors. Remind yourself you are making progress and that your committee, advisors, and professors feel fine about where you are. Do your work on the timeline that is best for you. It is easy to become overwhelmed when things don't go according to plan; if you are not careful, a small bump in the road can spiral you into a full-fledged detour because you have lost your bearings. The timelines that are created and communicated are made for students under the best grad school conditions, and it is very possible that your journey has a few bumps. Don't let this throw you into a downward spiral. Communicate regularly with your advisor and counselors, and work out a timeline that suits you.

Finally, while we have spent most of this section talking about your cohort, one of the most helpful resources in helping you navigate graduate school is actually the cohort ahead of yours. They recently have walked the path you are walking and have seen some things along the way—learn from that knowledge. Whether it is advice about what classes to take, how to find information about fellowships, or who the friendliest person in the financial aid office is, the cohort ahead of you is full of useful information. They can also, possibly, be a source of camaraderie, support, and friendship in a slightly different way because some of the dynamics around competition that may be present with your own cohort are removed. Of course, as you advance in your own academic trajectory, and once you are no longer the newbie, remember to be a helpful resource to the cohort behind you by making yourself available to them. Another important note: while it can be easy to stay focused on just your program and/or department, there are other graduate students in other disciplines on your campus. Some of the best relationships can be forged with students in other cohorts, other programs, and other disciplines. Take advantage of opportunities for cross-campus connections, and seek out these connections through shared identity centers and programming on campus.

Navigating Chisme

You know you are reading a book by your people and for your people when *chisme* appears in a subheading, right? Listen, you know what we are going to say, but I hope including this section is a push for you to reflect on your own chismoso/a/x tendencies and to figure out if there is some growth you need in this area. In your professional relationships, avoid chisme at all costs. Chisme breeds drama, and you do not need drama in your professional relationships.

Be especially wary of taking on your advisor's beefs with their colleagues, whether they are other faculty in your department, elsewhere on your campus, or at other institutions. You may encounter an advisor who openly dishes about their grudges with other academics, which may be based on opposing intellectual views or petty interpersonal conflicts that have been raging for decades. This behavior is problematic because of the power dynamics at play: when your advisor brings you into the gossip, you logically feel compelled to choose a side. As we have mentioned, academia is a small world, and you never know when your path may cross, even years after grad school, with the scholar whom your advisor is trashing. So, if you are working with someone who regularly spreads department chisme and talks shit about colleagues, remind yourself that there are parts of the story that you do not and may not ever know, and do your best to stay neutral.

I used to be in a political organization that had codes of conduct for members, and one of them was to avoid gossip and to deal with conflict in a politically principled manner. In the context of a political organization, this was about reinforcing the integrity of the organization against outside interference and disunity (read up on COINTELPRO and how this sort of tactic was used to disrupt political work in the 1960s and '70s). Let's learn a lesson here. If you hear someone has an issue with you, deal with it in a politically principled manner, not by talking shit. If you don't like someone, do your best to keep those sentiments out of your communication with others in your grad school and professional circuits. We do not need to belabor this point because you know exactly what we mean, but we felt it important enough to include here. Avoid chisme at all costs. Punto. Final.

Remaking Mentorship: Mentoring above You, to the Side, and Below

Mentorship is one of those words you hear a lot in certain spaces. Sometimes mentorship is formal, as in an institutional mentorship relationship with your dissertation advisor; at other times, a mentor is someone who informally looks out for you, helps guide you, and is a resource and support person for you. First-generation students often have a hard time navigating mentorship because it is one of those things we know we should be thinking about, but we often lack real guidelines for how to approach it. You may be blessed with a great mentor(s)—fantastic! However, if you are struggling to figure out what mentorship is and can or should look like, or if you have been assigned a mentor but are not really sure you are approaching the relationship right, this section may help you think this through a bit more. We are not going to talk about how to take care of good relationships with mentors because we laid out such considerations in the previous section.

Here we will talk about mentoring up, mentoring to the side, and mentoring down. We provide some brief, specific ideas about each of these categories, but more than anything we want to share that thinking of mentorship in these three categories is a helpful interruption to the prevalent idea that as a graduate student you need to find a mentor to guide you, or that you will find all the mentorship you need in one single person. That idea rests on mentorship as a unidirectional relationship (the mentee receives and the mentor gives), when we actually think that a solid mentorship is perhaps not reciprocal but certainly mutually beneficial. Additionally, this traditional understanding of mentorship positions the student as clueless and the mentor as the knowledgeable one. It's helpful to complicate that a bit, and as you can see in the next sections, we think that having a more nuanced relationship of the idea of mentorship is actually a responsibility we should step up to as Latinx scholars.

Mentoring Up: How to Mentor a Mentor Who Is Not Equipped to Mentor You

The reality is that not all faculty who are appointed as mentors are prepared to do so effectively. Moreover, not all faculty are prepared to mentor all students. It is possible you are put in a position to be mentored by someone who does not have experience mentoring junior scholars in general, or perhaps is only used to mentoring junior scholars who are middle class, white, and/or not first generation. This means you may have to mentor up, that is, mentor the person who is mentoring you. Remind yourself that grad school is a time when it is completely acceptable to ask questions and ask for guidance. I remember thinking, "Man, I don't want to ask about this. I should already know this." Dude, you are a student—the exact stage when it is okay to not know things! Your mentor may not know that there are certain things you do not know, so ask. Doing so not only helps you but also indicates to them that you need this guidance. So, if your mentor suggests it would be a good time for you to start applying for predoctoral fellowships and you have no idea what those are, why you would apply, or how to find such fellowships, then ask for clarification: "I am not familiar with that. Can you tell me more?" Such a statement may seem obvious in the abstract, but many students fumble their way through, trying to figure things out because they do not know how to ask for help or clarification. Remind yourself that sometimes your mentors do not know how to mentor you, and the way that you help them learn is by asking them to teach you, guide you, and support you in ways that you need. It is a win-win.

It is also important to name the structural elements at play here, particularly when you are mentored by Latinx (and Latina, in particular) faculty or other faculty of color. Faculty of color, as we have mentioned, often disproportionately carry the work of equity and inclusion on campus, and a part of that work is mentoring students of color. We are called to do this work; we want to do this work; we are moved by this work and feel a responsibility to it; also, this work can be all-consuming. When a professor, advisor, or mentor tells you they only have fifteen minutes to meet with you, takes a few days to reply to your email, or is late in returning your draft with feedback, keep in mind the weight they are carrying and, in particular, the institutional and structural reasons that weight is disproportionately placed on the shoulders of faculty of color, and women of color in particular. While you are mentoring up, also remember that your faculty members may be navigating burnout, receiving an unending stream of requests for their time, and also trying to attend to their own work—this is even more true for junior (untenured) and adjunct faculty members. Be proactive, but also be generous.

Mentoring to the Side: How Your Colleagues Are a Vital Tool

Pay attention to your relationships with classmates, your cohort, and colleagues in your program, including those who may not be classmates or cohort mates because they are perhaps a year or two ahead of you. Part of building collegial relationships is building a reciprocal culture in the program; one way you can do that is by thinking about those relationships as a part of mentorship. And no wonder: the process of reciprocation is how communities of color, poor communities, and other marginalized people have always gotten through shit—by working together. The same holds true in higher education. I have said many times that there are very few individual accomplishments in higher education; most of what we achieve comes about because other people have supported us along the way. On graduation day, when I am congratulating students and meeting their families, I always say, "Congratulations to you, too! This is a family achievement!"

Okay, so back to my point. If we think about building a reciprocal, collaborative culture in graduate school by thinking about how we mentor each other, this opens us up both to taking seriously the responsibility of supporting classmates and to seeing them as important sources of information, guidance, and advice. You need to be able to see them as people who have good information, insight, advice, and guidance. You also need to see yourself as someone who has insight, advice, and guidance that can benefit others.

Here is an example: I had a student in my MA class who came to office hours at the beginning of the semester because she was really struggling with one of the core assignments of the class, which requires students to exchange weekly reading responses with a small group of classmates. They read each other's work, then get in a small group to discuss the ideas as a start to each class session. The student had a deeply rooted fear about her classmates reading her work. When I talked with her about her reticence, I told her, "Look, in graduate school, you *need* to be able to see your colleagues as sources of guidance to work out ideas with and through. And they need to be able to see you in this way as well. I promise, you all will be better for it." In fact, it is one of the reasons I make this a core assignment in the class. At the end of the semester, she explained in her final class reflection how much she had learned from engaging in the activity—how she had grown by being pushed to share her writing with her classmates, as well as how she had surprised herself by being able to provide feedback to them. This muscle is important to develop—particularly around writing, but in general when it comes to interacting with peers—and having a mindset that understands how we can mentor to the side is key.

A quick note about the word *support*: support is often misconstrued as a blanket cheerleading for the other person. To be real, we need that positivity at times. Cheerlead and lift up and celebrate your peers and surround yourself with people who will do the same. But we also need the kind of support that is critical, constructive, and demands that we do better. And we need to provide that support for others.

Mentoring Down: Responsibility, Engagement,
and Lifting as a Latinx Grad Student

I will say this clearly, without apology and without mincing words: as a Latinx graduate student, you have the responsibility to mentor those who are coming up behind you. As I said before, no one who gets to graduate school did it alone. As a side note on that point: if you have some sort of narrative about how you got where you are because of your hard work and grit alone and nobody helped you along the way, I encourage you to rethink that bootstrap narrative, because it serves nobody and harms everybody. None of us got here alone, and while it can be hard to imagine yourself as the mentor and not the mentee in a mentorship relationship, remember that being a mentor does not mean that you know everything. Mentorship is the acknowledgment that you are farther along in the journey than others, and in being farther along, you have the ability to support others.

I actively encourage you to look for ways to serve as a mentor to Latinx students or other marginalized students who are behind you on the educational journey. This work can be done formally or informally. You can email students in the cohort behind you introducing yourself and letting them know that you are happy to serve as a resource as they get acclimated to graduate school. You can write down your experiences—for example, of assembling your dissertation committee or studying for your qualifying exams—and share that generously with others as they reach those milestones. You can look for explicit and formal ways to mentor others by joining a mentorship program at your local high school or volunteering to sit on the panel for preview days as new students check out the program. There is no shortage of ways to get involved in mentoring junior students; it is just a matter of seeking them out. It also bears saying that you can also get a lot out of these relationships and the practice of mentoring others. And to be clear, while we encourage you to take this obligation seriously and to appreciate the meaning to be found in mentoring down, you also need to guard against giving away so much of your time and energy that you lose focus on what you came to grad school to do. I encourage you to think about mentoring the scholars who come after you as a professional obligation. You have to hold the door open for folks behind you, just as you would do when walking into the grocery store.

Cultivating Relationships in the Academy beyond Your Institution

Cultivating relationships beyond your institution is also important. While we spent most of this section talking about your own little universe in academia, it is important to remember that your universe is not the only universe. Graduate school tends toward insularity—push against it. Consider networking in professional associations, in your field broadly, at conferences, and in other professional spaces as an important part of relationship building as well. There are no hard rules around this, but, in general, assume an environment of collegiality and camaraderie in academia as a whole and interact with it as such. That means that, when you read an article that you find really helpful to your own thinking, it is appropriate to send a quick email to that scholar (pretty much all of our email addresses are available online) to thank them for their work. It may be the start of a professional acquaintanceship, or it may go unacknowledged—which is also fine.

A word of warning here: some students approach networking like it is their job; they take a transactional approach, as if they will get paid for each name they add to their phone contacts. My suggestion is to reach out with generosity and gratitude to make actual connections and thank people for their work, not to simply say you know Dr. Hotshot Scholar or only to ask for something. It is wonderful to cultivate a broad network of mentors and contacts, but remember that your aim should not be self-promotion or to get them to help you. Your goal is to make a thoughtful connection and thank them for their work. Sometimes, a deeper connection can grow from these minor points of contact—you never know!

Remaking the Academy by Rethinking Academic Relationships

In sharing these concluding thoughts, I want to remind you all of the fundamental framing here: these are relationships. While it can be easy to focus on the minutiae of daily interactions like office hours or class discussions, remember that what we are talking about is how to care for relationships with other people. In thinking about this skill, the institution necessarily looms large. We navigate these relationships within and through the context of white supremacy and other forms of oppression that are endemic to the academy. Thinking of these relationships as relationships, though, can help us focus on the bigger picture, strategize about how to stay true to ourselves and our principles through this process, and remember that at the heart of all these interactions are complicated people finding their way through the institution in different and sometimes contradictory ways. Despite their difficulty, relationships you develop in graduate school with peers, professors, and mentors can be lifelong connections that continue to shape who you are as a scholar, teacher, mentor, and person for a long time.

Reflection Questions

1   Who are you in professional relationships? What are your strongest assets, and how will those translate to the graduate school context? In what ways do you need to grow? How will you approach that growth?

2   What is your relationship to critique? What can you do to cultivate an openness in receiving critique that is meant to uplift? What will you develop as a mantra to deal with critique that is meant to tear you down? What concrete practices will you build into your education to ensure you get substantive critique that will make you a better student and scholar?

3   What is your cohort helpful for? What can you give and receive from that space? What do you need to get elsewhere?

4   What has your experience been with mentorship? What can you bring from those experiences into your life as a graduate student? Give some thought to mentoring up, mentoring to the side, and mentoring down. What's your plan to integrate those three areas into your practice?

6 Navigating Personal Relationships in Graduate School

I entered graduate school when I was twenty-five years old.[1] Looking back, as I currently work with students of a similar age, I can see now that I was younger than I felt. I think this was in part because of my background. I always took school seriously, even as a young child, because the sacrifices my parents made so that my sister and I could go to college were never lost on me; this awareness lived just below the surface of all my academic endeavors. On a good day, the weight of the responsibility to live up to that sacrifice served as grounding and motivation to get the damn thing done; on harder days, it weighed me down with guilt and obligation. There were no spring break trips to the beach for me—I honestly never even considered that kind of frivolity, figuring it was the exclusive domain of rich frat boys and sorority girls. There was no money for expensive trips, and anyhow I used the break to get ahead on work in preparation for the end of the semester or to go home and see my parents, who were sad that we were so far apart. When I graduated with my BA, I did not lie around on the couch or backpack across Europe like recent (white) college graduates on TV do. Instead, I asked my supervisor at the nonprofit job in Oakland I had worked at for the previous two years if I could move from part-time to full-time, and I kept plugging along. I talked in the introduction about my journey to graduate school, so I will not retell that story here, but I share all this to say that I did not enter graduate school feeling young or new or like I was just getting started in life. My life felt pretty much in full swing with a forward momentum of its own even if I was not entirely sure where I was headed and what I would do professionally. A big part of why I felt so rooted is because of the relationships I had.

At the time, I was in a romantic relationship of seven years that was quite serious. We had begun dating when I was eighteen; early on, we both felt that we were meant for each other and that our partnership would be long-term. The relationship also had a seriousness because we had weathered a sad and significant life event together: the death of my partner's mother after a yearlong battle with brain cancer, during which time he was her primary caretaker. Her death brought many things into focus for us. We married when I was twenty-four and knew that we would have kids, probably soon. He was working as a community organizer, a stable job he had been in for years, when I started graduate school. Things in my personal life were solid and just felt right.

Early in my grad school journey, I encountered some research on trends related to family and children among successful graduate students that threw me for a bit of a loop. I learned that the most successful graduate students live in housing geographically close to campus, with other graduate students, so as to be immersed in a culture in which students could live and breathe graduate school, staying focused on the task at hand.[2] Graduate students should not work off-campus, the literature said. Some programs actually prohibit it, and the research generally shows that if graduate students need to work, they should do so on campus. Finally, I remember reading about women in tenure-track academic positions, and the research was quite clear that the women who are most successful getting tenure are those who wait until after tenure to have children. In writing this book, I have had a difficult time tracking down most of this literature, which makes me wonder exactly when and how I encountered it or if it is even still in circulation. The last point, though, about motherhood remains true to this day.[3]

Two weeks into graduate school, and I was already doing it all wrong. I did not live close to campus; I lived a public bus ride away in the adjacent city of Oakland, California, in an apartment building with reasonable rent and not another graduate student in sight. I lived with my husband, a community organizer who worked crazy long hours and always brought his work home with him. The challenges faced by the members of his organization—homelessness, racism, extreme poverty—also occupied my heart and mind because these were people I knew and loved. I still worked at my nonprofit job, having assumed the role of executive director. I had planned to transition out of my job the summer before starting graduate school, but the planned hire fell through, and I needed to stay on until we could bring on the right person. And what felt like the biggest blow—I knew that there was no way I would wait fifteen years (eight to finish graduate school, seven more in a tenure-track job) to have a kid. There was just no way.

I share this story because it perfectly illustrates how graduate school culture can often feel oppositional to the family and home cultures of Latinx students. While clearly there is no monolithic Latino culture, it is important to acknowledge that there are ways that the culture and ethos of graduate school—particularly around individual achievement—can feel oppositional to and even perhaps incompatible with Latinx family culture. This chapter attempts to make explicit some of those tensions, to talk through what resolving that friction can look like, and also to talk honestly and candidly about what it means to navigate graduate school while also navigating the important relationships in your life.

We want to explicitly state two fundamental ideas at the start because they are likely different from what you have heard from your institution. First, though graduate school is often imagined as a retreat from your relationships, this notion is completely false. It is imperative to hold on to those relationships as you go through graduate school, and the grad school context itself is filled with relationships you need to navigate. Once you understand and accept those realities, you can develop a grounded and thoughtful approach to these relationships. The second fundamental idea is that some basic principles related to cultivating, nurturing, and navigating relationships in graduate school are generalizable, but there are also some elements that are unique to academia and particular to the power relationships in higher education. Understanding these allows you to figure out how to be authentic and engage in ways that feel principled to you, while also pivoting for the particularities in this context. This chapter may feel geared more toward doctoral students simply because the time commitment of doctoral programs (which typically span five or more years) places a greater strain on personal relationships, but we think this chapter will also offer helpful insights to master's students. Also, the chapter ends with a brief but important conversation about your relationship with yourself, which is both relevant to and an important read for all.

Latinx Culture Is Relational: Busting the Myth
That Grad School Requires You to Hide at Home

In many disciplines, and at many institutions, there is an explicit or implicit cultural norm that once you are a doctoral student, your life should orbit around that identity. Elite programs are more likely to be this way than less elite programs, as the boundaries between insiders and outsiders are drawn in ways that structure daily life and (consciously or unconsciously) mark the elitism of the space. Commuter programs, or programs that are delivered on nights and weekends, catering to working adults, are less likely to adopt this all-consuming grad student culture. Nevertheless, the expectation that graduate school should be engrossing and that your membership in that space should define your identity is prevalent in many programs.

Yet the idea that you can be a successful doctoral student only if you shut yourself into your study, surrounded by books and a pristine desk, is a fallacy. The idea that writing your dissertation must be lonely and solitary is a myth. The idea that the academy is the place where the thinking happens and that its integrity is somehow safeguarded by maintaining it as a pure or separate space inherently distinct from—and better than—the community is bullshit. We come from and contribute to a relational culture, and we do not need to adopt this sort of pure, white supremacist, elitist way of doing graduate school. In fact, graduate school is filled with many different kinds of relationships, and navigating them can be key to figuring out how to make it through your program with confidence and grounding.

The immediate induction into a shared community can be helpful, of course. Building community with other people who understand the intricacies of this odd space is useful; they will nod empathetically when you speak of stress over things like qualifying exams or position papers, while these terms mean little to people outside of academia. Moreover, graduate school is difficult, so being connected to others who are walking the same journey builds mutual support, crafts structures of accountability, and enables you to share resources as you trudge through the difficult parts together. The insular nature of doctoral programs in particular fills a form and function, but it also reinforces the insular nature of academia as a whole, a dynamic that for many of us goes against our nature (more on that below) and forms a problematic divide between the academy and the community.

But here's the thing: we are not like this. Latino cultures are relational, connected, and strong. You may think I am making some sort of Hispanic Heritage Month argument about how we like to gather for fiestas and how all Latinos have seventy cousins and this is who we are as a people. Look, I am not saying that is not true (my small home is perpetually in a state of cleaning up from a large gathering or prepping for the next one, and seventy cousins may be lowballing it on my dad's side of the family), but that is not the argument I am making here. The idea that you should have to put your life on hold to pursue a doctoral degree does not resonate for many of us. Why?

Some of us are working and cannot pause our lives in any practical way. Some of us do work that actually fuels our intellectual curiosity rather than distracts from it. Some of us cannot simply move into an apartment near campus where we stay up all night devouring texts and writing memos to ourselves. We are raising children, being partners, living as members of multigenerational family units, or caring for elderly parents. These examples reflect the reality of being young and Latinx in this country that resonates with many of us—because of gentrification, systemic racism, legacies of exclusion, redlining and housing market discrimination, and the intergenerational transfer of poverty. So, yeah, we are connected to one another.

Romantic Relationships during Graduate School

Someone (not us) could probably write an entire book on navigating romantic relationships during graduate school. While we can't do justice to all the nuances and depths of the topic here, we do provide some basic tips and points for consideration to help you navigate this terrain. There is also a diversity of family and romantic configurations you may be experiencing. While we want to acknowledge that those different configurations exist, we also want to be honest that there is no way to really fully engage in all of those nuances in this space, nor do we feel like it is really necessary. If you are asexual or polyamorous or casually dating, for example, have fun, be safe, and do your thing! Along with our advice about the benefit of having a diverse social crew while navigating graduate school, not being in a serious relationship where you are trying to meet the needs of another person can also be a very good thing.

Our focus in this section is geared more to our hermanas/os/xs who are navigating a romantic relationship in a way that requires care and attention. Perhaps you are in a serious relationship that you began before grad school (and hope to stay in), or maybe you are in a less serious or newer relationship that you would like to grow into something that lasts for a while. We are not relationship experts, and there is no right way to do a relationship. Yet having a grounding in some basic principles will be helpful in navigating what can be a tricky situation if you have not put some thought into it.

Entering Grad School in a Serious, Committed Relationship

There are some statistics (and many memes) about how graduate school is the place that relationships go to die. Now, I am not going to tell you that that is a total fabrication, or that if you just work hard enough, the romantic relationship you are in when you start graduate school can totally be the relationship you have when you leave graduate school. While that is true in some cases, it does not adequately account for the real and unique stresses that accompany the graduate school experience, and some relationships cannot withstand that kind of strain. At the same time, your relationship is not doomed once you enroll in graduate school. Besides, not all relationships are meant to last forever: breakups do not need to be devastating, and sometimes moving on is what is best. What follows is a set of principles for you if you are in the position to be entering graduate school in a relationship, and you want to make that relationship work. These thoughts are crafted with the assumption that your partner is not also in graduate school (because we address that type of partnership later). Again, I am not saying we are relationship experts or anything, but these are probably good ideas regardless.

BE HONEST AND UPFRONT ABOUT MONEY AS EARLY AS POSSIBLE · If you are in graduate school, it is likely that your student status will cause some sort of recalibration of your finances. Perhaps you are taking a pay cut or trying to subsist on an income that consists of grants, fellowships, scholarships, and underpaid graduate student teaching or research assistantships. It may simply be increased strain caused by your tuition payments. Money can get tricky, especially if your finances are in any way wrapped up with your partner's (either in a formal way because you share a home together or in an informal way because you mix money when going out or buy joint gifts for friends). Be upfront about this reduction in income, the tightening of funds, and the general complication of finances so that together you can establish how you are going to navigate this new reality that impacts both of you. It is probably also helpful to explain a bit to your partner, if they do not know, about how graduate school funding can be unreliable.

It bears saying here that for many of us first-gen Latinx students, money stuff is complicated. If you have not gotten some financial education yourself—about budgeting in general and graduate school specifically—you should do so. We often make bad decisions because we do not know any better—for example, not truly understanding how student loans work and that if you pay the lowest possible payment, you are only paying the interest and not making a dent in the amount of your debt. So, educate yourself and craft a clear plan with your partner about how being in graduate school will impact your finances.

TRY YOUR HARDEST TO KEEP NORMAL WORKING HOURS · This can be tough. There are times when doing so will be easy, and others when it will be nearly impossible. However, the definite trend is for school to take up more and more of your life, and you will need to set boundaries on it; this holds true for your own health and well-being, as well as that of your relationship. Additionally, the open structure of graduate school can be quite destabilizing, especially if you are entering graduate school after leaving the workforce; you may find yourself with much more unstructured time in your day. Our strong recommendation is to not be lured by the siren call of this open structure. Sleep in until 11:00 a.m.? No problem when you don't have class until 3:30 p.m.! Catch up on some Netflix at noon and, oh wow, suddenly it is 3:00 p.m.? No problem, study group is not until 7:00 p.m.! Yeah—no. Don't fall for it. A solid structure to your day where you get up and start doing your schoolwork as if you were going to your job is good for both you and your relationship. Consider posting a large wall calendar in your home where you keep track of your academic deadlines and due dates. This tool can help you communicate with your partner, offering a visual reminder of the weeks that will be stressful for you or during which you may need to devote extra time to your studies. I also want to be clear that in some programs, and at some institutions, there can be a conscious or unconscious message that you should be working around the clock, day in and day out, throughout the weekend. That is not sustainable, nor is it necessary. While there may be times you have to work more or harder or stay up late because of an impending deadline, this should be the exception and not the norm. It can be hard, but it is important to push back on this sort of academic culture and to remember to take time to rest and recoup—for your relationship with yourself and your partner. Clear communication is key when it comes to managing your time with your partner.

SET ASIDE TIME TO FOCUS ON YOUR PARTNER AND RELATIONSHIP · Regardless of the previous point, make sure you set aside time—weekly or daily—when you can focus on your partner without the encroachment of grad school. I mean, this should be pretty obvious and is probably something you can find in any book on relationships, but it bears at least a brief mention here. Why? Because graduate school can be all-consuming; it is the culture of the institution, academia, and graduate education. I remember getting to a point in the second or third year of my graduate program where I realized that the only acceptable response to the question "How are you?" was some variation of "So busy!" Usurp that dynamic by deciding that you won't participate in it. Take time for yourself, and if this is a partnership you hope to hang on to, make time for your relationship and your partner.

INTEGRATE YOUR PARTNER INTO YOUR GRAD SCHOOL LIFE OR DON'T—JUST DON'T BE WEIRD ABOUT IT · There is no definitive right way to navigate this new social space with your partner. Do you invite her to join your cohort when you meet up at a bar on a Saturday night? Do you invite them to the holiday party sponsored by your department? What about a study session at a café because he also has something he needs to crank out for work and could benefit from some coffee and company? I don't know. Seriously, there is no right answer to that question. So instead of giving you some sort of blueprint that tells you the rules to invoke in this situation, I say do whatever makes sense for you and your partner—just don't be weird about it. If they are not invited, cool: be upfront and honest about why that makes the most sense. If you do bring them along, be cognizant that you are bringing a new person into a group dynamic and respect the balance: don't take up too much room as a couple or, conversely, act like your partner is not there. Again, just don't be weird about it.

BE CLEAR AND UPFRONT WITH YOUR PARTNER ABOUT WHAT SUPPORT YOU NEED · Be open to hearing what support your partner needs from you, and vice versa. Maybe you need a shift in your division of child-care labor; maybe you need to ask for certain hours of the day to be quiet in your apartment; maybe you need your partner not to ask, "How's the thesis coming? Are you almost done?" every day when they walk in from work. Be clear with yourself, and then clear with your partner. This conversation cannot be had only once. It is ongoing and open-ended. Both needs and wants will change over time, and good communication about those things is key to making relationships work.

Dating in Graduate School: Dating Another Graduate Student

There are, of course, pros and cons to dating other graduate students. It can be comforting not to have to explain the odd elements of grad school when you are stressing about comprehensive exams, assembling a thesis committee, or working on a grant application before the deadline. At the same time, when both of you are navigating similar terrain, you may be subjected to double the amount of stress around comprehensive exams, assembling a committee, and working on a grant application before the deadline. You will need to take care in managing those dualities. A few basic principles may amplify the good and minimize the challenges:

- Find ways to be helpful and supportive without taking on your partner's academic stress. You are partners, and mutual support is a critical part of a good relationship. At the same time, it is critical that you take steps to maintain boundaries—for example, your partner's impending final paper deadline should not give you an upset stomach. Channel the concern into support for your partner: bring them a cup of tea while they are working or give them a quick shoulder rub, but do not borrow their stress.
- Don't try to make your experience their experience. You are different people on different journeys, and what works for one of you will not automatically work for the other. More importantly, assuming that it will can lead to lots of strife.
- Get in the habit of asking, "Are you venting and want me to just listen, or are you asking for my advice?" It can be frustrating when someone gives you advice when you are not asking for it, and it can reinforce your anxiety that you can't handle things on your own. When you start venting (there is plenty of venting in graduate school), get in the habit of clarifying whether you are just letting off steam or whether you want advice—and when your partner is the one venting, ask them the same question.
- Build in ways to nerd out together—but also spend time together that is not about academics. Sharing your academic journeys can be fun. Build in study nights. Splurge on takeout if you can afford

it when you both turn in your final papers for the semester. Find ways to share the experience you are both navigating. And, also, make sure that all your together time is not academically focused so you can remember to enjoy and cultivate the other parts of your relationship. Watch trashy TV. Go on a hike. Cook a meal together. Have sex. Don't forget to be partners to each other.

If either, or both, of you aspire to get an academic job, there are additional complications once you near completion of your degrees. Academic jobs are few and far between (read more about this in chapter 7) and often require applicants to move across the country (or perhaps even internationally). It gets complicated, of course, if you are in a committed relationship and following your dreams of an academic job means uprooting the lives of two people, perhaps moving to a place that neither of you is particularly excited about. Another complication comes when you are in what is known as a dual-career academic couple, that is, when both partners are in academia. Others have written on the intricacies of this situation more, and we cover some of the considerations and tips for navigating this in chapter 7.[4]

Ethical Considerations Regarding Dating in Graduate School

Just as ethics are an important part of navigating a research relationship, they are also an important part of graduate school relationships. You may not be used to thinking of romantic relationships as ethical questions, but here's the deal: if you are getting into a relationship with someone you are in community with—whether you belong to the same grassroots political organization, are members of the same graduate program, attend the same church, or are in the same field or discipline—you are treading into potentially tricky territory, and your relationship must be treated with care. Consider the following two ideas.

First, picture the breakup. In the honeymoon phase of a relationship, it is easy to get caught up in the magic, rainbows, and sparkles, yet if you are in community with one another in any way, it is important to also envision the parting of ways. If you are considering sleeping with someone, imagine seeing her at a conference in your field in a year. Is it gonna be cool? If you are contemplating getting into a relationship with someone who attends the same school, what will it mean to be in classes with them for the next year and a half until you finish coursework if things don't work out? Issuing blanket advice like "Don't date anybody in your cohort" is a setup. It does not make sense as a one-size-fits-all solution for the multiple and varied ways that graduate school relationships can get complicated. And y'all wouldn't listen even if we did say that. Ha! So, instead, we encourage you to really think about what is at stake if you part ways or things don't work out. We encourage you to see through the rainbows and sparkles to envision things getting hard. Is this person mature enough to handle it with grace? Are you? Is there enough distance between you that the spaces you overlap would not feel stifling and unbearable if you had to be in them with a broken heart? Consider what is at stake, and then decide what you are risking if you choose to get into a relationship with that person.

Second, abide by the Campsite Rule. Sex/relationship advice columnist Dan Savage created the Campsite Rule, which says:

> If you're in a sexual relationship with somebody significantly younger or less-experienced than you, the rule that applies at campsites shall be applicable to you: you must leave them in at least as good a state (physically and emotionally) as you found them in. That means no STDs, no unwanted pregnancy, not overburdening them with your emotional or sexual baggage, and so on. Younger partners and particularly virgins will often take everything given to them by an older, more experienced partner as being "written in stone," and will carry around everything they learn from them for the rest of their life: so treat them right![5]

We encourage you to employ the Campsite Rule as a guidepost in ethically navigating relationships in graduate school with romantic partners. Leave that person in at least as good condition (physically and emotionally) as you found them. Let's be real: that takes maturity and discipline. If you are not ready for that, there's no shame in admitting it. We are all on our journeys, and we don't all start out there—but please do some deep consideration about whether that relationship makes sense for you. Be smart, be ethical, be intentional.

Graduate School and Kids

As soon as we started to conceptualize this book, I knew I wanted to include a section on kids and graduate school, in large part because, for many of us, kids are our invisible and unmentioned companions on the journey. I want to make them and the importance of our relationship with them visible. When I think back to my graduate school years, my kids are a huge part of that story. I also know that so many people—often white people—are surprised that I wanted to have kids while in graduate school. They are taken aback that I graduated from UC Berkeley with two young kids. They wonder, sometimes silently and sometimes quite audibly, why I did not heed the very well-documented warnings to women about waiting until after tenure to have kids. To put it simply, I knew that if I did not land an academic job, or if I did and then did not get tenure, having children would make my life happy and fulfilling. I also knew that if I never had kids, or if I waited to secure my career first but then it was too late or too complicated to have kids, that I would be filled with regret. For a beautiful and scholarly exploration of this topic, check out the *Chicana Motherwork Anthology*, a collection of "narratives that make feminized labor visible and that prioritize collective action and holistic healing for mother-scholars of color, their children, and their communities within and outside academia."[6]

Let me be very clear that this is not to say that everybody should have kids. I mean, I don't need to spell this out, right? Or maybe I do because you are getting the opposite message from your tías and your mom. If there was a nearby mountaintop, I would belt out a song that goes, "You do not need children to be happy. You do not need to have children to be whole. You do not need to have children to be a woman. You do not need to be a parent to nurture children." Also, if you have chosen, are choosing, or will choose not to have children, develop a mantra that you can repeat to yourself: "My body is mine to make decisions for; my life is mine to determine." Hell, everybody make that mantra!

Okay, moving on. I have known I wanted to have kids since I was a kid. As I got older, and then as I entered graduate school, I knew that I wanted kids soon. I walked across the graduation stage with a PhD, a newborn in my arms, and a four-year-old's hand in mine. To be honest, I also walked across that stage with a sense of pride in what I had accomplished because there was a little bit of "fuck you" mixed in, directed at the people along the way who had questioned my decision, who had looked down on me and my pregnant belly making my way across campus, and who had assumed that I would not finish once the first baby appeared, let alone once that baby had a little sister. I do like a good "fuck you."

CONSEJO #8   My daughter was born at the end of my second year of classes and my son after I completed a draft of my dissertation. What I had not realized beforehand is the wonderful side of having children while a student—that they would distract me from the stress of grad school and give me sweet breaks, that their due dates provided huge incentives to finish papers/chapters, that it's relatively manageable to revise a dissertation with a sleeping infant, that children love the amenities of nice hotels when you take them to conferences, and so much more. While it was really challenging and I had to fend off assumptions that I wasn't committed to my career, my children were blessings.

Pat Zavella, Department of Latin American and Latino Studies, University of California, Santa Cruz

Discrimination, Leave, and Navigating Graduate School While Pregnant

Let's go ahead and state the obvious here, something that most books about preparing for or navigating graduate school will not say: if there is one image that mainstream white US society finds easy to look down on, it is the young, pregnant Latina. It can feel like you are fulfilling a stereotype if you are indeed a young(ish) and pregnant Latina. I bring this up because I want to be clear that (1) you should not let that stereotype steal your joy from the anticipation of welcoming a kid into your family, and (2) you will very possibly experience discriminatory behaviors if you walk around campus pregnant. Some of those may be mild, like people assuming you are an undergraduate (which is a backhanded assumption that someone who is pregnant can't possibly be a graduate student), and some may be more serious (a faculty member who decides not to work with you because she thinks your pregnancy signifies that you are not a serious student).

Here is what I can say about all this: decide early on that you will shut out the haters, and learn what your rights are as a parent-to-be. Pay attention to departmental policy, university policy, state policy, and federal policy. Figure out what you are entitled to and what you are required to do. If your health insurance is through your university, meet with the correct folks on campus early on to figure out exactly what is covered and make sure that you are setting up care within your network. Things you should investigate are parental leave, the policies around extending that leave if necessary, stopping the clock (if there are grants at your institution that give you a certain amount of money if you meet benchmarks that are deemed normative, you may be able to stop the clock and get more time added to meet those benchmarks), and childcare options on campus. If there is a student-parent center on campus, consult with them about what resources exist and what you should know about. Yes, this center will likely be geared toward undergraduate students, but that does not matter. Maybe some of those undergrad student parents can teach you a thing or two. Be open and ready to learn.

One thing that is likely true across campuses is that the institution is not going to bend over backward to make sure you know about your rights as a pregnant student, student parent, or adoptive parent. You will have to seek the information out. It will take effort, but you and your kid deserve it. It is better to proactively figure out the policies and resources that exist than to wait until you need that information urgently.

The Value of Kids in Latino Culture and Incompatibility with Graduate School

As we have said in other places in this book, despite the way white America views us, there is no such thing as a monolithic Latino culture. Take it from this Chicana married to a Puerto Rican. But for real, it is complicated (and often problematic) to talk about one Latino culture because our nationalities and ethnic origins are so diverse. And now I will contradict myself—or, rather, I am going to ask you to suspend that grounded critique so I can say the following: Latinos love babies and kids. We just love and cherish them! In Latino culture, we value children. Always? No. Everybody? No. But I think you get my point. We hold our children in high regard, which can sometimes feel incompatible with graduate school.

This (feeling of?) incompatibility is both cultural and structural. Structurally, we are expected to set everything aside and make graduate school the first priority. The de facto assumption is that graduate students do not have children or dependents. Culturally, there is a lot about graduate school that is not conducive to parenting. Heading out to drinks with your cohort mates after class is often impossible if you have to get home to relieve the sitter, and yeah, you can't bring the preschooler to the bar. The culture around conferences and travel is fundamentally difficult for people with small children, frequently cost prohibitive, and logistically impossible. You can't afford to bring the kid with you, but you can't afford to leave them behind. I guess this is where I acknowledge that there are no good solutions. It is more an attempt to say clearly what is stated in the section header: graduate school can sometimes feel and be incompatible with parenting. We just deal with it, and we do our best. And also, more and more, student parents are pushing the institution to be more accountable to and supportive of students who have children. We should applaud, and join, these efforts. But also, it is hard. And each day we get up and try to do better, both as graduate students and as parents, and there is really nothing more that we can ask of ourselves.

What the Research Says and Why the Research Can Go Fuck Itself (Just Kidding. Sort Of.)

As rigorous (or aspiring) researchers and thinkers, we can be tempted to go down the rabbit hole of reading what others have written about how to be most successful in graduate school as a parent, or with children, or in relation to getting pregnant. To a certain extent, reading firsthand accounts can be grounding; it is always helpful to learn from people who have walked the path before us. At the same time, if you look at the research, especially if you are a woman, then the situation is pretty grim. We already know that less than 3 percent of professors are Latinx/a/o.[7] If you separate that by gender—because, yes, women still do most of the reproductive and caretaking labor in the family unit—the number drops even lower. It is estimated that less than 4 percent of tenured or tenure-track female faculty members in the United States are Latina.[8] I cannot find a figure for how many of those Latinas are mothers, but we can be sure that the numbers take another meaningful dip.[9] And, yes, Latina motherhood is different from white motherhood. The research on having children in academia is pretty clear: if your goal is achieving tenure at a four-year institution, the best time to have children is after you have earned tenure. Did you catch that? If your goal is to get tenure, it is best for you to not have kids until you have reached that goal. If this is the path that women in academia face— and we can assume that most of these are white women who at least have the privilege of their whiteness—then we can make some deductions about the much harder path faced by Latina mothers.

Now, you may be wondering, perhaps with slight annoyance, why I am focusing on mothers in this section as opposed to parents. Well, the research shows that for men in academia, having children can actually benefit them.[10]

While academic mothers are assumed to be flaky, distracted, and unreliable, their male counterparts with children are seen as more stable, honorable, and hardworking. I don't need to state the obvious here, but that has not stopped me before, so here I go: this, comadres, is patriarchy at work. And that's some bullshit.

So here is where I am going to ask you to set aside your research-minded trust in the literature because, honestly, fuck the research. I mean, okay, not really. You should look at it, and you should understand why mothers have so much trouble succeeding in academia (spoiler alert: it is institutional and systemic biases) and the pressures on working mothers in every profession. This is why so many people recommend waiting to have children, and our position is essentially that you should read this research so that you can go into any decisions (to get pregnant, to pursue adoption, to continue a pregnancy, etc.) with your eyes wide open. Moreover—and this next point is something that not enough advisors say to their students and not enough books about navigating graduate school mention—your personal choices should not be determined by your professional path unless you decide they should. There is nothing wrong with deciding that you are going to pursue parenthood even when it is proven to make that path harder.

Let me conclude this section with a brief story that may help you think about this decision in your own life. I have mentioned before that my dissertation advisor was a hard-ass. I had my son at the end of my MA program and was ready to get pregnant again when I was in the middle of data collection (my kids are four years apart). I had a few bad experiences when I was assembling my dissertation committee while pregnant; some professors whose classes I had performed well in and who had expressed an openness to being on my dissertation committee clearly lowered their regard for me once I decided to get pregnant during the dissertation journey. They communicated their judgment in sometimes subtle, other times explicit ways. So, though I assumed that my committee chair, Dr. Roy, would be supportive, I was a bit nervous to talk with her for fear that her view of my seriousness as a student would also falter if she discovered that I was hoping to get pregnant again.

I asked to meet with her, and she invited me to lunch at the faculty club on campus. As we started to wrap up and ordered tea and coffee, I mustered my courage. "I, um . . . I . . . I wanted to check in with you because . . . well, I'm . . . I am considering trying to get pregnant again." Dr. Roy set down her tea, looked me right in the eyes, and asked, "Have you had this conversation with any other members of your committee yet?" I told her I had not and braced for her to admonish me for even considering getting pregnant at this pivotal time. In that split second, I anticipated that she would tell me that she was glad I had not talked this over with anyone else, that we could bury this silly little idea of mine and pretend we had never had this conversation.

Instead, she said, "Good. I'm glad you haven't talked to anyone else about this yet because the way you talk about it needs to change. You do not need *anyone's* permission to make a decision about your family. Not *anyone's*. Your tone is apologetic. What are you apologizing for? So you will finish this degree as a mother with two children. Of course, it will be challenging, but what isn't challenging? You can do it. That's wonderful news. But stop apologizing." She set her tea down. And that was it. I have thought about that conversation many, many times over the years. The baby that was just a glimmer in my eye and a song in my heart at that time will be a teenager by the time you are reading this book. But the conversation has stayed with me because it serves as a reminder that I do not need anyone's permission to make decisions about my family, and I should not apologize for putting my family's needs first. Is it always that simple? Of course not. But it is true all the same.

Relationships with Your Kids during Graduate School

The reality is that caring for anything and anybody while doing graduate school is hard. But it is workable, and there are also some distinct upsides. I had both of my kids while I was a graduate student. I drank too much coffee, slept too little, and exercised not enough; I don't know that my body will ever truly recover from that period when I was doing so much, burning the candle at both ends, and trying my best to make it all work. Being a parent meant that I missed out on school events that were held in the middle of the day when I could not make it over to campus. It also meant that my social time was basically nonexistent; even though I had a supportive partner who really did do an equal share of the parenting work, the truth is that I always wanted to get back home to my kids after being away for a few hours. Looking back, that was the hardest part. I quantified the time away from them; it felt like a betrayal. I now know that that was not the case, but my young mama heart felt that it was. There were no late-night hangout sessions with cohort mates or social events for me. In many ways, having kids during a period when most people are very truly unattached meant that I missed out on different aspects of campus life—which, as a graduate student, also meant missing out on some professional development and networking opportunities. At times I was out of the loop on things like fellowship opportunities and campus events not because the information was being deliberately kept from me but because I simply was not around when people were chatting. All of the challenges of navigating graduate school with children are compounded if your kid has special needs, if you are a single parent, if you do not have or cannot afford childcare help, or if a traumatic childhood brings up additional emotional labor and trauma when parenting your own kids.

At the same time, having my kids while I was in graduate school gave me a kind of flexibility with my time that would have been impossible with a traditional full-time job. I could move things around to be free during the preschool Mother's Day event on a random Friday morning. I was able to flag things that needed my attention, and then sit down and hammer them all out when the baby was napping, leaving the morning free to go for a long walk, play in the park, or do a messy art project. Having a cute toddler in tow made for a much easier entry into new research sites and made the facilitation of relationships and connections easier. Having kids during this period was also a permanent anchor for me. I would start to stress out about a paper or begin to ruminate about an interaction with a professor—then, suddenly, I would be holding a feverish baby in my arms and all of my priorities would fall into place, allowing me to remember, over and over again, what was truly important and what was just noise.

As we talk about relationships with advisors, professors, peers, and intimate partners, remember that our relationships with our children also deserve attention. Children are neither a burden to manage nor an appendage to account for. They are people with whom we build relationships, and these relationships will either flourish or flail. It is important to nourish this relationship when in graduate school, especially if you are in a place where not many of your peers have children or if there is hostility to having children in graduate school. We are sometimes expected to pretend that our children are not there—but they are, and we should not be made to feel embarrassed or ashamed of that. If there is a student-parent community at your campus, that may be a place for you to feel connected.

Regardless, do not sacrifice a strong relationship with your kid to be a stellar graduate student. Or, perhaps more precisely, to be seen as a stellar graduate student. My son was an infant when I was studying for my oral qualifying exams. One day, my partner, in nursing school at the time, was caught in traffic coming back from his clinical site, which was eating into my studying time because it meant that the baby handoff was delayed. Desperate to keep my study schedule, I remember lying in bed with my infant boy, nursing him to sleep while some index cards that mapped out Marxist theory were propped up on a pillow behind his head. I don't know what caused this moment of introspection, but all of a sudden I saw myself— really saw myself—and recognized the absurdity of the situation. I looked at my sweet nursing babe, thought about how fleeting these moments are (something I am acutely aware of now that, at 6 feet 4, he towers over me and is beginning to think about life after high school) and realized that sometimes you must put down the Marx index cards and just be in the moment, enjoying your baby.

Finally, consider that as a student parent you may feel that you are constantly working against assumptions about you, and while your impulse may be to try to take up as little space as possible and fly under the radar, you have certain rights, and you should feel emboldened to make sure those rights are respected. Do not hesitate to get support from federally funded programs like Supplemental Nutrition Assistance Program (SNAP) or Special Supplemental Nutrition Program for Women, Infants, and Children (WIC) to support your family. Consider the power you have as a graduate student with children, and do not hesitate to hold the university accountable in this regard. If you are teaching as part of your fellowship and need a place to pump while on campus, ask for it. While it is fine for some department events to be held at bars, don't be shy to ask the planners if some can be held at family-friendly restaurants. Your power as a student will be magnified if you join with other students who have children to collectively assert your rights and shift the culture in your program.

The last thing we want to mention is geared toward the nonparents who are reading this. The marginalization graduate students with children are subjected to by the institution is hard to deal with—please do not compound this by marginalizing your colleagues with children. Even if they seem constantly bogged down with childcare obligations and tight schedules, continue to invite them to gatherings. Consider getting together as a cohort at a park instead of a bar on the weekend. While your colleagues with kids may continue to turn down your invitations, do not stop inviting them.

CONSEJO #9   Please don't be the person who stops inviting the new parent to social gatherings because they are visibly pregnant or just had a baby. Please keep inviting them. They will probably say no, but stopping the invitations adds another layer of banishment and isolation that is not cool. Maybe say, "I know you are probably very busy with Baby'sName, but I wanted to let you know that some of us are getting together at the local spot and you are welcome to join us if you can." Again, they will probably decline, but please make an effort not to ghost them!

Esther Díaz Martín, Latin American and Latino Studies and Gender and Women's Studies, University of Illinois at Chicago

Communicating with Your Family

In my first year of my MA program, I took a class that put me in the mix with students in the School of Education at UC Berkeley more broadly, not just in my social justice–oriented program. I can't even really remember what the class was about, but there was a moment that has stuck with me for almost twenty years. Education, as you may know, is a field dominated by white women. White femininity and fragility as an educational approach unfortunately has deep roots in the field. Anyway, back to this moment: While discussing what is widely referred to as "the achievement gap," a young white woman, who was preparing to be a school counselor if I remember correctly, sighed with exasperation and said with a hint of authority, "I mean, there are just some kids who don't want to learn. It starts with the family." The audacity of this white woman talking about brown and Black children in this way made me feel ill. This idea that parents of color do not value their children's education is deeply ingrained in educational philosophy and policy in the United States.[11] And, importantly, this deficit framing of familial relationship to schooling is a cornerstone of this idea.[12]

Without going too far afield, let me say very clearly that this idea that Latino families do not value education is simply a perversion of the reality that Latino families, and other marginalized people, are repeatedly and systemically devalued by educational institutions, and therefore any sort of disengagement or distrust we see has to be interpreted through that lens. In short, Latino families are told in both explicit and implicit ways that our children are not smart, that our culture and our language are deficient, and that who we are will never be enough. So yeah, don't shit on us and then act surprised or outraged when we don't show up with flowers of gratitude.

I say all of that as an entry point into the conversation about communicating with your family about your decision to pursue a graduate degree. Those of us who are first-generation specifically may find this conversation complicated. "¿Más escuela? ¿Pero porqué?" "¿No te graduaste ya?" "¿Cuando vas a terminar?" "¿Pues, está bien, pero porqué tan lejos?" are some of the common refrains when we decide to go to graduate school, each time we go home for Christmas, or when we call Mom to check in after she gets home from mass on Sunday. Though it can often come across as indifference or frustration, it is often just a lack of understanding. When we pursue graduate degrees—especially when we do so with the elusive goal of "getting a master's" or "getting a PhD" as opposed to "getting certified to be a social worker" or "getting my teaching credential so I can be a teacher"—there is a disconnect between the world of work that most of our parents have occupied and the one we are navigating. This is, and can turn into, a class difference as well. And because, more and more, there is a disconnect between going to school for a graduate degree and getting a good-paying job, the decision to do so can be even more confusing to our families.

I want to impress upon you the importance of not consciously or subconsciously reverting to that deficit framing that blames our parents for not valuing education if you run into the manifestations of this disconnect. Observe it, study it, acknowledge it, and try to move on from it. There may also be some particular dynamics you have to navigate with your family members, especially if you live nearby. Your mom may assume that because you have class from 3:00 to 6:00 p.m. on Wednesdays, you will be available if she calls you at noon and asks for a quick ride to the mercado. It is difficult for outsiders to understand that the work of a graduate student is different than that of someone who works as a receptionist or in retail; just because you are not in class does not mean you are not working. It can be important to clearly, and kindly, communicate your boundaries and needs to your family around your work schedule—and calling it a "work schedule" is a helpful place to start. Also, learn to be okay with some level of disconnection. They do not need to understand and appreciate every nuance of your grad school experience. At the same time, check yourself before you wreck yourself: make sure that you do not take on an air of superiority because you are pursuing an advanced degree. That shit smells from blocks away.

Still, for some, the relationship between the academy and your family of origin may be truly, unequivocally at odds. Perhaps your family rejects or denigrates your academic goals or ridicules your professional aspirations. In these situations, there may be no possibility, or value, in trying to bridge that chasm. When my kids were smaller and would squabble about silly things, we established a rule I learned from a friend: don't argue with someone who is wrong. So when his little sister insisted it was Wednesday when it was actually Saturday and my logical son was floored by her audacity, his gut impulse was to argue it logically to her. We'd shrug and say, "Remember? Don't argue with someone you know is wrong." When my daughter had a different memory of something that happened than her older brother and started to dig into the details to convince him that her memory was reliable, we'd shrug and say, "Remember? Don't argue with someone you know is wrong." I know it is not that simple, but if your academic pursuits are truly at odds with your family of origin's beliefs and values, remind yourself that there are structural and institutional realities that are relevant in this situation, try to compartmentalize this experience, and figure out a way to relate to your family outside of your professional and academic self, even if this is limited. Resolve to not argue with someone you know is wrong. It is best for your health, your well-being, and the relationship.

Family Caretaking Responsibilities

For some readers, your relationship with your family while in graduate school may be even more complicated because you play a primary caretaking role. Perhaps you live at home and are the de facto childcare provider for your younger siblings, or your mom lives with you because she is not in good health, or you took in your cousin after he came out to his parents and home was no longer a safe place. Being a caregiver for a family member is complicated in the graduate school context because even though student parents face a hard road with little institutional support, people of all class and racial backgrounds have a way to understand parenting as a responsibility. Caring for or taking in a family member, or living with members of the family unit, is common in many Latino families, but that is not necessarily true for all your classmates. To put it bluntly, they may find it odd.

The important points here are that (a) you should feel justified in doing whatever you need to do to support your family members; (b) others may not understand that; and (c) that does not matter. You will have to feel out the dynamics in your department, program, and school, but if caretaking holds a significant place in your life, you will need to be even more on top of your obligations, timelines, and responsibilities. Make use of all the tools we have provided here so that you can use your time well, be intentional and strategic about what takes up your energy, and remember that you do not need to apologize to anyone for taking care of your family.

Your Relationship with Yourself: Mental Health, Self-Love, and Prioritizing Wellness

The anchor of all these relationships—both personal and professional—is your relationship with yourself. You could fill an entire library with books on this topic, but here we just want to say your relationship with yourself is a priority. There are many messages within the culture of graduate education, both implicit and explicit, that encourage us to deprioritize our mental and physical health in service of our graduate work. And while I could claim that I rose above this and saw through that BS when I was a student, I would be lying. In fact, my years in graduate school were marked by too little sleep and too much coffee—a reality that for many years I was proud of. Not sleeping enough should not be a point of pride. We are worthy of care, and we are the ones who are responsible for getting it. Embracing this sentiment will mean going against the grain at times, but it is worth it.

The question of mental health deserves particular attention here. This is compounded for Latinx/a/o students because (a) we may attribute getting this far to hard work, and at times caring for oneself and working hard can feel or be in opposition; (b) as a result of racism (and patriarchy, and heterosexism, and . . .), we have to work twice as hard to get half as far; (c) many of us come from families where hard work is valorized, and therefore engaging in self-care can feel frivolous or vain; and/or (d) we come from a community that has historically distrusted therapy, and sweeping mental health issues under the rug is an outgrowth of this distrust. You may even have an (e) and (f) to add to this list. This territory is loaded; it is common to revert to the practices that have served us in the past—head down, work hard, ignore the other stuff. But this strategy does not work in the long term, and we should not valorize it. We want to be full, whole people—not at some abstract point in the future but right now. Caring for our mental and physical health is a critical part of that process.

Many graduate students struggle with mental health issues, the most common being anxiety and depression. While many of us struggle, it is easy to feel alone because there is often stigma associated with needing mental health support. One of the very best things you can do for yourself is to utilize the mental health services that are available to you. Virtually every campus has mental health support for students that you pay for with your tuition dollars. Those support services exist for a reason. Use them. If you need more support or individualized support, investigate what you are entitled to as a part of your student or employer health plan, and prioritize getting care. Stigma is eroded when we decide that there is no shame in claiming what we deserve, and being grounded and healthy in mind, body, and spirit is something we all deserve. We live in a world that is quick to tell us that we are not deserving. Deciding to love ourselves enough to care for ourselves is a transgressive act for Latinx/a/o people. Do it. Be proud of doing it. This part of academia is entirely in our power to change.

CONSEJO #10   One of the best pieces of advice I got while in grad school was that balance, or trying to find balance amid so many responsibilities, is a fleeting reality that often leaves us spread so thin, burnout is inevitable. Instead, what I started to learn in graduate school was the importance of having priorities. What are your priorities? What do you want your life to be like, feel like, look like? Are you prioritizing what you need to manifest this vision for your life? Who are you doing this for? What kind of impact do you want to have? What intentions and goals can you set to meet these priorities, both personally and professionally? What is getting in the way of meeting said priorities? Maybe you don't know what your priorities are because grad school provides a rigid and narrow ideal of what is possible and where you should be after you graduate, or maybe because, like myself as a first-generation, trans/queer, poor, child of immigrants, it's hard to dream up a vision for your life when you're just trying to survive. So slow down, take time to look inward, and ask yourself, what am I doing this all for? Check in with yourself, rest, and remember everything you need to thrive already exists within you; your job is to muster the courage day in and day out to show up as imperfectly perfect as you are.

Jack Cáraves, UC Chancellor's Postdoctoral Fellow, Department of Gender and Sexuality Studies, University of California, Riverside

Reflection Questions

1   Who are you in personal relationships? What are your strongest assets, and how will those translate to the graduate school context? In what ways do you need to grow? How will you approach that growth?

2   Which relationships are most important to you? What steps will you take to concretize and prioritize those relationships while you are in your graduate program?

3   What are your personal goals for this period of your life? How will these connect to your professional goals? What are likely to be points of tension or friction between these two sets of goals? What principles can you hold on to while you navigate those areas of friction?

4   Are there any personal relationships that you worry will suffer under the strain of being in graduate school? What will you do to weather that strain?

5   Take stock of your mental, physical, and emotional health. What do you do well in this regard? Where do you need support? How can you get it? What practices—big and small—do you need to integrate into your daily life to prioritize your wellness?

7 Life after Graduate School

When I (Magdalena) was nearing the end of graduate school, I did not feel jubilation over completing my PhD.[1] Far from it. I felt burned out and lost. The pressure of writing a dissertation had zapped my love of writing; the act of writing that I had once pursued for pleasure now gave me a feeling of pure dread. Meanwhile, my teaching hadn't been transformative for me or for the students; in fact, years after my first experience as a teaching assistant, I ran into a student from that class in a bookstore, and he caused bystanders to turn and stare when he shouted, "You were the *worst* teacher I ever had!" (I could easily have shouted back that he was the worst student I ever had, but instead I kept it classy.) I had spent seven years preparing to be a professor, only to realize that the two activities central to faculty life, writing and teaching, were apparently not my calling. Yet I had been on the pathway to a faculty career for so long and had not explored other interests and opportunities, so I could not imagine what else I could do with my degree, which now felt pretty useless. At the time, I figured I could continue working in higher education, the only environment I had known, but instead of being a professor, I imagined working as an academic advisor or at a campus cultural center. As you may recall from the introduction, I ended up getting accepted into a postdoctoral teaching fellowship that initially interested me only because it was renewable for up to three years. I had no idea that the opportunity would change my life and help me realize that teaching was my calling after all.

The moral of the story is that just because you are completing your degree does not mean that your next steps are clear. If you are nearing the end of your program and feeling a little panicked, like, "I should have this figured out by now but I haven't!," know you are not alone. This chapter will walk you through some self-reflection questions and help you identify concrete steps that will, eventually, lead you to greater clarity, if you take deep breaths and trust the process. If you are on the other end of the spectrum, feeling confident that you know what you want to pursue next and what it will take to get there, then great! You will also find the self-reflection and planning useful.

Either way, it is critical to be clear-eyed about what grad school does and doesn't do for you. The skills you come away with are often imparted through the doing, the process of being in graduate school, and not the actual course content per se. Very likely, it will be up to you to figure out what you take away from your degree program and how you want to apply it moving forward—meaning, your grad program or institution may not have specific supports in this area. This chapter intends to help you begin mapping out next steps to figure out what you will do with your postgrad life, understanding that there are multiple pathways. If you are earning a PhD and dreaming of a faculty career, the reality is that most doctoral programs prepare you to be a researcher, not to do the real day-to-day work of managing teaching, research, and service all at once. While that type of how-to deserves its own book (and there are many), we do provide guidance on how to apply for faculty jobs.

Preparing to Be Postgrad

For now, let's start by thinking about this time of transition: just as you had to mentally prepare to enter grad school, you must similarly prepare to leave it. The experience of grad school can be so intense and, whether you are wrapping up a master's or a doctorate, you might have burrowed so deeply into a particular area of expertise that you may have lost sight of what this experience has meant for you. This transitional time is a key opportunity for self-reflection, one that takes you beyond the specific highs and lows of grad school, the bonding experiences and dramas within your cohort over the years, and the feedback from your faculty. At the end of this chapter, you will find a set of big-picture reflection questions that can help you to articulate the new concept of self that you have gained throughout grad school.

Let's talk about crafting a mission statement for your postgraduate life. What do you want to stand for and contribute to? In a master's capstone class that I taught, students developed a mission statement by brainstorming a list of their personal values; scholarly interests; knowledge and skills gained from their time in the program; the experience and abilities they gained before and/or outside of the program; their long-term goals (what many people like to call soul goals); and who they represent and show up for, and why. Drawing upon the insights that emerged in their list making, they each crafted a mission statement that captured what they wanted to work toward, meaning the broader, longer-term questions and issues to which they could apply their knowledge from the master's program.

This mission statement is a key tool because so often—especially in contexts in which we are marginalized—we tend to define ourselves "in opposition to," in terms of what we are against. But what would happen if we shifted our frame to instead focus on what we stand for? How might that shift enable us to work from a space of proactivity rather than reactivity? What is our insistence, rather than our resistance? Keeping an eye on this bigger picture is a critical means for preserving your attention and energy for the projects and opportunities that sync with your values and commitments.

It is also important to take time to reflect because you need to distill the skills gained in grad school and translate them into an applied career path. Here are two examples from my experience: in the months before applying to grad school, I had a job at a company named Salco that made parts for railcars. The railroad company would contact the company's engineers to, say, request a design for a new hatch cover. My job was to take that design and solicit quotes from local manufacturers, then organize the information to determine who could produce it the fastest and cheapest for Salco. You might wonder how I ended up at that job because, if you recall, I was an English and Latin American Studies major. Well, I was hired because I had research experience and strong communication skills—everything else, including highly technical engineering and manufacturing terms, I learned on the job. As another example of this adaptability, earlier in grad school I had to find a summer job. I was hired at Broadvision, a company that specialized in e-commerce software, and my job was to enroll clients in software training classes. Obviously, Broadvision's focus had nothing to do with early twentieth-century American cultural studies. Yet again, what got my foot in the door were my communication skills and ability to organize information and work independently.

I hope you can see where this is going: reflect on what you have really learned in grad school, the core concepts, skills, and tools that you can apply in a variety of career fields. In fact, when you think about it, grad school gives you a wide array of possible tools:

- Communication skills across various modes, from research briefs and executive summaries to detailed reports and longer narratives
- Presentation skills, being able to walk both novices and experts through important information
- Teaching and discussion-facilitation skills
- Methodological skills, such as interviewing and transcribing, data collection online or in archives, coding data sets, statistical analysis
- Content areas: understanding certain populations, cultures, histories, trends
- Reading, interpreting, and analyzing highly technical information
- Collecting and organizing information chronologically or thematically
- Ability to distinguish key information from that which is less important
- Ability to guide a large project from concept to completion while working independently

When you step away from your specialized area(s) of expertise and identify the core competencies gained in grad school, you'll be able to do two important things: understand the totality of what you have learned in your graduate program, and translate those competencies into skills that employers in any career field are seeking. In turn, that opens you up to considering and applying for a number of job opportunities, getting you past the belief that your degree only leads down a single path (a master's in psychology means that you have to become a counselor, or a doctorate in sociology means that you can only become a sociology professor). Remember that you are more than your degree, and while earning an advanced degree is something you should absolutely be proud of, your degree does not define you. It is simply a tool that prepares you to do other, bigger things.

Picking a Preliminary Pathway: Industry, Nonprofit, or Academia?

Now that you have engaged in self-reflection and mapped out your concrete skills, you are prepared to hunt for a job. The search may take you down one of three paths: industry, that is, corporate roles; nonprofits; or academia. When you are deciding which path to follow, you should revisit the question explored in chapter 1: Where is the real work done? The reality is that educated Latinx/a/os are needed in every job sector, and, like turtles who carry their homes on their backs,[2] we bring our commitments to justice and equity wherever we go. Wherever you are is where the real work is being done. If you are still feeling angsty about which sector to work in, then reread that earlier discussion.

This is not a decision you make once and then stick with the rest of your life. You may start off in the corporate world for a few years, then decide it's time to move in a different direction and switch to the nonprofit sector . . . and maybe years after that, you develop an interest in turning toward higher education. There is no single or right pathway, and what is right for someone else is not necessarily right for you, so explore all the possibilities in front of you.

This time of transition is another opportunity to engage in a fresh round of informational interviews, connecting with folks who are in career paths that look interesting to you. Take the time to have those conversations and learn what the actual day-to-day work looks like in different fields. Meanwhile, tune up your résumé or cv to reflect those skills and highlight examples that showcase your experience. Take advantage of your university's career center for support, as it likely offers one-on-one coaching and guidance, workshops, networking events, and job fairs. They may offer specific support for graduate students. If you are unsure where you want to head next, that is even more reason to seek out their offerings to discover careers you may be unfamiliar with—especially if you are a first-generation professional, many types of jobs may not seem obvious or even be on your radar.

To get started in any of those three broad sectors, you do need to prepare a strong résumé that makes clear your core competencies and highlights your experience. You also need to dust off your networking skills. You should develop what some refer to as an elevator speech: imagine you are riding in an elevator with someone who could be a great career contact, and you only have thirty seconds to give them a snapshot of your interests, skills, and what motivates you. An elevator speech is a way to practice giving your pitch in a concise and understandable way (avoid using jargon). Your pitch should help someone understand what you studied in grad school, why it matters, and the applied meaning, or how your skills and knowledge help to address interesting questions or issues.

Navigating the Academic Job Market

Many students are drawn to graduate school—doctoral programs, specifically—with the hope of becoming a professor. However, just because you have a professional research degree does not mean that you are guaranteed a faculty position—in fact, far from it, as only "between 5 and 35 percent of PhDs will ever get even a single tenure-track job offer."[3] Moreover, so much about the process of navigating the academic job market is under the cloak of darkness. There are a lot of reasons for that obscurity, but here we lay out important information to help you navigate what ends up being, for many, one of the hardest parts of the graduate school journey. This section is largely oriented toward doctoral students, though students in master's programs who are considering adjunct teaching/lecturing may also find utility in the following advice.

Understanding Key Terms and the Organizing Principles of the Academic Job Market

First, what do we mean by the "academic job market"? By and large, this term relates to professor job positions. In some fields, this term can also be used to describe research-focused jobs in the academy, but for the most part we are talking about jobs working as a professor, which would mean that your work is defined by a combination of teaching, research, and service. Three kinds of job postings generally fall into this category: assistant professor, associate professor, or open-rank positions. When I (Genevieve) was a young graduate student just starting out, someone at a conference gave the advice to start looking at job posts in my field to get a sense of what was out there, what the expectations were, and so on. Lord almighty, I didn't even know what I was looking at or how to understand the difference between these different job ads—it was mostly just intimidating and not at all enlightening. So this information may feel too basic for some of you, but I suspect it will be new (and useful) for others.

You may remember the following explanation from earlier chapters, but it is worth repeating here. An assistant professor position is the lowest level of entry and comes without tenure—these jobs are aimed at people who are just starting out in academia; this role would either be your first job or one that you got in your first few years on the tenure track if you change institutions. By contrast, a job ad for an associate professor is aimed at someone who is already tenured and is looking to move to a new institution. So if you are looking for your first academic job, an associate professor post is not aimed at you. An open-rank position is what it sounds like: the department is open to hiring someone who is just starting out or someone who is a seasoned professor. While that may sound like a joke to you—how is it possible that someone just starting their academic career could compete with a seasoned professor?—there are a lot of reasons this can happen. Maybe, for example, they are looking for someone with a particular specialty, and that expertise means more to the search committee than the precise status of the applicant's career. The takeaway is this: you should, with very few exceptions, apply at the level that corresponds to your status—a fundamental organizing principle of the academic job market, and one that I had no idea about for my first several years in graduate school.

There is another specific component to job ads and job rank that is important to know: the distinction between tenure-track and non-tenure-track jobs. A tenure-track job is a job that is on a six- or seven-year track, by which point you are expected to meet certain benchmarks and are evaluated by a committee of your peers (generally on your campus, as well as beyond your campus) to assess if you have sufficiently met those benchmarks. If you are determined to have met those criteria, you are granted tenure, which is essentially a "guarantee" of job security. I put *guarantee* in quotes because we have seen the erosion of the tenure system in recent years, a hallmark of the neoliberal trend in higher education—but that is a conversation we cannot fully have in this space.[4] If you are not granted tenure, you lose your job.

The other important thing to note about the tenure system is that it is a fixed period of time. You generally go up for tenure (meaning that your materials are reviewed) at the start of your sixth year on campus. In other words, with few exceptions—such as parental leave, paid family leave, or sick leave—the tenure clock runs from the time that you set foot on campus in your new position. You must meet the criteria by the time the clock runs out (you cannot, for example, just decide you would like to wait another year). In short, in the tenure process you are expected to meet a set of benchmarks (some explicit, some implicit) by a certain period of time (difficult! stressful!), and the reward for doing so is an incredible amount of job security that in this day and age is relatively unparalleled in other sectors (ideal! amazing!).

There are also clinical positions that may fall in the open-rank category, though those positions are generally focused on teaching. This does not mean that people who have clinical positions do not engage in research or scholarly work, but rather they are not compensated for it or professionally assessed on it. At least speaking from the field of education, a clinical position is often one where an expert in the field is hired to teach on that practical basis. Each campus thinks and talks about this sort of position differently, so check the specifics of the institution when you see a job post like this. They are also compensated differently across institutions; in some places they are compensated very similarly to a tenure-track full-time professor position, and in other places they are closer to adjunct pay. Do your homework and figure out the specifics if you are going to apply for a clinical or term position.

The Tenure System

Let's step back here to talk a bit more about the broader questions: Why tenure? What's the other option? And why is any of this important? The tenure system is designed at its heart to protect academic freedom. This idea is rooted in the concept of the university as an institution that houses critical thinking and the potential for social change. It is no secret that societal change and counterhegemonic thinking are often met with resistance. The tenure system is, in essence, a manifestation of the principle that someone who is championing unpopular or controversial work or research or thinking or writing should not be vulnerable to firing as a result of doing that work—that is what academic freedom means.

To give a concrete example, let's say a particular university (*cough cough* UC Berkeley) is the beneficiary of corporate giving (*cough cough* British Petroleum), meaning they get tax write-off donations from the company. Then an environmental disaster that is squarely the fault of that corporation (*cough cough* British Petroleum's Deepwater Horizon oil spill in the Gulf of Mexico in 2010) happens, and it has broad and deep environmental impacts (the Deepwater Horizon oil spill is considered one of the largest environmental disasters in US history). We would want UC Berkeley environmental scientists to have the ability to write about this, research this, and educate the public about this without fearing for their jobs and their livelihood. Right? Of course. So, though the tenure system is often bad-mouthed because people equate it with teachers and professors who are doing the bare minimum because they do not need to worry about losing their jobs, it is important to note that in our experience, those professors are few and far between, and the vast majority of tenured professors take their work very seriously and meet a set of high expectations despite the fact that their job is not threatened. Furthermore, the fundamental principle of academic freedom is one that we should safeguard.

You may also see job ads for non-tenure-track employment, a short- or long-term professor position that does not come with the stress of performing on a set timeline on a tenure track but also does not offer the protections of tenure. These positions will most often be called contract or clinical positions. This means you are brought in, generally with a contract that can range from one year to ten years or more, but there is no track that you are moving forward on. Often, you are not expected to perform in all three areas of the tenure review process—research, teaching, and service—but, like we said, it also means that you are vulnerable to your contract not being renewed.

This is different from an adjunct position, which is generally when you are brought in to teach one or two classes at a time and your contract is semester-to-semester. Let me also say two things really clearly. First, this means that the university system upholds a two-tier system—between tenured and nontenured professors, between full-time professors and adjunct professors—and those tiers often correspond with different kinds of compensation. That reality is fucked up, inherently unfair, rooted in capitalism, and should be resisted at every turn. Second, despite the fact that this distinction is rooted in unequal power relationships, there is nothing wrong or lesser about working as an adjunct or as clinical/term/contract faculty. I say that because these structural dynamics steeped in inequality can transfer into personal and interpersonal dynamics, with full-time faculty looking down on adjunct professors, tenure-track faculty looking down on non-tenure-track faculty, and so on. Not only is that fucked up, elitist, and counterproductive for collegial relationships, collaboration, and political solidarity, it also makes people generally regard those positions with less respect than is due.

Adjunct teaching can be fantastic for people who want to keep teaching but are also pursuing other professional endeavors. I (Genevieve) have a friend who works as an attorney in a nonprofit legal organization but who loves teaching and connecting with students; adjunct work allows her to keep a foot in the teaching world while also advancing her other professional goals. I have many colleagues who work in their field and also work as clinical faculty; they appreciate that they do not have research obligations or publication expectations; they want to do the work and teach, and being clinical faculty is perfect for that goal. I share these examples because I want to sharply draw out the point that just because these sorts of positions are debased within the capitalist structure of the neoliberal university does not mean that we should debase them in our professional practice. I worked for two years as an adjunct faculty member between finishing my doctorate and securing my tenure-track position. Those were some of the best years of my teaching life, in a department with colleagues that I developed a connection to (my coauthor of this book is one of them), and teaching incredible students, many of whom I am still connected with today, more than a decade later. Those years helped shape me as an educator and gave me confidence in the university classroom that grounded me when I moved into my tenure-track position at the University of San Francisco.

Let me say one last thing about the tenure system. Like all other things in higher education, it is inscribed with questions of power, privilege, hierarchy, and oppression, including white supremacy, patriarchy, classism, and heterosexism. The tenure system works differently on each campus (including the basis on which candidates are being assessed and evaluated, and by whom), but it is not an overstatement to say that there are many times in which this inherently hierarchical and judgmental system falls in line with the system it is a part of and unfairly targets people based on race, class, gender, political affiliation, and other axes of oppression. We do not have enough space to go into this here, and there are many other books, scholars, and works that discuss this with much more detail and finesse than we can manage here, so frankly we feel it is best to leave it to them.[5] We did not want to close this section, though, without acknowledging this fundamental truth about the tenure system particularly because, though fundamental, this truth is often not acknowledged, and it targets people like us. There are many examples of failed tenure cases along these lines, and despite this overwhelming evidence, there remains a cultural sense of shame for someone who does not get tenure. The misguided belief persists that if you did not get tenure, it must be because you screwed up somehow. That is not true, and the individual blame game will never be a sufficient explanation for structural and institutional inequality; the sooner we realize that, the better off we all will be.

The Job Search, a.k.a. Explaining to Your Tía Why You Can't Just "Get a Job Near Your Mom's House por si Acaso"

The academic job search is tough because of one fundamental reality that comes down to a simple math equation: far more doctoral degrees are conferred each year than there are jobs for those newly minted PhDs to fill. This result is part of the academy's overreliance on cheaper, more exploitable adjunct labor.[6] If you plan to enter the academic job search, you are likely competing with many others for the same jobs. This scenario is even wilder when you think about how having an academic specialty means that many of us know each other because of overlapping professional interests and spaces—which means that, for the most part, when you are working on your application materials for a position as an education scholar with an Ethnic Studies background who works on Black and Latina girls and the school-to-prison pipeline, you probably have a good sense of the other people who are also applying for that position. This imbalance between newly minted PhDs and open positions means that it is a widely accepted and not often challenged reality that if you are serious about finding a job in the academy, you have to be willing to travel anywhere. Your dream position may be in Kansas or Oklahoma or Florida or some other place you have never imagined living, and if you want to be a professor, the insinuation and assumption is that you gotta go. And, yes, it is hard to help people outside of academia understand this. Don't get frustrated with family members who don't understand your decision to move to Kansas or who can't see why you can't simply move back home because there's a college nearby where they are sure you can find a job. The pursuit of academic jobs is a complicated and nuanced process, and though we become acculturated to it in the academy and start to think of it as normal, it is really not, and you should take time to think about how you will relate to it.

What this comes down to is a deeply personal question: Are you open to moving to an all-white college town or to the opposite coast from your family? The concerns that surface will depend on the particularities of your life. If you are single and want to be partnered, you may ask yourself about the potential for finding a mate in this place. If you have children, you may ask yourself how you feel about uprooting your children of color to go to another place. There is no right way to do this, but it is important to determine your comfort and then construct your job search accordingly. When I (Genevieve) was job searching, I had young children whom we were going to great lengths to raise as Spanish speaking. I knew raising them in a community with Spanish, access to bilingual or two-way dual-immersion education, and other communities of color was critical to me. I had also spent two decades building community in the area where I was living. I decided that my job search would be a local one. I did so understanding the gamble I was taking, and I decided that I would rather not work as a professor and find another job in higher education here than work as a professor somewhere that I did not want to live and raise my children. That was a personal decision for me, not necessarily the right decision for anyone else, and I am lucky it worked out. My point is that although the common practice in looking for an academic job is that you need to be willing to cast the net wide and go anywhere and do anything, you should take the time first to figure out your ideal scenario and what your nonnegotiables are, and you should do that without feeling shame or judgment or that you are not a serious scholar—but also understanding the risk you are taking in a tight and competitive market. In their reflection piece about being first-gen academics navigating the job market together, scholars Esther Díaz Martin and José García write poignantly about wondering, "Have we made it? Or rather: ¿Valen la pena nuestros sacrificios?"[7]

The Logistics of the Academic Job Market

If you are at the point of preparing for the academic job market, get some specific instruction in preparing your materials. There are numerous resources that will be helpful in those efforts.[8] While we do not delve deeply into all the specifics here, we lay out the basics of understanding a job ad and how to think about preparing job materials, because this is often assumed knowledge that many of us lack as first-generation Latinx students (and is a necessary precursor to the deeper dive necessary when you actually begin to prepare).

First, study the job ad carefully. Search for clues about what they are looking for. Some jobs will be a stretch, and some, we hope, will feel like a perfect fit. When I was applying for jobs, I was doing so having completed a dissertation about political activism among undocumented college students. Policy was not necessarily an intentional focus of my research work, but because much of the activism at that time was focused on the campaign to pass the DREAM Act, there was an (unintentional) focus on policy in some parts of my work. I applied for, and got, an adjunct position that was focused on policy analysis and the Chicano/Latino community; the policy focus was a bit of a stretch, but one I felt I could work at and be comfortable with. On the other hand, there were jobs that focused on the Latino community and immigration but also had an explicit focus on health and wellness. That felt like too much of a stretch, so I did not apply. You will have to make this call as you review job ads, figuring out where the lines exist between a post that feels like it was designed for you, something that feels like a reasonable stretch, and something that feels like too far a stretch, where positioning yourself as a perfect fit would be a misrepresentation.

The components of a faculty job application typically include the following:

- CV (curriculum vitae), which is a long-form résumé. Essential components (and suggested headings) of your CV are education, professional experience, teaching experience, publications, honors/awards/fellowships, and presentations/conference proceedings. You may have additional sections, or alterations of these components, depending on the specifics of your experience.
- Cover letter, which is like a normal job cover letter, though for an academic cover letter make sure that you clearly explain your fit with the position, talk briefly about your relevant experience, your research area of focus and research trajectory, and your institutional fit.
- Diversity statement, which should do two things: situate you as a person who can bring diversity to the department and university, and explain how you approach the integration of diversity in your research, teaching, and professional work.
- Teaching statement, or overview of your experience as a teacher, as well as your teaching philosophy and how that manifests in your teaching practice.
- Research statement: for junior scholars who are just starting out, this should provide not only an overview of the research you have done but also an explanation of your research trajectory—meaning that you talk about what you have done as well as where you see the arc of your research heading. This greater context is important to situate yourself as a scholar who has plans to be productive over a longer period of time, rather than someone who has not thought past her dissertation.

You also want to consider the type of institution you are applying to, as a big public research university (these are often called R1s, despite the fact that this is a somewhat outdated term rooted in the old Carnegie Classifications)[9] will place a large emphasis on your trajectory and potential as a scholar and less emphasis, generally speaking, on teaching. A smaller liberal arts school or regional comprehensive university, however, will place a heavy emphasis on teaching, mentoring, and working with students. You cannot use the same materials for different types of institutions; you'll have to tailor your materials to fit the institutional context and priorities. Consult sources listed above, as well as scholars in your field who are a couple years ahead of you, for specifics about pulling these together. The last thing I will add is that there are some universalities, but some things tend to be more discipline-specific—so when possible, seek guidance from people in your specific area.

After you submit materials, you can expect to wait. Sometimes, the wait is long. Applications are reviewed by a search committee, which is composed of current faculty members, usually in the hiring department, although sometimes an outside faculty member is also included for diversity of opinion. Most of your interaction in the job application process will be with the hiring committee, and communication outside of the on-campus interview will likely happen with the chair of the committee and/or the administrative staff person. Now, I know I don't need to say this because we are the children of housekeepers and janitors and gardeners, and so I know you all know this, but it is very important to treat the administrative staff person with the same level of respect and courtesy with which you treat the dean. This is both because it is the right thing to do, and also because it is a true reflection of character, which the search committee may be assessing. Here's how the process generally works: you submit materials, and the committee reviews them and whittles the list of candidates down to a select group for a first-round interview (sometimes called the "long short list." I know. Academia is funny). The long short list will then, as a result of the interviews, be cut down to three finalists who are invited to campus for an interview. We call this smaller group the "short short list."

The campus interview is traditionally a daylong interview that is often preceded by dinner with the search committee. This is a supposedly informal part of the process that is very much part of the interview and should be treated as such. The daylong interview is a series of meetings with different people—the search committee and the dean are a given, but likely also a group of students, a larger group of faculty not on the search committee, and perhaps other campus partners. You will also be expected to do a job talk, which is a research talk, often held as a semipublic event that all are invited to and may be a mix of students, faculty, staff, and administrators. You may also be asked to do a teaching demo, which is essentially like running a miniclass with a small group of students so that they can see your teaching style. Assume that everyone you interact with all day is being solicited for feedback about their impressions of you. You may still have to wait several weeks after the on-campus interview before you hear anything about the job. Keep in mind that they are likely interviewing three candidates, and in the event that you are the first candidate to visit campus, you may have to wait for the other candidates to complete their visits, as well as for the committee to consult. Patience is required on the academic job market.

CONSEJO #11   When I was in graduate school, I learned to openly discuss authorship norms, particularly on joint collaborations. Publications can play an important role when on the job market (depending on the field) and yet often reinforce privilege in academia. Before you begin a research and writing project (particularly if there will be publications), I suggest the group should come to a consensus of what authorship rules they will follow. Ideally, if there is a mix of professor and graduate students on the project, this discussion would be modeled for you by the professor. This is particularly important for Latino students who may not fully understand the nuances of publishing (e.g., sole authored, first authorship) and its relationship to getting a tenure-track position and tenure. I had a mentor who showed me how to operate within a "publish or perish" world of academia but also encouraged us to consider whose voice most often gets published and whose voice does not. By discussing the critical role publications have, we can better strategize how to share and dole out authorship, particularly when folks are about to apply for tenure-track positions.

Ursula Aldana, **Department of Leadership Studies in the School of Education, University of San Francisco**

The Really Hard Stuff: Competition, Self-Doubt, and the Realities of the Academic Job Market

It is also important to acknowledge that sometimes you don't have to navigate the process laid out above because you don't get the job. It is totally possible that despite being stellar, despite being a perfect candidate, you won't get the call to interview. There is a lot of talk about not taking things personally in academia and developing a thick skin, and I wish I could tell you otherwise, but you will fail a lot of times. You will be turned down for many things you apply to. As cliché as it is to say, you do need to learn how to dust yourself off and try again. Yet, contrary to how some people talk about this, this is not a switch you turn on or off. You may feel like you are not wired to easily brush off disappointment like others are. As with writing, taking rejection in stride is not an innate ability nor a personality trait; it is a skill you develop, and like all other skills, it is developed through practice. (Re)read the section on critique if you need to, but the best way to think about developing this skill is to develop a rejection practice that you do whenever you get turned down for something—a journal article gets rejected; you don't get the fellowship you applied for; you don't get the job. I suggest a rejection practice that combines a mantra of some sort ("I'm smart and capable, and things will come together") with some reflective practices that allow you to engage in self-critique and self-celebration. Each rejection has a lesson and an opportunity for improvement, but you need to look for it.

It's also important to note that who gets the job and who does not is often way outside the bounds of who you are and what you can control. Getting the job requires you to have good solid materials, good solid skills to navigate the application and interview process, and a good solid research trajectory, research project, and profile as a scholar. But even with all those things, you can be unlucky on the job market. Who gets the job is a mixture of luck and other stuff. As I already said, there are far more qualified people than there are jobs to give them. Moreover, you could be passed up for a job because there is already someone in the department who is a labor theorist like you, or they really need a quantitative methodologist and you are an ethnographer. It really does come down to luck sometimes or other things outside of your control. When you map that onto the general volatility and fickleness of the academic job market, it can be nearly impossible. The year you are looking, for example, there may not be any jobs that match your field and expertise. I remember saying to my partner the first year I was on the job market, "Too bad I did not get a degree in zoology, because it really seems like that would have been the ticket this year!"

As we mentioned earlier, there is also a likelihood that you will be competing for positions with people that you know, maybe even friends of yours. There is no way to get around it: this situation can be difficult. The best advice we can offer is to try to do this in a way that acknowledges the awkwardness embedded in the situation and do your best to be gracious, honest, and forthcoming in the process. The degree of collaboration you engage in is up to you and will depend largely on the quality of your relationships and your ability to depend on the other people who are applying for the same position. A good rule is to engage with colleagues whom you may be competing against in the way you would want them to engage with you. Be forthcoming, be honest, be generous, and if this is a relationship you are invested in for personal or professional or intellectual reasons beyond this job, keep that in mind and use that as a continual touchstone for your engagement with them through the process. At the same time, not all colleagues or acquaintances are trustworthy enough to be regarded as collaborators, and that is okay too.

Finally, we encourage you to respect and honor yourself through the process of engaging with the academic job market. Despite what I said earlier about developing a thick skin, rejection is fucking hard, even more so when you map rejection onto the weight most of us carry around because we are attempting to do all of this within the context of an institution that is hostile to us and our people and steeped in white supremacy. Only you will be able to determine what honoring yourself in this process looks like, but we suggest that you consciously and thoughtfully consider the challenges involved in going on the job market. Build practices into your daily life that allow you to reflect on your accomplishments, that make clear that being turned down for a job does not mean you are unworthy or unemployable, and that you do the things that make you happy, healthy, and whole. Easier said than done, but when you know better, you can do better. If you are not even thinking about this stuff, you surely won't do it. So do it!

Even when you get a job, there are still moments of self-doubt and the need to remember that this is *your* life; you are making choices based on *your* values and priorities. For example, I (Magdalena) was thrilled to receive a tenure-track job offer from San José State University because I wanted to be at a teaching-centered HSI. After signing my letter, I attended a talk by a visiting scholar from a big-name Ivy League school. Everyone at the table had to introduce themselves, so when it was my turn, I announced, "This fall, I will be an assistant professor at San José State." The folks in the room smiled and murmured congratulations. A colleague from my postdoctoral fellowship spoke next, saying, "I have a visiting assistantship at Fancy Private Liberal Arts University." The room erupted into applause and expressions of amazement. I sat there thinking, "Am I missing something here? I'm the one with the tenure-track job!" Yet, to the elite scholars in the room, having a temporary job at an elite school was more impressive than a tenure-track role at a public state school. All I could do was shrug and remind myself that their hierarchies and values are not mine, and my career plans did not need their validation.

Alt-Ac Route, or Let's Return to the Start of This Chapter

The last thing we want to discuss in relation to the job market is what is often referred to as the "alt-ac" (or alternative to academia) route, which means completing your doctoral degree and then deciding not to continue to work in academia, to instead go into a different sector. There are many resources to check out if that option speaks to you, either because you have been on the job market for several cycles and have not successfully secured a position or because you simply do not want to pursue a traditional academic job.[10] This decision is consequential because, with a few exceptions, it is very difficult to come back to the academy after leaving. The *Professor Is In* blog, written by a former academic who left the academy to do consulting work with academics, is particularly instructive on this question.[11] We will not attempt to cover the content that these other sources do perfectly well, but we do want to say that you should not feel ashamed or embarrassed to pursue a life and career outside of academia. Depending on your institution and institutional culture, you may have gotten the message explicitly or implicitly, but listen to us when we say that that is a construction of academia that you may have a hard time seeing around right now but in a few years will see for what it was: a mirage and nothing more. A very happy and fulfilling life can be made outside of academia.

Whether or not you pursue a career in higher education, there is no shame in your game. You worked hard for your degree, and now you need to make it work hard for you. And you can start to do that by engaging in the deeper reflection on what you gained in graduate school and how you will help others—and yourself—understand the new skills, preparation, and, ultimately, the fortitude that enabled you to make your way through an advanced degree from start to finish. ¡Adelante!

Reflection Questions

1 Who was I when I entered grad school? Who am I now? What has changed for me, what hasn't, and why?
2 What experiences and skills did I hope to gain when I started this program? Did I gain those? Did I come away with additional or different experiences and skills than I had anticipated and, if so, what are those?

3 What readings, assignments, conversations, and connections have been most meaningful during my time in the program? Why did these resonate with me? How might I apply those concepts and methods in the next chapter of my journey?

4 What did I learn in grad school that I want to carry forward and share with others? And what anxieties arose during this time that I can release and put past me?

Conclusion

FIVE MANDAMIENTOS FOR REMAKING
THE ACADEMY

As we generated the first draft of this book, the world as we knew it was forever changed by COVID-19.[1] As we all know, the pandemic disrupted nearly every aspect of daily life, with particularly devastating consequences for marginalized communities across the United States. In the halls of the ivory tower, classes and meetings abruptly shifted online, a massive change for the vast majority of faculty and students. Unprepared faculty did their best to keep their courses going—though that often meant forging ahead without changing the pace of their syllabi and assignments, acting as though taking a class online simply meant doing the same synchronous work via videoconference. Some faculty even increased their readings and assignments under the assumption that students surely had more time to study now that they were homebound. And many of us struggled deeply, as we attempted to balance schooling our kids, caring for our elderly parents, and also caring for our students, who needed us in more ways than ever before.

Students, meanwhile, faced a host of challenges. They not only navigated concerns for their loved ones' physical and financial well-being, they also struggled to figure out how to be students while also attending to the crisis around them. Many of those living in multigenerational households or with several roommates did not have a quiet space to log in to class, a dedicated study space or private bedroom to do their work, and/or reliable internet access. Even those who did have home internet and a place (e.g., a corner of the kitchen table) where they could log on could not necessarily show themselves on screen. Courses that required students to have their cameras on emerged as a source of stress for those who did not want to reveal their home conditions or who needed to conserve data on their cell phones. Although I (Magdalena) was not one of those professors who required cameras on, one student in my Chicana/o literature course felt compelled to explain that she was embarrassed to turn on her camera because her bathtub was the only space she could claim when all of her roommates attended class at the same time. Another student kept a folding chair in his truck so that he could park on campus to access Wi-Fi and use his tailgate as a desk to work on his assignments. Many of our students took on new jobs or additional hours to supplement family income as their family members lost their regular work in the early months of the pandemic.

These examples reveal the numerous ways that the pandemic both brought to light and exacerbated long-existing inequities around who can access higher education and the options that are available to them. These realities resulted in a wide range of choices: some students made the pivot to fully online education, discovering that, by doing so, they could move to more affordable areas or take on extra shifts at work. Others missed face-to-face instruction and preferred to pause their progress until classes in that mode of instruction resumed—or felt discouraged by the enormity of the pandemic and left school altogether because trying to manage it all was too much.

For Latinx educators and students, the pandemic forces us to think creatively about how we engage in intentional community building with the new tools we are being forced to use. We have long faced numerous challenges as we seek to educate ourselves—not the least of which is the fact that publicly funded education has been under siege for many years as lawmakers seek to defund public schools and make education a privatized resource. It is no coincidence that as greater numbers of Latinx and other marginalized students begin accessing higher education in greater numbers, tuition and fees have become increasingly expensive.

As we confront this crossroads together, we want to leave you with some final thoughts about how we can approach the work ahead of us as we seek to transform higher education through our growing presence. We urge you to follow these five mandamientos (commandments) as you pursue your pathway through academia.

1. Our Work Is Needed Now More Than Ever

Again, given the scope of the inequities heightened by the pandemic, our intellectual engagement and critical analyses are needed to generate possible solutions. Our voices absolutely must be heard in addressing the issues that impact our families and our communities. We deserve to access the training and tools that will enable us to be intellectual leaders within and beyond the academy. We need to arm ourselves with the theories, scholarship, and methods that will provide us with a strong foundation to engage in dialogue with others who work to tackle these issues.

2. We Have a Responsibility to Claim Pieces of the Institution for Ourselves and for Our Community

It is imperative that we move away from visions of success that are individualistic; our achievements are meaningless outside of community. So always strive to be a bridge—between other scholars, between the community and the academy, between your home culture and academic culture. Reach out to students who are behind you in the journey, and seek out those who have walked the pathway before you. Don't try to do this work alone or try to claim credit all to yourself.

3. Aim to Be a Lantern Mentor

Scholar Monisha Bajaj writes about two types of mentors. The first is a street sign mentor, someone who tells you how to get from point A (say, starting your graduate program) to point B (completing your degree) by offering specific, turn-by-turn directions, expecting you to follow the same path they took. By contrast, a lantern mentor shows you the entire map, inviting you to find your route between those points.[2] So share with others your understanding of the institution and encourage them to find the pathways to success that suit their learning and career goals.

4. Remain Part of a Community of Learners

No matter what levels of education and experience you achieve, try to hold on to a learner's perspective, being mindful of how much we all still have to learn. Be open-minded and generous in spirit with other folks—in and beyond academia—because you never know what important insights and lessons they can teach you. As you engage in conversation, always be on the lookout for angles that are not being addressed, perspectives that are not being included or considered, and do your best to acknowledge and make space for those.

5. Remember That Your Life Is Happening Now

Many graduate students tell themselves, "I'll start doing [fill in a meaningful project, hobby, area of personal growth] once I finish my degree." For those who intend to pursue academic careers, this sentiment easily turns into, "I'll begin [X] once I become an assistant professor," and then later, on the tenure track, "once I get tenure," and so on. You end up deferring major decisions, life events, great opportunities for some later date whose arrival always shifts. Well, guess what? Life is short, and it is taking place now! You can find ways to both do grad school and pursue other important goals if you have a community of support and have done your homework to understand your options (case in point: Genevieve's discussion of having kids in grad school). Be all the parts of you that you want to be and allow them to inform your educational commitment.

....

Writing this book was an emotional experience as well as a labor of love. As we spoke to the faculty colegas who did an early reading of the draft manuscript, as well as the former students we have worked with and taught who also provided preliminary feedback, there were many moments we had to take a breath as we remembered the difficulty, the challenges, the trauma, and the moments we contemplated throwing in the towel. We also reflected on the mentors who shaped us and the gratitude we can still feel deep in our bones for the ways they believed in us, the triumphant moments in which we surprised ourselves with how strong and smart we are, and the incredible privilege going to graduate school is. We hope that this book upheld its promise of being a love letter, a manifesto, and a flashlight.

You know how when you are leaving a family party, your tía sends you off with a bendición? It is gratitude for the time you have spent together, a blessing of well wishes, and a plea to God/the universe to keep you protected. We now end this book with our bendición to you. Thank you for trusting us, even though most of you have not met us. Thank you for the vision for yourself and your community that has pushed you to pursue education with ganas, with purpose, and with intention. Thank you for the ways you will reshape our community and our society by doing the work you will do, by insisting it is done with integrity, and by mentoring the next generation of Latinx scholars coming up behind you even while the identity of "Latinx scholar" may be one you still have difficulty applying to yourself. We hope that as you read these last lines, you feel not only the weight of responsibility to your community on your shoulders but also the arms surrounding you, holding you up. Your Latinx/a/o faculty members are cheering you on. We love you. We believe in you. We are inspired by you.

We wrote this book because we believe in education as a tool for transformation and that we can use our Latinx cultural values to approach our intellectual engagement in ways that not only bring to light but also challenge harmful practices long perpetuated within the academy. This book represents our commitment to your success and to the promise of higher education as a tool for liberation. We enter this work with our eyes wide open and invigorated by the energy and potential you bring, especially in this most challenging moment. We believe in you; we believe in us; and we believe in the vision we are creating together. Vamos.

CAROLINA VALDIVIA, PHD

———

UndocuGrads

UNDOCUMENTED AND APPLYING TO GRAD SCHOOL (FAQS)

Navigating the educational system as an undocumented student, including three years of graduate school, I encountered multiple challenges. Thankfully, I had a community to support me along the way. This experience motivated me to create the blog *My Undocumented Life* (https://mydocumentedlife.org/) in 2011 to support fellow undocumented students. The FAQs here stem from my work with undocumented students, which spans over a decade, including facilitating UndocuGrads workshops and blog post series about the grad school application process while undocumented.

If I'm undocumented, can I apply to grad school?

Yes! However, depending on the institution, where it's located, as well as whether you have Deferred Action for Childhood Arrivals (DACA), Temporary Protected Status (TPS), or neither, there will be variations in eligibility requirements, funding, and access to professional licensing postgraduate school.

Should I apply to public or private schools?

It's good to keep your options open. While private schools are often more expensive, they may have greater financial opportunities available for undocumented students. Check with individual programs you are interested in applying to and inquire about their funding opportunities at the institutional and department levels.

Can I apply to out-of-state schools for grad school?

Yes. Two important things to keep in mind are funding and safety. As of this writing, at least twenty-one states and the District of Columbia have tuition equity policies in place, which allow eligible undocumented students to pay in-state tuition fees when pursuing higher education (as opposed to paying out-of-state tuition fees, which can be three times as much as in-state fees). Moreover, thirteen states currently have policies that allow eligible undocumented students to receive state financial aid. States also have different policies around obtaining a driver's or professional license while undocumented, so it's important to research the state you're considering moving to for grad school and to ask the specific program and/or school what kind of funding support is available to undocumented graduate students. For the latest information on state policies, I recommend the National Immigration Law Center's website (https://www.nilc.org/). Another issue is travel safety and whether you will need to board an airplane, cross a checkpoint, or drive long distances to get to school. It can be helpful to connect with fellow undocumented graduate students (both those who stayed close to home and those who traveled out of state) to hear their experience, advice, and tips.

I do not qualify for Deferred Action for Childhood Arrivals (DACA). Can I still receive funding for grad school?

There are fellowship and scholarship opportunities that are open to graduate students regardless of immigration status (to learn about up-to-date resources, I recommend the blog *My Undocumented Life*). There are also graduate programs that may have internal funding opportunities that do not require a Social Security number or work authorization. If you can, it's helpful to connect with the various programs you're considering and to ask about their support for undocumented students without DACA. You can also reach out to your mentors and/or potential advisor(s) for help as you navigate these conversations.

I qualify for DACA, but I'm worried about the uncertainty of the program. Any advice on whether I should delay applying to grad school?

This will depend on multiple factors, including your personal and family circumstances, and there is no one way that works for everyone.

Nevertheless, know that this is a valid concern, and there are undocumented students who may opt for working while DACA is still in place and applying to grad school once there's greater certainty. There are also undocumented students who may pursue grad school right after graduating from college to gain a sense of some certainty, however limited it may be. As you weigh your decision, seek support from others (e.g., your mentors, fellow undocumented students, family, and friends). If you do take a few years before applying to grad school, it's also possible to be actively engaged in work or research opportunities that can strengthen your grad school application in the future, so it's good to discuss your circumstances and options with your support network. You may also want to reach out to the specific programs you are considering and inquire about funding options with or without DACA. It may also be helpful to have conversations about institutional support if DACA were terminated, especially if funding in the program is predicated on having work authorization.

Should I disclose or conceal my immigration status when applying to grad school?

This will also depend on multiple factors, including your personal and family circumstances, and there is no one way that works for everyone. There are also different approaches. Some undocumented students may opt to disclose their immigration status only in their personal statement (e.g., as it relates to their passion for pursuing grad school), and some may disclose their status during conversations about financial aid. A mentor can help you navigate specific questions or concerns (e.g., they may contact the specific program or school on your behalf without revealing personal information). The best thing to do is to seek advice and support from others. I recommend connecting with fellow undocumented graduate students so you can learn more about how they approached the decision to disclose or conceal their status during the application process and/or once enrolled in the program.

How can I connect with fellow undocumented students who are applying to or attending grad school?

Immigrant rights organizations (either on campus or in the broader community) are a great way to connect with fellow undocumented folks or allies. The blog *My Undocumented Life* features the UndocuGrad series where you can learn more about undocumented graduate students from various fields, including their experience and advice. *My Undocumented Life* also facilitates both online and in-person UndocuGrads workshops, which are great venues to connect with others who are getting ready to apply to grad school. Mentors can also help connect you with fellow undocumented graduate students. The key here is not to be afraid to ask for help. Even if someone doesn't have all the answers, they can connect you with someone else, or they can work with you to support you along the way.

Four Key Resources for Undocumented Students Applying to Grad School

1 *My Undocumented Life* features up-to-date information for undocumented students, including advice and funding opportunities for those pursuing graduate school (https://mydocumentedlife.org/).
2 Pre-Health Dreamers is a rapidly growing network and community of over one thousand health career–bound undocumented students, and their allies, across the United States, representing various career interests (https://www.phdreamers.org/).
3 Immigrants Rising provides resources to undocumented young people, including a list of fellowship opportunities available to undocumented graduate students (https://immigrantsrising.org/).
4 The *Undocu-Grad School Guide*, created by the New York State Youth Leadership Council, has 104 pages of information and advice about applying to and funding grad school across the United States (https://www.nysylc.org/s/UndocuGradSchoolGuideFinal.pdf).

Glossary of Terms

ABD (all but dissertation). A term for doctoral students who have completed their coursework, qualifying exams, and dissertation proposal, and who now only need to complete and defend a thesis in order to earn a PhD.

adjunct. An instructor who teaches at a university on a contractual basis. Also known as lecturer. These faculty are paid significantly less than probationary or permanent faculty and often teach at multiple universities to earn a living.

assistant professor. A professor who is on the tenure track, typically a six-year timeline toward job permanency. Also referred to as junior faculty or probationary faculty.

associate professor. A professor who has earned tenure and has been promoted from assistant. Also referred to as midcareer faculty, they are often in the process of working toward promotion to full professor.

backward planning. The technique of creating a project plan starting from the day it is due, then mapping each step backward in time.

code-switch. To alternate speaking in different languages or adapting the words you use for particular audiences so that they can be better understood. It can also refer to your personal style and how you choose to present yourself differently depending on the context.

community cultural wealth. The idea, coined by scholar Tara Yosso, that Latinx/a/o students may not bring traditional social capital, in the form of social networks and familiarity with the norms of graduate school, but they do bring family and cultural values—such as strong aspirations, ability to speak more than one language, and navigational know-how from supporting family in other contexts (such as translating for an abuela at the doctor's office) that contributes to their academic success.

cv (curriculum vitae). Latin for "curricular life," this is a multipage academic résumé that records your educational experiences, publications, courses taught, honors and awards, associations you belong to, and more.

department chair. A faculty member who serves as the head of the department, typically for a three- to four-year term. They are responsible for establishing a department's course schedule, advising structure, personnel processes, and more.

dissertation committee. A group of three to five faculty who supervise and provide feedback on your dissertation, the book-length research project that leads to completing a doctoral degree. It is headed by a chair or cochairs, the faculty whose own research interests or methods mostly closely align with yours.

dissertation proposal. A brief essay that outlines the topic and methodological approach of your dissertation.

for-profit institution. A university owned by private corporations or investors that primarily operates to generate money for its owners. The revenue does not get funneled back into the university. Often predatory, these institutions leave students with high debt and poor job placements.

full professor. A professor who is well established in their field and has been promoted to the highest professional rank. Also referred to as senior faculty.

graduate advisor. A faculty member who has been appointed to head the graduate program, overseeing the admissions process, making sure students are meeting benchmarks in a timely way, helping to complete paperwork for submitting a thesis, and so on.

graduate researcher. A paid role in which a grad student supports a faculty member's research through activities such as tracking down readings from the library, helping to proofread articles, and so on.

Hispanic-Serving Institution (HSI). A federal designation for institutions of higher education whose full-time student population is at least 25 percent Hispanic.

impostor syndrome. The nagging feeling that you may not be qualified to undertake an important endeavor, such as an exam, a graduate degree, or a new job. This concept was coined by psychologists Pauline Clance and Suzanne Imes in the 1970s.

microaggression. A form of racism expressed in subtle, seemingly innocuous comments that make you uneasy yet leave you wondering whether you are reading too much into the interaction or being overly sensitive. Accumulating over time, these jabs can wear you down just as much as overtly racist comments.

neoliberal university. Neoliberalism, as defined by Henry Giroux, is an ideology that "construes profit-making as the essence of democracy, [and] consuming as the only operable form of citizenship, and upholds the irrational belief that the market cannot only solve all problems but serve as a model for social relations." Expanding on this definition, the neoliberal university is a way to understand the corporatization and commodification of higher education, which reduces a college degree to a commodity to be purchased and devalues the act of learning and the importance of knowledge more broadly. The effects include skyrocketing tuition costs, a decrease in financial aid, increase in corporate contracts, the defunding of arts and humanities, and academic leadership positions being held by businesspeople rather than educators.

nepantla. A term coined by Chicana theorist Gloria Anzaldúa to describe the experience of straddling multiple cultural worlds, a state of "in-betweenness" from which Latinx/a/os draw creativity and insight.

nonprofit institution. University run by an appointed board of trustees who do not profit from the revenue. The funds generated by tuition and fees are put back into the educational programs and are often supplemented by support from state and federal governments, as well as private donations. These schools are seen as more reputable than their for-profit counterparts.

normative time. The perceived normal timeline for meeting graduate program benchmarks and/or time to graduation.

position paper. Longer theoretical or research paper used in some doctoral programs to indicate readiness to take one's qualifying exams.

predoctoral fellowship. A fellowship or form of funding open to doctoral students who are still working to complete their dissertations.

qualifying exam. A benchmark exam common in many doctoral programs that often takes the form of a two- to three-hour oral exam, which may have written components, to test your research preparedness. Once you pass it, you qualify as a doctoral candidate. In some programs, this benchmark may be a qualifying paper, a long research essay that shows your preparation to take on a full dissertation.

sabbatical. A formal period of leave that enables faculty to focus on their research and have a break from teaching and service.

socialization theory. The idea that graduate students progress through a series of distinct stages as they advance through their graduate education. Entering a new stage makes you feel unbalanced at first but is not a sign that you are inadequate; it is simply a part of the process. See Weidman, Twale, and Stein, *Socialization of Graduate and Professional Students in Higher Education*, and Twale, Weidman, and Bethea, "Conceptualizing Socialization of Graduate Students of Color."

teaching assistant. A paid position through which grad students assist faculty with their teaching by grading papers, leading discussion sections, and the like.

tenure. A system through which faculty earn permanent employment at a university. Tenure gives faculty the freedom to pursue their research and teaching agendas without fear of reprisal. Once a professor has tenure, they can only be terminated under extreme circumstances.

Notes

Introduction

1 We use the term *Latinx* to follow the lead of scholars and thinkers who have encouraged its use to challenge the gender-binary system that assumes everyone is either man or woman. At the same time, there is not universal consensus around the use of *Latinx*, and at times we use it as an accompaniment to the terms *Latina* and *Latino*. We are uninterested in the critiques of the term that emerge from a homophobic or transphobic analysis, although we do understand the critiques that are concerned with the fact that *Latinx* is difficult to pronounce in Spanish and is largely used in U.S.-centric higher education circles at this time. We use the term freely through the text, also alongside the more conventional *Latina* and *Latino*, in solidarity with the transgender and nonbinary community and also in acknowledgment that as a community we are still grappling with the best way forward.

2 A short note on the term *first generation* to avoid any confusion: you can talk about first generation both in the context of immigration (the first generation to be born in this country) and in the context of higher education (the first generation to go to college). Members of our Latinx community may be first generation in one sense but not the other, first generation in both contexts, or neither. Because this book focuses on higher education, when we use the terms *first generation* or *first-gen students*, we are using the second definition: the first generation to go to college, meaning a student's parents did not attain a college degree. Some parents earned college degrees in their home countries, yet, for the most part, their children are also considered first-generation college students. This is because of both the specificity of the US higher ed context and the difficulty associated with having one's degrees recognized in the United States, which often means that trained professionals in other countries migrate to the United States and work in service-sector or low-wage work, therefore rendering their children functionally first-generation college students.

3 Latina Feminist Group, *Telling to Live*.

4 Anzaldúa, *Borderlands*.

5 HoSang, *Racial Propositions*.

6 For *ninas*, see Garcia and Barrera, "Supporting Latinx Scholars."

7 Yosso and Solórzano, "Leaks in the Chicana and Chicano Educational Pipeline"; Hispanic Association of Colleges and Universities, "2019 Fact

Sheet"; Rivas et al., *Latina/o Transfer Students*; Snyder, de Brey, and Dillow, *Digest of Education Statistics*.

8 Hurtado, Ramirez, and Cho, "The Current Latinx/a/o Landscape."

9 Perez Huber et al., *Still Falling through the Cracks*.

10 Covarrubias, "Quantitative Intersectionality."

11 Hurtado, Ramirez, and Cho, "The Current Latinx/a/o Landscape."

12 Contreras and Gandara, "The Latina/o Ph.D. Pipeline"; Snyder, de Brey, and Dillow, *Digest of Education Statistics*.

13 Hurtado, Ramirez, and Cho, "Current Latinx/a/o Landscape"; Snyder, de Brey, and Dillow, *Digest of Education Statistics*.

14 Yosso, "Whose Culture Has Capital?"; Rendón, Nora, and Kanagala, *Ventajas/Assets y Conocimientos/Knowledge*; Ramirez, "'¿Qué Estoy Haciendo Aquí?'"

15 Dowd, Sawatzky, and Korn, "Theoretical Foundations."

16 Gutiérrez y Muhs et al., *Presumed Incompetent*; Karabel, *The Chosen*.

17 Marchevsky and Theoharis, *Not Working*, vii.

18 Machado, "Caminante, No Hay Camino."

Chapter 1. To Grad School or Not to Grad School?

1 Though collaboratively written, this chapter was principally drafted by Magdalena Barrera; thus the use of *I* in this chapter refers to her.

2 Kelsky, "The Tenure-Track Job Search," 16; Nelson, "Contingency," 285.

3 Cottom, *Lower Ed*.

4 One other caveat here is that the COVID-19 pandemic has caused a recalibration of how standardized tests like the GRE are regarded in the higher ed world. Many campuses suspended the requirements for standardized tests during the 2020–22 shutdowns simply because of logistical reasons, but some of those suspensions may be causing lasting changes in policy. At the time of publication (2022), the future of standardized tests remains to be seen.

5 Anthony Ocampo, "Typical Statement of Purpose Template," email to author, September 12, 2017.

6 Hernández, *La Virgen de Guadalupe*.

7 Adapted from Luck and Oakes, "Why and How to Email Faculty."

Chapter 2. Learning to Be a Grad Student

1 Though collaboratively written, this chapter was principally drafted by Magdalena Barrera; thus the use of *I* in this chapter refers to her.

2 Clance and Imes, "The Impostor Phenomenon in High Achieving Women."

3 Jaremka et al., "Common Academic Experiences No One Talks About"; Bauer-Wolf, "Feeling Like Impostors"; Ramirez, "Developing an Academic Identity."

4 Simmons, "How Does Impostor Syndrome Impact Students of Color?"

5 Ahmed, *On Being Included*.

6 San Miguel and Valencia, "From the Treaty of Guadalupe Hidalgo to *Hopwood*"; Rendón, Nora, and Kanagala, *Ventajas/Assets y Conocimientos/ Knowledge*.

7 Tichavakunda, "Understanding Microaggressions."

8 Weidman, Twale, and Stein, *Socialization of Graduate and Professional Students*; Twale, Weidman, and Bethea, "Conceptualizing Socialization."

9 Barrera, "Hottentot 2000."

10 Anzaldúa, "Border Arte."

11 Yosso, "Whose Culture Has Capital?"

12 Ramírez, "Developing an Academic Identity," 23.

Chapter 3. Essential Skills in Graduate School

1 Though collaboratively written, this chapter was principally drafted by Magdalena Barrera; thus the use of *I* in this chapter refers to her.

2 Goodson, *Becoming an Academic Writer*, 1–11.

3 Evans et al., *Disability in Higher Education*; Connor et al., *DisCrit*.

4 Fritzgerald, *Antiracism and Universal Design for Learning*.

5 Rockquemore and Laszloffy, *The Black Academic's Guide*.

6 Dorothy Duff Brown, "Dissertation Workshop," Stanford University, Stanford, CA, November 21, 2003.

7 Kelsky, "Why You Need a 5-Year Plan."

8 Adachi, "How to Bullet Journal."

9 Tompkins, "We Aren't Here."

10 hooks, "Theory as Liberatory Practice," 1.

11 Brown, "Dissertation Workshop."

12 Tompkins, "We Aren't Here."

13 Goodson, *Becoming an Academic Writer*, 16–17.

14 Goodson, *Becoming an Academic Writer*, 6–9.

15 Abrego and Negrón-Gonzales, *We Are Not Dreamers*.

16 Negrón-Gonzales, "The Power of the Pen."

17 Cisneros, "The House on Mango Street."

18 Teju Cole (@tejucole), "Writing as writing. Writing as rioting. Writing as righting. On the best days, all three," Twitter, April 11, 2014, 8:45 a.m., https://twitter.com/tejucole/status/454646310994710528.

19 Belcher, *Writing Your Journal Article*, 33.

20 Goodson, *Becoming an Academic Writer*, 16.

21 Belcher, *Writing Your Journal Article*, 26–38.

22 Goodson, *Becoming an Academic Writer*, 30–31.

23 Goodson, *Becoming an Academic Writer*, 142.

24 Belcher, *Writing Your Journal Article*, 8.

25 Lamott, "Shitty First Drafts."

26 Booth, Colomb, and Williams, *Craft of Research*.

27 Rockquemore and Ocampo, "Dealing with the Curse."

28 Belcher, *Writing Your Journal Article*, 151.

29 Smith and Choi, "Carmen Giménez Smith vs. Amplification."

30 Mohr, *Playing Big*, 101.

31 Barrera, "Domestic Dramas."

32 Brown, "Dissertation Workshop."

33 Germano, *From Dissertation to Book*.

Chapter 4. Unwritten Rules of the Academy

1 Though collaboratively written, this chapter was principally drafted by Genevieve Negrón-Gonzales; thus the use of *I* in this chapter refers to her.

2 Bledstein, "The Culture of Professionalism."

3 Nash, "Entangled Pasts"; Wilder, *Ebony and Ivy*.

4 Karabel, *The Chosen*.

5 Hu-DeHart, "The History, Development, and Future"; Dong, "Third World Liberation."

6 Bonilla-Silva, *Racism without Racists*.

7 Villenas, "The Colonizer/Colonized Chicana Ethnographer"; Pearce, "A Methodology for the Marginalised"; Solórzano and Yosso, "Critical Race Methodology"; Omanović, "The Emergence and Evolution of Researcher Identities"; Finefter-Rosenbluh, "Incorporating Perspective Taking in Reflexivity."

8 Tcheng Wing, "Building Bridges across Difference."

9 Tuck and Yang, "R Words"; Saavedra and Perez, "An Introduction."

10 Flores and Olcott, "A Few Rules of Thumb," 45.

11 Petrzela, "Navigating Social Media"; Connolly, "My Social Media Philosophy."

12 Iwamoto and Chu, "The Emotional Impact of Social Media"; McLean Hospital, "The Social Dilemma."

Chapter 5. Navigating Professional Relationships in Graduate School

1 Though collaboratively written, this chapter was principally drafted by Genevieve Negrón-Gonzales; thus the use of *I* in this chapter refers to her.

2 Hurston, *Their Eyes Were Watching God*.

3 For vivid glimpses of faculty life, check out Kelsky, "The Tenure-Track Job Search," 12; and Deutsch, "Surviving the Dream."

4 Flaherty, "Beyond Naming to Shame."

Chapter 6. Navigating Personal Relationships in Graduate School

1 Though collaboratively written, this chapter was principally drafted by Genevieve Negrón-Gonzales; thus the use of *I* in this chapter refers to her.

2 Schudde, "The Causal Effect of Campus Residency"; LaNasa, Olson, and Alleman, "The Impact of On-Campus Student Growth"; and Kuh et al., *What Matters to Student Success.*

3 Kulp, "Parenting on the Path to the Professoriate"; Armenti, "Women Faculty Seeking Tenure."

4 Bird and Bird, "In Pursuit of Academic Careers"; Pixley, "Differentiating Careers from Jobs"; Morton and Kmec, "Risk-Taking in the Academic Dual-Hiring Process"; Durkac, "The Relationship between Marital Satisfaction and the Division of Housework."

5 Q, "Savage Love Readers."

6 Caballero et al., *The Chicana Motherwork Anthology.*

7 IES NCES, "Fast Facts."

8 Nuñez and Murakami-Ramalho, "The Demographic Dividend."

9 Mason, "The Pyramid Problem."

10 Hodges and Budig, "Who Gets the Daddy Bonus?"

11 Quiocho and Daoud, "Dispelling Myths about Latino Parent Participation"; Chavkin, "Debunking the Myth about Minority Parents."

12 Gorski, "Unlearning Deficit Ideology"; Olivos, "Racism and Deficit Thinking."

Chapter 7. Life after Graduate School

1 This chapter was collaboratively drafted by both authors, so the use of *I* in this chapter shifts and is clarified in the text.

2 Anzaldúa, *Borderlands/La Frontera.*

3 Kelsky, "The Tenure-Track Job Search," 16.

4 Winslow, "The Undeserving Professor"; Posecznick, "Introduction"; Betensky, "'Tenured Allies.'"

5 Fenelon, "Race, Research, and Tenure"; Griffin, Bennett, and Harris, "Marginalizing Merit?"

6 Bousquet, "The Rhetoric of 'Job Market'"; Pfannestiel, "It's Not Just a Job"; Samuels, *Why Public Higher Education Should Be Free.*

7 Díaz Martín and García, "'Si pega, bueno.'"

8 Kelsky, *The Quick and Relatively Painless Guide*; Moore, "Timing a First Entry"; Vick and Furlong, *The Academic Job Search Handbook*; Kelsky, *The Professor Is In*; Greeson, "From PhD to Professor."

9 Kosar and Scott, "Examining the Carnegie Classification."

10 Cornthwaite, "What Nobody Tells You"; Caterine, *Leaving Academia*; Caterine, "A Virtual Guide to *Leaving Academia*"; Wallis, "Embracing an Alt-Ac (Alternative Academic) Career Path"; Sanders, "Going Alt-Ac"; Linder, Kelly, and Tobin, *Going Alt-Ac*; Greenlee, "The Dangers of Doing Other Things."

11 Kelsky, "Pearls of Wisdom."

Conclusion

1 This chapter was collaboratively drafted by both authors, so the use of *I* in this chapter shifts and is clarified in the text.

2 Bajaj, "Lanterns and Street Signs."

UndocuGrads

We are grateful to Dr. Carolina Valdivia for contributing this resource that draws from her extensive knowledge of and work in the area of undocumented student education.

Bibliography

Abrego, Leisy, and Genevieve Negrón-Gonzales, eds. *We Are Not Dreamers: Undocumented Scholars Theorize Undocumented Life in the United States*. Durham, NC: Duke University Press, 2020.

Adachi, Kendra. "How to Bullet Journal: The Absolute Ultimate Guide." *Lazy Genius Collective* (blog), November 11, 2021. https://www.thelazygeniuscollective.com/blog/how-to-bullet-journal.

Ahmed, Sara. *On Being Included: Racism and Diversity in Institutional Life*. Durham, NC: Duke University Press, 2012.

Anzaldúa, Gloria. "Border Arte: Nepantla, el Lugar de la Frontera." In *Chicano and Chicana Art*, edited by Jennifer González, C. Ondine Chavoya, Chon Noriega, and Terezita Romo, 341–50. Durham, NC: Duke University Press, 2019.

Anzaldúa, Gloria. *Borderlands/La Frontera: The New Mestiza*. San Francisco: Spinsters/Aunt Lute, 1987.

Armenti, Carmen. "Women Faculty Seeking Tenure and Parenthood: Lessons from Previous Generations." *Cambridge Journal of Education* 34, no. 1 (2004): 65–83. https://doi.org/10.1080/0305764042000183133.

Bajaj, Monisha. "Lanterns and Street Signs: Effective Mentoring for Greater Equity in the Academy." In *The Truly Diverse Faculty: New Dialogues in American Higher Education*, edited by Stephanie Fryberg and Ernesto Martínez, 235–63. New York: Palgrave Macmillan, 2014.

Barrera, Magdalena. "Domestic Dramas: Mexican American Music as an Archive of Immigrant Women's Experiences, 1930–1950." *Aztlán: A Journal of Chicano Studies* 37, no. 1 (2012): 7–35.

Barrera, Magdalena. "Hottentot 2000: Jennifer Lopez and Her Butt." In *Sexualities in History: A Reader*, edited by Kim M. Phillips and Barry Reay, 407–17. London: Routledge, 2001.

Bauer-Wolf, Jeremy. "Feeling Like Impostors." *Inside Higher Ed*, April 6, 2017. https://www.insidehighered.com/news/2017/04/06/study-shows-impostor-syndromes-effect-minority-students-mental-health.

Belcher, Wendy. "Solutions to Common Academic Writing Obstacles." *Wendy Laura Belcher* (blog). Accessed March 19, 2022. https://wendybelcher.com/writing-advice/solutions-common-writing-obstacles/.

Belcher, Wendy. *Writing Your Journal Article in 12 Weeks: A Guide to Academic Publishing Success*. Newbury Park, CA: Sage, 2009.

Betensky, Carolyn. "'Tenured Allies' and the Normalization of Contingent Labor." *Academe* 103, no. 5 (2017): 25–27. https://www.aaup.org/article/tenured -allies-and-normalization-contingent-labor#.YMoxhZNuerc.

Bird, W. Gloria, and Gerald A. Bird. "In Pursuit of Academic Careers: Observations and Reflections of a Dual-Career Couple." *Family Relations* 36, no. 1 (1987): 97–100. https://doi.org/10.2307/584656.

Bledstein, Burton. *The Culture of Professionalism: The Middle Class and the Development of Higher Education in America.* New York: W. W. Norton, 1976.

Bonilla-Silva, Eduardo. *Racism without Racists: Color-Blind Racism and the Persistence of Racial Inequality in the United States.* Lanham, MD: Rowman and Littlefield, 2006.

Booth, Wayne C., Gregory G. Colomb, and Joseph M. Williams. *The Craft of Research*, 2nd ed. Chicago: University of Chicago Press, 2003.

Bousquet, Marc. "The Rhetoric of 'Job Market' and the Reality of the Academic Labor System." *College English* 66, no. 2 (2003): 207–28. https://doi.org/10 .2307/3594266.

Caballero, Cecilia, Yvette Martínez-Vu, Judith Pérez-Torres, Michelle Téllez, Christine Vega, and Ana Castillo, eds. *The Chicana Motherwork Anthology.* Tucson: University of Arizona Press, 2019.

Caterine, Christopher L. *Leaving Academia: A Practical Guide.* Princeton, NJ: Princeton University Press, 2020.

Caterine, Christopher L. "A Virtual Guide to *Leaving Academia*." Princeton University Press, September 23, 2020. https://press.princeton.edu/ideas/a -virtual-guide-to-leaving-academia.

Chavkin, Nancy Feyl. "Debunking the Myth about Minority Parents." *Educational Horizons* 67, no. 4 (1989): 119–23. https://www.jstor.org/stable/42924788.

Cisneros, Sandra. "The House on Mango Street—Inspiration." Knopf Group, April 1, 2009. YouTube video, 3:50. https://youtu.be/nXO8a6HYttw.

Clance, Pauline, and Suzanne Imes. "The Impostor Phenomenon in High Achieving Women: Dynamics and Therapeutic Intervention." *Psychotherapy: Theory, Research and Practice* 15, no. 3 (1978): 241–47.

Connolly, N. D. B. "My Social Media Philosophy in (Roughly) One Thousand Words." In *The Academic's Handbook*, 4th ed., edited by Lori Flores and Jocelyn Olcott, 258–60. Durham, NC: Duke University Press, 2020.

Connor, David, Beth Ferri, and Subini Annamma, eds. *DisCrit—Disability Studies and Critical Race Theory in Education.* New York: Teachers College Press, 2015.

Contreras, Frances, and Patricia Gandara. "The Latina/o Ph.D. Pipeline: A Case of Historica and Contemporary Under-representation." In *The Latina/o Pathway to the Ph.D.: Abriendo Caminos*, edited by Jeanett Castellanos, Alberta Gloria, and Mark Kamimura, 91–112. Sterling, VA: Stylus, 2006.

Cornthwaite, Christopher. "What Nobody Tells You about Leaving Academia." *Roostervane: Careers with Purpose*, May 9, 2019. https://roostervane.com /nobodytellsyou/.

Cottom, Tressie McMillan. *Lower Ed: The Troubling Rise of For-Profit Colleges in the New Economy*. New York: New Press, 2017.

Covarrubias, Alejandro. "Quantitative Intersectionality: A Critical Race Analysis of the Chicana/o Educational Pipeline." *Journal of Latinos and Education* 10, no. 2 (2011): 86–105.

Deutsch, Sarah. "Surviving the Dream." In *The Academic's Handbook*, 4th ed., edited by Lori Flores and Jocelyn Olcott, 56–66. Durham, NC: Duke University Press, 2020.

Díaz Martín, Esther, and José García. "'Si pega, bueno': Testimonio of a First Generation Latinx Dual-Career Academic Couple Navigating Family and Profession." In *Amplified Voices, Intersection Identities*. Vol. 2, *First-Gen PhDs Navigating Institutional Power in Early Academic Careers*, edited by Jane Van Galen and Jaye Sablan, 18–24. Boston: Brill Sense, 2021.

Dong, Harvey. "Third World Liberation Comes to San Francisco State and UC Berkeley." *Chinese America: History and Perspectives* (2009): 95–106.

Dougherty, Sean Thomas. "Why Bother?" In *The Second O of Sorrow*. Rochester, NY: BOA Editions, 2018.

Dowd, Alicia, Misty Sawatzky, and Randi Korn. "Theoretical Foundations and a Research Agenda to Validate Measures of Intercultural Effort." *Review of Higher Education* 35, no. 1 (2011): 17–44.

Durkac, Judith. "The Relationship between Marital Satisfaction and the Division of Housework and Child-Care Tasks among Dual-Career Couples." PhD diss., University of San Francisco, 1987.

Evans, Nancy, Ellen Broido, Kirsten Brown, and Autumn Wilke. *Disability in Higher Education: A Social Justice Approach*. San Francisco: Jossey-Bass, 2017.

Fenelon, James. "Race, Research, and Tenure: Institutional Credibility and the Incorporation of African, Latino, and American Indian Faculty." *Journal of Black Studies* 34, no. 1 (2003): 87–100. https://doi.org/10.1177/0021934703253661.

Finefter-Rosenbluh, Ilana. "Incorporating Perspective Taking in Reflexivity: A Method to Enhance Insider Qualitative Research Processes." *International Journal of Qualitative Methods* 16 (2017): 1–11. https://doi.org/10.1177/1609406917703539.

Flaherty, Colleen. "Beyond Naming to Shame." *Inside Higher Ed*, September 20, 2018. https://www.insidehighered.com/news/2018/09/20/why-one-academic-spends-hours-week-putting-together-spreadsheet-documented.

Flores, Lori, and Jocelyn Olcott. "A Few Rules of Thumb about Conference Presentations and Invited Talks." In *The Academic's Handbook*, 4th ed., edited by Lori Flores and Jocelyn Olcott, 45–46. Durham, NC: Duke University Press, 2020.

Fritzgerald, Andratesha. *Antiracism and Universal Design for Learning: Building Expressways to Success*. Wakefield, MA: CAST, 2020.

Garcia, Alicia, and Magdalena Barrera. "Supporting Latinx Scholars through Academic Ninos." *Inside Higher Ed*, June 14, 2018. https://www.insidehighered.com/advice/2018/06/14/benefits-specific-type-relationship-between-latinx-graduate-students-and.

Germano, William. *From Dissertation to Book*. Chicago: University of Chicago Press, 2005.

Giroux, Henry. *Neoliberalism's War on Higher Education*. Chicago: Haymarket, 2014.

Goodson, Patricia. *Becoming an Academic Writer: 50 Exercises for Paced, Productive, and Powerful Writing*. Newbury Park, CA: Sage, 2012.

Gorski, Paul C. "Unlearning Deficit Ideology and the Scornful Gaze: Thoughts on Authenticating the Class Discourse in Education." *Counterpoints* 402 (2011): 152–73.

Graff, Gerald, and Cathy Birkenstein. *They Say, I Say: The Moves That Matter in Academic Writing*. New York: W. W. Norton, 2014.

Greenlee, Cynthia. "The Dangers of Doing Other Things: Why I'm a Scholar but Not an Academic." In *The Academic's Handbook*, 4th ed., edited by Lori Flores and Jocelyn Olcott, 32–37. Durham, NC: Duke University Press, 2020.

Greeson, Johanna. "From PhD to Professor: Advice for Landing Your First Academic Position." *The Muse*, June 18, 2021. https://www.themuse.com/advice/from-phd-to-professor-advice-for-landing-your-first-academic-position.

Griffin, Kimberly A., Jessica C. Bennett, and Jessica Harris. "Marginalizing Merit? Gender Differences in Black Faculty D/discourses on Tenure, Advancement, and Professional Success." *Review of Higher Education* 36, no. 4 (2013): 489–512. https://doi.org/10.1353/rhe.2013.0040.

Gutiérrez y Muhs, Gabriella, Yolanda Flores Niemann, Carmen G. Gonzalez, and Angela P. Harris, eds. *Presumed Incompetent: The Intersections of Race and Class for Women in Academia*. Logan: Utah State University Press, 2012.

Hernández, Ester. *La Virgen de Guadalupe Defendiendo los Derechos de los Xicanos*. 1975. Etching and aquatint on paper. Smithsonian American Art Museum, Washington, DC. https://americanart.si.edu/artwork/la-virgen-de-guadalupe-defendiendo-los-derechos-de-los-xicanos-86123.

Hispanic Association of Colleges and Universities. "2019 Fact Sheet: Hispanic Higher Education and HSIS." HACU Office of Policy Analysis and Information, July 11, 2019. https://files.eric.ed.gov/fulltext/ED600629.pdf.

Hodges, Melissa J., and Michelle J. Budig. "Who Gets the Daddy Bonus? Organizational Hegemonic Masculinity and the Impact of Fatherhood on Earnings." *Gender and Society* 24, no. 6 (2010): 717–45. https://doi.org/10.1177/0891243210386729.

hooks, bell. *Black Looks: Race and Representation*. Boston: South End, 2009.

hooks, bell. "Theory as Liberatory Practice." *Yale Journal of Law and Feminism* 4, no. 1 (1991): 1–12.

HoSang, Daniel Martinez. *Racial Propositions: Ballot Initiatives and the Making of Postwar California*. Berkeley: University of California Press, 2010.

Hu-DeHart, Evelyn. "The History, Development, and Future of Ethnic Studies." *Phi Delta Kappan* 75, no. 1 (1993): 50–54. http://www.jstor.org/stable /20405023.

Hurston, Zora Neale. *Their Eyes Were Watching God*. Philadelphia: J. B. Lippincott, 1937.

Hurtado, Sylvia, Joseph Ramirez, and Katherine Cho. "The Current Latinx/a/o Landscape of Enrollment and Success in Higher Education." In *Latinx/a/ os in Higher Education: Exploring Identity, Pathways, and Success*, edited by Angela Batista, Shirley Collado, and David Perez II, 3–22. Madison, WI: National Association of Student Personnel Administrators, 2018.

IES NCES. "Fast Facts: Race/Ethnicity of College Faculty." Institute of Education Sciences, National Center for Education Statistics. Accessed in 2020. https://nces.ed.gov/fastfacts/display.asp?id=61.

Iwamoto, Darren, and Hans Chu. "The Emotional Impact of Social Media in Higher Education." *International Journal of Higher Education* 9, no. 2 (2020): 239–47.

Jaremka, Lisa, Joshua Ackerman, Bertram Gawronski, Nicholas Rule, Kate Sweeny, Linda Tropp, Molly Metz, Ludwin Molina, William Ryan, and S. Brooke Vick. "Common Academic Experiences No One Talks About: Repeated Rejection, Impostor Syndrome, and Burnout." *Perspectives on Psychological Science* 15, no. 3 (2020): 519–43. https://doi.org/10 .1177%2F1745691619898848.

Karabel, Jerome. *The Chosen: The Hidden History of Admission and Exclusion at Harvard, Yale, and Princeton*. Boston: Houghton Mifflin Harcourt, 2005.

Kelsky, Karen. "Pearls of Wisdom—the Blog." *The Professor Is In* (blog), February 14, 2020. https://theprofessorisin.com/2020/02/14/introducing -pearls-of-wisdom-the-blog/.

Kelsky, Karen. *The Professor Is In: The Essential Guide to Turning Your Ph.D. into a Job*. New York: Crown, 2015.

Kelsky, Karen. *The Quick and Relatively Painless Guide to Your Academic Job Search*. Washington, DC: Chronicle of Higher Education, 2014.

Kelsky, Karen. "The Tenure-Track Job Search, Start to Finish." In *The Academic's Handbook*, 4th ed., edited by Lori Flores and Jocelyn Olcott, 9–17. Durham, NC: Duke University Press, 2020.

Kelsky, Karen. "Why You Need a 5-Year Plan." *The Professor Is In* (blog), May 2, 2014. https://theprofessorisin.com/2014/05/02/why-you-need-a-5-year -plan.

Kosar, Robert, and David W. Scott. "Examining the Carnegie Classification Methodology for Research Universities." *Statistics and Public Policy* 6, no. 1 (2019): 1–12. https://doi.org/10.1080/2330443X.2018.1442271.

Kuh, George D., Jillian Kinzie, Jennifer A. Buckley, Brian K. Bridges, and John C. Hayek. *What Matters to Student Success: A Review of the Literature*. Washing-

ton, DC: National Postsecondary Education Cooperative, 2006. https://
nces.ed.gov/npec/pdf/Kuh_Team_Report.pdf.

Kulp, Amanda M. "Parenting on the Path to the Professoriate: A Focus on
Graduate Student Mothers." *Research Higher Education* 61 (2020): 408–29.
https://doi.org/10.1007/s11162-019-09561-z.

Lamott, Anne. "Shitty First Drafts." In *Language Awareness: Readings for College
Writers*, edited by Paul Eschholz, Alfred Rosa, and Virginia Clark, 93–96.
Boston: Bedford/St. Martin's, 2005.

LaNasa, Steven M., Elizabeth Olson, and Natalie Alleman. "The Impact of
On-Campus Student Growth on First-Year Student Engagement and
Success." *Research in Higher Education* 48, no. 8 (2007): 941–66. http://www
.jstor.org/stable/25704536.

Latina Feminist Group. *Telling to Live: Latina Feminist Testimonios*. Durham, NC:
Duke University Press, 2001.

Linder, Kathryn E., Kevin Kelly, and Thomas J. Tobin. *Going Alt-Ac: A Guide to
Alternative Academic Careers*. Sterling, VA: Stylus, 2020.

Luck, Steve, and Lisa Oakes. "Why and How to Email Faculty Prior to Applying to
Graduate School." *Luck Lab* (blog), UC Davis Center for Mind and Brain,
September 17, 2018. https://lucklab.ucdavis.edu/blog/2018/9/17/emailing
-faculty.

Machado, Antonio. "Caminante, No Hay Camino / Traveler, There Is No Road."
Favorite Poem Project. Accessed March 19, 2022. https://www.favoritepoem
.org/poem_CaminanteNoHayCamino.html.

Marchevsky, Alejandra, and Jeanne Theoharis. *Not Working: Latina Immigrants,
Low-Wage Jobs, and the Failure of Welfare Reform*. New York: NYU Press, 2006.

Mason, Mary Ann. "The Pyramid Problem." *Chronicle of Higher Education*, March 9,
2011. https://www.chronicle.com/article/the-pyramid-problem/.

McLean Hospital. "The Social Dilemma: Social Media and Your Mental Health."
Accessed February 9, 2021. https://www.mcleanhospital.org/essential/it
-or-not-social-medias-affecting-your-mental-health.

Mohr, Tara. *Playing Big: Find Your Voice, Your Mission, Your Message*. New York:
Avery, 2014.

Moore, David Chioni. "Timing a First Entry onto the Academic Job Market:
Guidelines for Graduate Students Soon to Complete the PhD." *Profession*
(1999): 268–74. http://www.jstor.org/stable/25595691.

Morton, Sarah, and Julie A. Kmec. "Risk-Taking in the Academic Dual-Hiring Process: How Risk Shapes Later Work Experiences." *Journal of Risk Research* 21,
no. 12 (2018): 1517–32. https://doi.org/10.1080/13669877.2017.1313761.

Nash, Margaret A. "Entangled Pasts: Land-Grant Colleges and American Indian
Dispossession." *History of Education Quarterly* 59, no. 4 (2019): 437–67.

Negrón-Gonzales, Genevieve. "The Power of the Pen: Writing Mentorship and
Chicana/o M.A. Students." *Journal of Latinos and Education* 13, no. 1 (2014):
62–70. https://doi.org/10.1080/15348431.2013.800819.

Nelson, Cary. "Contingency." In *The Academic's Handbook*, 4th ed., edited by Lori Flores and Jocelyn Olcott, 285–94. Durham, NC: Duke University Press, 2020.

Nuñez, Anne-Marie, and Elizabeth Murakami-Ramalho. "The Demographic Dividend: Why the Success of Latino Faculty and Students Is Critical." *American Association of University Professors*, September 25, 2015. https://www.aaup.org/article/demographic-dividend.

Olivos, Edward M. "Racism and Deficit Thinking." In *Counterpoints*, edited by Joe L. Kincheloe and Shirley R. Steinberg, 41–59. New York: Peter Lang AG, 2006.

Omanović, Vedran. "The Emergence and Evolution of Researcher Identities: Experiences, Encounters, Learning and Dialectics." *Qualitative Research in Organizations and Management* 14, no. 2 (2019): 119–38. https://doi.org/10.1108/QROM-09-2017-1566.

Pearce, Ruth. "A Methodology for the Marginalised: Surviving Oppression and Traumatic Fieldwork in the Neoliberal Academy." *Sociology* 54, no. 4 (2020): 806–24. https://doi.org/10.1177/0038038520904918.

Perez Huber, Lindsay, Maria Malagon, Brianna Ramirez, Lorena Camargo Gonzales, Alberto Jimenez, and Veronica Velez. *Still Falling through the Cracks: Revisiting the Latina/o Education Pipeline*. Los Angeles: UCLA Chicano Studies Research Center, 2015.

Petrzela, Natalia Mehlman. "Navigating Social Media as an Academic." In *The Academic's Handbook*, 4th ed., edited by Lori Flores and Jocelyn Olcott, 255–57. Durham, NC: Duke University Press, 2020.

Pfannestiel, Todd. "It's Not Just a Job, It's an Indenture: Graduate Students and the Academic Job Market." *Academe* 84, no. 1 (1998): 44–47. https://doi.org/10.2307/40252288.

Pixley, Joy E. "Differentiating Careers from Jobs in the Search for Dual-Career Couples." *Sociological Perspectives* 52, no. 3 (2009): 363–84. https://doi.org/10.1525/sop.2009.52.3.363.

Posecznick, Alex. "Introduction: On Theorising and Humanising Academic Complicity in the Neoliberal University." *Learning and Teaching* 7, no. 1 (2014): 1–11. https://doi.org/10.3167/latiss.2014.070101.

Q, Dan. 2008. "Savage Love Readers Talk about the Campsite Rule." *DanQ* (blog), May 14, 2008. https://danq.me/2008/05/14/campsite/.

Quiocho, Alice M. L., and Anette M. Daoud. "Dispelling Myths about Latino Parent Participation in Schools." *Educational Forum* 70, no. 3 (2006): 255–67.

Ramirez, Elvia. "'¿Qué Estoy Haciendo Aquí? (What Am I Doing Here?)': Chicanos/Latinos(as) Navigating Challenges and Inequalities during Their First Year of Graduate School." *Equity and Excellence in Education* 47, no. 2 (2014): 167–86.

Ramírez, Yuridia. "Developing an Academic Identity: Lead with 'You.'" In *The Academic's Handbook*, 4th ed., edited by Lori Flores and Jocelyn Olcott, 18–23. Durham, NC: Duke University Press, 2020.

Rendón, Laura, Amaury Nora, and Vijay Kanagala. *Ventajas/Assets y Conocimientos/Knowledge: Leveraging Latin@ Strengths to Foster Student Success.* San Antonio, TX: Center for Research and Policy in Education, 2014.

Rivas, Martha A., Jeanette Pérez, Crystal R. Alvarez, and Daniel G. Solórzano. *Latina/o Transfer Students: Understanding the Critical Role of the Transfer Process in California's Postsecondary Institutions.* Los Angeles: UCLA Chicano Studies Research Center, 2007.

Rockquemore, Kerry A., and Tracey Laszloffy. *The Black Academic's Guide to Winning Tenure—without Losing Your Soul.* Boulder, CO: Lynne Rienner, 2010.

Rockquemore, Kerry Ann, and Anthony Ocampo. "Dealing with the Curse of the Blank Page." *Inside Higher Ed*, October 11, 2018. https://www.insidehighered.com/advice/2018/10/11/advice-getting-past-writers-block-opinion.

Saavedra, Cinthya, and Michelle Perez. "An Introduction: (Re)envisioning Chicana/Latina Feminist Methodologies." *Journal of Latino/Latin American Studies* 6, no. 2 (2014): 78–80. https://doi.org/10.18085/llas.6.2.0645634738372v66.

Samuels, Roberts. *Why Public Higher Education Should Be Free: How to Decrease Cost and Increase Quality at American Universities.* New Brunswick, NJ: Rutgers University Press, 2013.

Sanders, Ashley. "Going Alt-Ac: How to Begin." *Inside Higher Ed*, January 26, 2014. https://www.insidehighered.com/blogs/gradhacker/going-alt-ac-how-begin.

San Miguel, Guadalupe, and Richard Valencia. "From the Treaty of Guadalupe Hidalgo to *Hopwood*: The Educational Plight and Struggle of Mexican Americans in the Southwest." *Harvard Educational Review* 68, no. 3 (1998): 353–412.

Schudde, Lauren T. "The Causal Effect of Campus Residency on College Student Retention." *Review of Higher Education* 34, no. 4 (2011): 581–610. https://doi.org/10.1353/rhe.2011.0023.

Silvia, Paul. *How to Write a Lot: A Practical Guide to Productive Academic Writing.* Washington, DC: American Psychological Association, 2007.

Simmons, Dena. "How Does Impostor Syndrome Impact Students of Color?" *TED Radio Hour*, March 16, 2018. https://www.npr.org/transcripts/593873586.

Smith, Danez, and Franny Choi. "Carmen Giménez Smith vs. Amplification." Interview with Carmen Giménez Smith. *VS* (podcast), May 25, 2021. https://podcasts.apple.com/us/podcast/carmen-gim%C3%A9nez-smith-vs-amplification/id1249005448?i=1000523003805.

Snyder, Thomas, Cristobal de Brey, and Sally Dillow. *Digest of Education Statistics 2017.* Washington, DC: National Center for Education Statistics, 2019.

Solórzano, Daniel, and Tara Yosso. "Critical Race Methodology: Counter-Storytelling as an Analytical Framework for Education Research."

Qualitative Inquiry 8, no. 1 (2002): 23–44. https://doi.org/10.1177
/107780040200800103.

Tcheng Wing, Breanne. "Building Bridges across Difference through International Summer Immersion Programs: A Narrative Inquiry in Racial Identity and Social Justice Orientation." PhD diss., University of San Francisco, 2018.

Tichavakunda, Antar. "Understanding Microaggressions." In *The Academic's Handbook*, 4th ed., edited by Lori Flores and Jocelyn Olcott, 203–7. Durham, NC: Duke University Press, 2020.

Tompkins, Kyla Wazana. "We Aren't Here to Learn What We Already Know." *Avidly*, September 13, 2016. https://avidly.lareviewofbooks.org/2016/09/13 /we-arent-here-to-learn-what-we-know-we-already-know/.

Tuck, Eve, and K. Wayne Yang. "R Words: Refusing Research." In *Humanizing Research: Decolonizing Qualitative Inquiry with Youth and Communities*, edited by Django Paris and Maisha T. Winn, 223–47. Newbury Park, CA: Sage, 2014.

Twale, Darla, John Weidman, and Kathryn Bethea. "Conceptualizing Socialization of Graduate Students of Color: Revisiting the Weidman-Twale-Stein Framework." *Western Journal of Black Studies* 40, no. 2 (2016): 80–94.

Vick, Julia, and Jennifer Furlong. *The Academic Job Search Handbook*, 4th ed. Philadelphia: University of Pennsylvania Press, 2008.

Villenas, Sofia. "The Colonizer/Colonized Chicana Ethnographer: Identity, Marginalization, and Co-optation in the Field." *Harvard Educational Review* 66, no. 4 (1996): 711–32. https://doi.org/10.17763/haer.66.4.3483672630865482.

Wallis, Todd. "Embracing an Alt-Ac (Alternative Academic) Career Path." *Inside Scholar*, April 18, 2018. https://insidescholar.org/alt-ac-career-path/.

Weidman, John, Darla Twale, and Elizabeth Stein. *Socialization of Graduate and Professional Students in Higher Education: A Perilous Passage?* Washington, DC: Jossey-Bass, 2001.

Wilder, Craig Steven. *Ebony and Ivy: Race, Slavery, and the Troubled History of America's Universities*. London: Bloomsbury, 2013.

Winslow, Luke. "The Undeserving Professor: Neoliberalism and the Reinvention of Higher Education." *Rhetoric and Public Affairs* 18, no. 2 (2015): 201–45. https://muse.jhu.edu/article/584315.

Yosso, Tara. "Whose Culture Has Capital? A Critical Race Theory Discussion of Community Cultural Wealth." *Race, Ethnicity, and Education* 8, no. 1 (2005): 69–91.

Yosso, Tara, and Daniel G. Solórzano. "Leaks in the Chicana and Chicano Educational Pipeline: Latino Policy and Issues." *Latino Policy and Issues Brief*, no. 13. UCLA Chicano Studies Research Center, March 2006.

Index

patriarchy, 24, 195, 202, 214

pedagogy, 4, 9, 12, 146. *See also* teaching

perfectionism, 98

personal relationships, 18, 65–66, 76, 180–204

position papers, 169, 183

postdoctoral fellowships, 11, 167, 171, 205

predoctoral fellowships, 122, 174

pregnancy, 8, 54, 190–96, 199

Pre-Health Dreamers, 232

private institutions, 40–41, 44, 221, 229

privilege, 123, 147–48, 153, 214, 219; educational, 1; racial, 7, 194. *See also* elitism

procrastination, 10, 84, 98

professional associations, 85, 133, 136, 138–39, 177. *See also* conferences; networking

professional dress/attire/appearance, 68, 123, 126–29

professional relationships, 17, 145–79

promotion, 4–5, 12, 39. *See also* tenure

Proposition 187 (CA), 6

Proposition 209 (CA), 6

provosts, 4

public institutions, 6, 40–41, 44, 53, 217, 221, 225, 229

public intellectuals, 142

publishing, 11, 107, 112, 125, 140, 149, 162, 219. *See also* academic journals; revise and resubmit (R&R); tenure; writing

Puerto Ricans, 12, 71, 98, 193

Purdue OWL, 152

qualifying exams, 168, 177, 183, 198; oral exam portion, 84, 92, 171

qualifying papers, 34, 112

quarter *vs.* semester system, 82

Quo Vadis, 85

R1 institutions, 14, 217

racial justice, 6–7

racism, 4, 29, 43, 68, 122, 139, 181, 202; of academia, 4–5, 24, 146, 164; environmental, 170; and unwritten rules, 122–25, 129, 146–47. *See also* microaggressions; white supremacy

reading (skill), 10, 16, 77, 102, 208; grad *vs.* undergrad, 16, 24, 42, 85, 88; reading responses, 11, 176; systems for, 10–11, 16–17, 63, 82–85, 88–97, 113–14, 117–18; and time management, 17, 79; and writing, 81–83, 99–109, 113–15. *See also* note taking

readings (texts), 61, 64, 72, 86, 93–96, 107, 113, 153, 156, 161, 168, 223; challenges of, 11, 66–67, 69; and COVID-19 pandemic, 224; load of, 77; reading responses, 11, 176; and writing, 81–83

regional comprehensive universities, 217

rejection, 49, 56–57, 161, 201, 220–21

research assistants, 42, 53, 185

research statements, 217

rest, 46, 82–84, 104, 119, 186, 203

résumés, 46, 49, 209, 217. *See also* CV (curriculum vitae)

revise and resubmit (R&R), 161

sabbatical, 39

San José State University (SJSU), 3–4, 12, 85, 203

SB1 (CA), 6

SB2 (CA), 6

scholarship (research), 5, 12, 97, 99, 116, 130, 142, 226. *See also* publishing

scholarships (funding), 9, 53, 55, 87, 138, 185, 230

Scrivener, 113, 118

self-care, 65, 76, 85, 114, 202. *See also* mental health

senior faculty. *See* full professors/senior faculty

sexism, 2

Shut Up & Write!, 101, 103, 118

slavery, 2, 13, 123

small liberal arts colleges (SLACs), 217

socialization theory, 68–69

social media, 17, 37–39, 83, 87, 98, 123, 140–44, 169. *See also* online presence; *individual platforms* social sciences, 13, 15, 31–32, 40, 51, 87, 111

Sociology of Education Conference, 136

software, 64, 105, 207; citation management software, 63, 75, 92, 116; Dabble, 113, 118; Microsoft Word, 63, 113; OneNote, 113; Scrivener, 113, 118

Special Supplemental Nutrition Program for Women, Infants, and Children (WIC), 198

spousal hires, 14

Stanford University, 10–11, 15, 59–61, 66, 70, 114

stipends, 24, 34, 41, 53, 79, 87–88

student centers, 38, 70, 139

student loans, 40–42, 87, 186

student organizations, 38

Sunday meetings, 82–83

Supplemental Nutrition Assistance Program (SNAP), 198

support centers, 38

teacher-scholars, 12

teaching, 70, 94, 100, 105, 139, 171, 174, 198, 208; and careers, 31, 38, 153–54, 206, 210–14, 217–18; devaluation of, 163; in graduate programs, 45, 126, 147, 157; of Latinx students, 3–6, 9, 12, 15, 19, 154, 160; and professional relationships, 178; respect for, 150; teaching credentials, 200; teaching fellowships, 11, 205; teaching styles, 164; of writing, 99. *See also* pedagogy; tenure

teaching assistants (TAS), 5, 11, 41–42, 53, 55, 85, 87, 185, 205

teaching-centered institutions, 12, 142, 221

teaching statements, 217

Telling to Live: Latina Feminist Testimonios, 3

Temporary Protected Status (TPS), 229

tenure, 4, 9, 32, 39, 127, 133, 139, 154, 175, 210, 212–14, 227; and children, 181–82, 191, 194; tenure clock, 193, 211. *See also* associate professors/midcareer faculty

tenure track, 2–5, 28, 112, 175, 194; jobs, 28–29, 143, 160, 181–82, 210–14, 219,

221. *See also* assistant professors/junior faculty

theses. *See* dissertations/theses

thesis defenses, 84, 115

TikTok, 142

time management, 10, 17, 63, 87–88, 119; and dissertations/theses, 11, 17, 80, 83–86, 111–16, 149, 158; and writing, 11, 81–82, 84–86, 101, 158. *See also* backward planning; calendars

trailing spouses, 14

translation, 17, 131, 135, 178, 204, 207–8

tuition, 9, 40–41, 87, 185, 203, 225; tuition equity policies, 230

tuition remission, 42

Twitter, 140–41

Uncalendar, 85

undergraduate degrees. *See* associate's degrees; bachelor's degrees

UndocuGrads, 43, 229–32

Undocu-Grad School Guide, 232

undocumented migrants, 6

undocumented students, 9, 13, 19, 35, 38, 43–44, 98, 129, 139, 216, 229–32

University of California, Berkeley, 6–8, 15, 191, 199, 212

University of Chicago (UChicago), 9–10, 38

University of San Francisco, 3, 5, 214; University Task Force to Support Undocumented Students, 9

unwritten rules, 1, 17, 121–44, 146

Valdivia, Carolina, 43; *My Undocumented Life* blog, 229–32

values: cultural and familial, 13, 17, 71, 193, 199, 201, 228; personal, 73, 207, 221

wait lists, 55–56

white supremacy, 2, 4, 24, 29, 123–25, 146–48, 178, 183, 214, 221

Write or Die, 102, 118

writer's block, 11, 99

writing, 62, 68, 79, 96, 130, 134, 151, 155–56, 170, 177, 181, 219–20, 227; and advisors, 12–13, 119, 132, 157–58, 167, 171–73, 195; arguments in, 11, 17, 29, 97, 103–5, 107–9, 118–20, 160; for class assignments, 11, 71, 77–78, 82, 93; creative, 31; of a dissertation/thesis, 8, 11–13, 31, 69, 85–86, 110–20, 132, 143, 157–58, 167, 171–73, 183, 195, 205; and editing, 81, 103–4, 109–10, 113–15; and fear, 10, 67, 99–100, 162; feedback on, 17, 50, 89–90, 109–10, 153, 158–62, 176; of letters of recommendation, 48, 56, 58, 145, 158, 163; of mission statements, 73; as a process, 82, 98–120; and reading, 89–92; shitty first drafts, 103; on social media, 141; and tenure, 212; of this book, 1, 3–4, 19–21, 24, 78–79; and time management, 11, 81–82, 84–86, 101, 158; tools for, 63–64, 117–18; writer identity, 16–17, 98–100. *See also* note taking; publishing

writing centers, 37, 46, 85, 109

writing groups, 37, 86, 101–4

writing samples, 43–47, 50

xenophobia, 29, 43

CPSIA information can be obtained
at www.ICGtesting.com
Printed in the USA
LVHW081654160723
752584LV00041B/820